A New Strength,
A New Song

The Journey to Women's Priesthood

MARGARET WEBSTER

MOWBRAY

Mowbray
A Cassell imprint
Villiers House, 41/47 Strand, London WC2N 5JE
387 Park Avenue South, New York, NY 10016–8810

First published 1994

British Library Cataloguing-in-Publication Data
A catalogue entry for this book is available from the
British Library.

Library of Congress Cataloging-in-Publication Data
Applied for.

ISBN 0–264–67320–4

Phototypeset by Intype, London
Printed and bound in Great Britain by
Mackays of Chatham PLC

Contents

Illustrations

Preface

This is an account of a journey in which countless people have taken part, and I am honoured to have been asked to write it. It is a record, not only of developments and events, but also of some of the feelings that accompanied the more recent stages of this movement into change. Perhaps it is a little like the biography of a family, written by a family member.

I have been greatly helped by conversations and interviews too numerous to mention. That time, so generously given, has been invaluable, filling in background and stimulating reflection. I have been very aware, during all this process of focusing and recollection, of the great company of women and men who have made this journey. They have worked and prayed with courage, hope and faith. To them the Church owes a great debt.

I would like to thank in particular Sr Hilary CSMV for close attention to the text, acute comment and much encouragement, and the Revd Pamela Fawcett for undertaking the index. Caroline Davis, MOW's Executive Secretary, and Jenny Standage in the office have unfailingly kept me going in my eastern outpost. And I think it is not out of place to thank my own family who, by being interested and by offering a variety of support, have enabled me to go on asking questions.

Lastly, I must beg the understanding of our Free Church and Roman Catholic and Church of Scotland friends in that, for the sake of brevity, I have frequently referred to 'Church' when meaning 'Church of England'. But they have been our companions along the way, and aspects of the struggle have shown us glimpses of the Church of the future.

MW
November 1993

Abbreviations

ABM   Advisory Board for Ministry
ACC   Anglican Consultative Council
ACCM   Advisory Board for the Church's Ministry
         (ABM's predecessor)
AGOW   Anglican Group for the Ordination of Women
ARCIC Anglican–Roman Catholic International Commission
CACTM Central Advisory Council for the Ministry (ACCM's
         predecessor)
CCWCW Central Council for Women's Church Work
CIO   Church Information Office
CMS   Church Missionary Society
CWMC   Council for Women's Ministry in the Church
GS   General Synod
JB   Jerusalem Bible
MOW   Movement for the Ordination of Women
NEB   New English Bible
PCC   Parochial Church Council
PWO   Priests for Women's Ordination
SCM   Student Christian Movement
SMWC   Society for the Ministry of Women in the Church
USPG   United Society for the Propagation of the Gospel
WAOW   Women Against the Ordination of Women
WCC   World Council of Churches

For all those who have worked for the ordination of women as priests in the Church of England and especially for Alan, the great encourager.

1   *Hearing good news*

Since the Measure has obtained the required majorities, we now pass on to the next business . . .

The Archbishop of Canterbury's momentous announcement came muted, gentle even, into the silence of the General Synod, as it waited for the result of the final vote on the ordination of women as priests in the Church of England.

Only the intake of breath was audible in response—no shouts inside the Chamber, no cheers, no tears. Even in the gallery people sat dazed, perhaps hanging on to their neighbour; but no fireworks, no abseiling down whether in protest or in joy. Only outside, on the grass of Dean's Yard, could people fling their arms round each other, as the television screen continued to relay the proceedings of the Church of England's General Synod on the late afternoon of Wednesday, 11 November 1992.

The announcement made its impact beyond the 566 members of the Synod and the hundreds standing outside. Not since Synod had debated *The Church and the Bomb* in 1983 had so much interest been directed at a Church of England debate. Every kind of newspaper had been making its own comment or analysis in the preceding days and weeks, and the list of media staff attending the debate, whether in the Press Gallery or in the overflow room, runs to four closely printed pages. Included are representatives from far-flung TV channels such as Nippon TV, Channel 7 Australia, and Canadian TV; photographers and reporters from *Time* magazine, the Andes agency, the *Toronto Star*, many US Episcopal Church papers, and European secular newspapers. The theological discussion between bishops, clergy and lay women and men made a deep impression on millions in Roman Catholic countries where the Church's decision-making is still wholly male. Before, during and after the debate, everything was buzzing.

The buzz even affected Dean's Yard, Westminster. Church House runs along the south side of the quadrangle of grass belonging to the Abbey, which also gives homes to offices, Abbey staff and Westminster School. Small boys play around, music practice floats up from basements. Twice a year one is more conscious of briefcases than clarinets as nearly 600 men and women gather from all over England, weighed down with papers, hopeful, anxious or determined as the case may be.

In the Church of England decisions are reached, not by a fiat from archbishops or bishops, but through a system of synods, gatherings of elected church people. Proposals take time, some would say an unconscionable time, to go through the various stages. So on the day that women's ordination as priests was finally passed, the rejoicing was all the more intense for the experience of waiting that had gone before.

It was now eight years since the latest stage in the process to enable the Church of England to ordain women priests had been set in motion. Behind this lay a long, long history as women from the days of the early Church onwards struggled to find a voice. Some had emerged as mystics, prophets, anchor-women; many more had been silenced or edited out of the story. From the small part of that history which is covered in this book it will be clear that the movement for ordination is just one aspect of the search on the part of women for their true place, whether ordained or lay, in a Church where all are valued, all voices heard. Women and men together have walked this often stony path.

In November 1984 Ronald Bowlby, Bishop of Southwark, had presented to the General Synod the motion 'that this Synod asks the Standing Committee to bring forward legislation to permit the ordination of women to the priesthood in the Provinces of Canterbury and York'. It had taken eight years to go through the various stages after that first successful proposition. During that time the legislation had been worked out, negotiated over, despaired over, revised, debated, revised again, and debated by the Church as a whole. Finally it had come back to Synod. We had just seen the Archbishop of Canterbury receive the voting figures and had heard him announce the result. The necessary two-thirds majorities in all three Houses—Bishops, Clergy, Laity—had been achieved.

Many people outside the immediate church context who saw this result as obvious and right found it difficult to understand why there had been any doubt at all about the outcome. After all, there were already more than 1,400 ordained women deacons, the majority of whom believed they were called to be priests and were offering their gifts in the service of the Church. Sympathetic observers of the Church of England recognized that by barring women from the priesthood the Church was depriving itself of a precious source of energy and devotion. Such observers were not in the least surprised that opinion in the Church of England as a whole had now expressed itself in favour of the change; surely there could be no doubt that this would be reflected in the General Synod?

Inevitably, however, anxiety was in the air. Five months before there had been an upset of expectations: a vote of lay members of Synod, meeting on their own, had failed to reach the necessary 66% majority. Everyone had been wondering if the balance could be shifted. Would the whole process be brought to nothing by just one or two votes short in the House of Laity?

From the point of view of the media, this uncertainty was meat and drink. The November result became more interesting because of this turn of events and the journalists loved making dire prognostications and diagnoses. But it was not just an interest in seeing the Church wrestle itself in and out of knots; the whole matter had become one of those issues like slavery, or apartheid, on which Christians realized the Church was being judged.

The result, therefore, fell out into a world which was a great deal more interested in this than in most church issues. It was rightly perceived as an issue which touched women, and men too, far beyond those most immediately involved. With a defeat, it was felt, all women would be diminished; and the credibility of the Church of England would be gone for the foreseeable future. There could be no more talk about justice or truth if it failed to put right its own glaring injustice, failed to acknowledge the 'new-grown occasion'. If 'the world outside' was already regarding the

Church and its hesitancies with disbelief, the recently-launched Decade of Evangelism would hardly stand a chance if the vote did not go through.

The changes in the recognized status of women, even in the Church, had been going on for decades. The process of raising consciousness among women and men about sexist issues had been continuing and the many lids keeping women down were creaking more and more painfully at the hinges.[1] The number of women MPs had nearly doubled in the 1987 election; women were more evident in high office; we had had a woman Prime Minister; and women were exercising authority in the judiciary and in virtually every area of public life. However much church people agreed that this *alone* was not a reason for women proceeding to priesthood, they could now see that the old arguments against it on grounds of unsuitability could not be maintained.

A 'new-grown occasion'

More important was the theological thinking which required that the Church should move forward. Professor Stephen Sykes, now Bishop of Ely, was one who had been addressing the question of the ordination of women to the priesthood with theological seriousness and academic rigour. In a lecture to his diocese, given in September 1990 (shortly after his appointment) he explored two objections put forward by those who opposed women priests: the authority of Scripture, and tradition. The bishop drew attention to the much revered classical theologian Richard Hooker,[2] and while not enlisting Hooker as a champion of women's ordination, emphasized one of Hooker's very important insights:

> At least 400 years ago there were already sharp arguments between Anglican theologians . . . about whether everything in the Church was to be organised strictly in accordance with the Scriptures, and if not how you could tell what parts of Scripture were merely for the times and what parts were intended to be permanent. The major theologian of the day, Richard Hooker, argued for two extremely important theses: first the fact that something was ordained by God did not, of itself, imply that it was so ordained for all time; and secondly, that you had to use God-given and God-inspired natural reason, in order to tell what parts of Scripture had which kind of authority.

He went on to make his own position very clear: 'I have come to the conclusion that the authority of the Scriptures, as Anglicans have traditionally taught, is neither threatened nor undermined by the proposed change.' He then introduced a wonderful phrase of Richard Hooker. Hooker said that there were new ways which would not have been God's will at earlier times: 'What has happened is "some new-grown occasion" which has made the old way, right in its own time, the wrong course of action at present.'

Such an understanding of God's 'new-grown occasion' had in fact, over many years, been filtering through to church people against a background of faithful, patient and sometimes perplexed prayer and meditation flowing from the word of God in Scripture. As they reflected on the significance of women as well as men in the scheme and purpose of creation and incarnation, the conviction had grown that the theological reasons for the change were compelling.

The Church feels its way

As these theological convictions became more and more compelling, the Church found that some new patterns of working together began to develop. In hospital, prison and industrial chaplaincies, on college staffs, and in ecumenical teams, collaborative ministry was being explored. This experience in turn gave rise to further theological reflection, as groups of colleagues began to understand very well that their work needed some of the women to be priests. The people to whom they ministered understood that too.

One example among many was the team ministry in Southampton where, in 1990, eight women were working full time for the church in that area, and one part time. Five were deacons in the Church of England, the others were from the Methodist and United Reformed Churches. Between them, they were responsible for churches and congregations, University chaplaincy, hospital chaplaincy, and a sector of the City Centre Team Ministry. This was in a parish showing extreme deprivation. As one parishioner wrote, 'There is no doubt that those women are capable of doing whatever job they have been called to do—they lead worship, do the admin., minister to the sick and the well, baptize, marry, bury the dead, teach the young and the not-so-young. But the Anglicans cannot celebrate the Eucharist.'[3]

These women, and countless others like them, knew about collaborative ministry, both between clergy and between clergy and lay people. In many parts of the country congregations were beginning to work together in a new way. Arguments against women's ordination as priests melted away in the face of the work the women were actually doing; and since 1987 their presence as clergy on all the synods had been crucial.

In addition to this new experience of collaborative ministry, there had been an explosion of fresh theological thinking, developed first in the United States, and taking place equally dramatically in England in the 1980s. *Sexism and God-Talk* by Rosemary Ruether and *In Memory of Her* by Elisabeth Fiorenza are just two titles out of the important body of writing that came from feminist theologians in the States.[4] English women theologians and biblical scholars were exploring in their own field: *The New Eve in Christ* by Mary Hayter, *Redeeming the Dream* by Mary Grey, *Women Before God* by Lavinia Byrne, all enabled a new approach to be made in this country to the questions surrounding ministry.[5]

Another section of the jigsaw puzzle was being fitted into place by other parts of the Anglican Communion. World-wide there were now almost 1,400 women priests serving the different branches of the Anglican Church. And on 11 February 1989, the Episcopal Church of the United States had become the first Anglican Province to consecrate a woman bishop, Barbara Harris, in the diocese of Massachusetts. In 1991 an Englishwoman, Penny Jamieson, had become Bishop of Dunedin, in New Zealand. At the time of the English vote on women priests, a third woman, Jane Holmes Dixon, had been elected bishop, and would take up her post as an Episcopal Church bishop in Washington in the middle of November.[6] Somehow this put the English vote into a new perspective: if other Anglican Churches were now consecrating women to the episcopate, this was surely a sign that their years of women priests had worked well, that the clock ticking so loudly in our ears could not be put back. And in the very week of the vote, the Province of Southern Africa encouraged us by voting wholeheartedly for women priests. By joining Kenya,

Uganda, Burundi, West Africa, Brazil, Hong Kong, Puerto Rico, Cuba and the Philippines, South Africa proved once and for all that this was no 'white women's club' but a universal, gradual, leading of the Spirit.

This was the context of the decision taken on 11 November 1992. The first chapters in this book explore some of the history and landscape of the struggle. Other chapters tell the story as some of us have lived through it, from the point of view of one who was closely involved with the Movement for the Ordination of Women, in touch with developments and present at many of the important moments. It is a book written with the heart as well as the head.

Both heart and head raise questions about attitudes to change, about attitudes to women, about the way in which the Church of England deals with controversy. As the story unfolds, a clearer picture emerges of the strange background to this much needed change in the Church's life. Against this background women and men come into focus who have over decades endured, worked, prayed and finally rejoiced.

Notes

1   Interest in women's abilities in non-traditional roles is reflected in films such as *The Life and Times of Rosie the Riveter* (1980), a film about women in shipbuilding during the Second World War; and the entertaining BBC2 'Play for Today' *The Sudden Wrench* (transmitted 23 March 1982), in which the wife of a plumber, growing desperate about her husband ever installing their own central heating, sets to herself, eventually achieves it and becomes a registered plumber.

2   Richard Hooker, Anglican divine and author of *The Laws of Ecclesiastical Polity*. Hooker's work was described by Pope Clement VIII as having in it 'such seeds of eternity that it would abide till the last fire shall consume all learning'.

3   Paper by Ann Lewin, Southampton 1990.

4   Rosemary Radford Ruether, *Sexism and God-Talk: Towards a Feminist Theology* (SCM, 1983); Elisabeth Schüssler Fiorenza, *In Memory of Her* (SCM, 1984).

5   Mary Hayter, *The New Eve in Christ: The Use and Abuse of the Bible in the Debate about Women in the Church* (SPCK, 1987); Mary Grey, *Redeeming*

the Dream (SPCK, 1989); Lavinia Byrne, *Women Before God* (SPCK, 1988).

6 In 1993 two other women were elected bishop: Mary Adelia McLeod, Diocesan Bishop of Vermont in the Episcopal Church of the United States, and Victoria Matthews, suffragan in the diocese of Toronto, Canada.

2   *The hidden gallery*

Your influence does not lie in public life and never will. It lies in the power you exert over men, individually and personally.[1]

As I walk down the stairs of church establishments, stern men meet my eye. The pictures on our walls are said to show what we love and think important, but many women look with a heavy heart at the huge portraits of bishops that hang in theological colleges, in the headquarters of the missionary societies, in Church House, Westminster. Even the faded black and white or sepia photographs of former vicars that are nailed to vestry walls can be depressing. But why? Haven't they got every right to be there; think how they laboured, how they were respected, maybe even loved? Well, yes, the conversation goes on in my head, but were they the *only* people who laboured? Where are the women? Where is there a portrait of the first woman sent out as a missionary by the Church Missionary Society in 1820 to Freetown, Sierra Leone? Or of Miss Sarah Coomes, sent to Sarawak in 1857 by SPG, the Society for the Propagation of the Gospel?

On the one hand, these women and others like them were absolute pioneers (within the context of the Church of England) with no models and scant support. On the other hand, they may have felt, awe-ful as their calling may have been, the strength of the womanspirit that was beginning to move and stir in the Church. Did they have friends in the Free Churches, Methodist women preachers, Quaker women giving ministry in their Meeting? Some, like Gladys Aylward of China ('The Small Woman'), knew the call of Jesus, and set out with a Bible into the blue; others would go to join established male missionaries, their wives

9

and families. Of the first two CMS women, Mary Bouffler, a London schoolmistress, died within five months; the other, Hannah Johnson, served for two years before marrying a widowed colleague. She then, like the other women who married, ceased to be counted on the CMS List of Female Missionaries. The CMS history, *Proclaim the Good News*,[2] makes it clear that this was a common pattern: 'Single women who went abroad, especially to Sierra Leone, did not often survive long. But those who did were likely to marry either a bachelor missionary or a man whose wife had died, often in childbirth.' No matter how much work these women may have done alongside their husbands, they only re-surface on the list of missionaries if they survived their husband's death and continued. Mrs Mary Beale went to Sierra Leone in 1840 to marry a missionary, and after his death in 1856 she stayed on as a teacher till her own death in 1866. Murray comments on this 27 years—a remarkable length of time in those days.

These women setting off as missionaries were just one aspect of an upsurge of devotion, courage and commitment among women right across the church spectrum. It was not a 'party' phenomenon in Anglicanism: just as the Movement for the Ordi-nation of Women (MOW) in our day was made up of many shades of opinion and church tradition, so in the nineteenth century women's ministry was developing in a variety of situations. From the London Bible-Women to the sisterhoods, a highly sig-nificant work of prayer, relief, nursing and teaching was under-taken, much of it among those whom the Church was notoriously failing to reach.

One considerable influence was the Lutheran Kaiserwerth Institution for Deaconesses in Germany, which included a hospi-tal, a 'lunatic asylum', an orphanage and two schools. Its work became well known; there deaconesses were trained for teaching, parish work and the care of the poor, and it was influential in the restoration of the Order of Deaconesses in the Church of England. One Evangelical visitor, John de Liefde, voiced reser-vations about 'the ecclesiastical stamp' on women living in any-thing approaching a monastic order, as well as about their wearing of special badges or uniform; but later he reassures himself and his readers with a comment which resonates today. Apparently thinking about his compatriot Englishwomen he writes: 'The

Reformed Protestant woman is trained in a spirit of independence of human authority in matters of religious concern, and is ... jealous of her liberty as a free child of God, who has to obey but one Master and to listen to no voice but that of her own conscience.'[3] At that time, Kaiserwerth was keeping going 'not less than 96 stations, where 293 deaconesses are labouring'. It is perhaps not surprising, therefore, that among other distinguished visitors to Kaiserwerth were Florence Nightingale and the notable Vicar of Wantage, W. J. Butler, who founded the Community of St Mary the Virgin in his Berkshire parish.

As women were becoming more educated, horizons other than husband and family were opening up for some. The religious orders for women began to become a reality, taking root from 1845 onwards. These communities, inspired by the Anglo-Catholic Oxford Movement, were dedicated to a life of prayer and care, especially for women and girls. The first was founded by Dr Pusey in West London: 'For at least six years Dr Pusey had realized that the social conditions of the industrial towns of England needed the services of dedicated women.' He was convinced 'that there must be something very wrong with Anglicanism if it could not produce religious communities, such as had existed in all ages of the Catholic church and in all parts of the world.'[4] Other sisterhoods followed, and towards the end of the century there were, in Charles Booth's words, 'Sisterhoods without number', trained and organized, wearing distinctive dress. In London alone, by 1900, there were many sisterhoods and six Institutions of Deaconesses.

The Deaconess Community of St Andrew was the first, founded in 1860 in Notting Hill by Elizabeth Ferard, who was commissioned and supported by Bishop Tait of London, later Archbishop of Canterbury. He helped to bring about the revival and restoration of the Deaconess Order in England. Deaconesses worked specifically in parishes alongside the clergy. Other bishops followed Tait's lead, in a very higgledy-piggledy way, and in spite of some suspicion of Romish influence (and no doubt also of *women's* influence) a deaconess house sprang up in one diocese after another. This spontaneous development may have caused problems later for the deaconesses, since the Church never really thought out the status of the Deaconess Order *vis-à-vis* the clergy.

In the mid-twentieth century, as we shall see later, statements were issued from Lambeth Conferences and from Archbishops' Commissions which see-sawed between declaring that deaconesses were, or were not, in holy orders.

As they started up, however, the pressing concerns were the immediate ones. Sometimes the work made dramatic demands: two deaconesses from the Mildmay Mission (at that time an independent rather than an episcopal foundation) went to help in the cholera epidemic at the request of the Vicar of St Philip's, Bethnal Green; more often it was sacrificial work, unhonoured and unsung, based on a life of discipline and prayer. At this time, the communities were growing, and many sisterhoods took on a huge amount of outside work—educational, nursing and social—mainly with women, children and the sick. By 1875 there were 18 sisterhoods working in 95 centres. In 1897 the Lambeth Conference found itself passing a resolution recognizing 'with thankfulness the revival alike of Brotherhoods and Sisterhoods and of the office of Deaconess within our branch of the Church'.

The calling of lay women

There is an interesting connection between the development of women's ministry, as expressed in the growth and activity of the religious orders, the deaconesses and parish workers, the women missionaries, and the expansion of the role of lay people in general in the Church of England. Alongside the new 'professional' role of churchwomen with the commitment which that entailed, there grew up a new awareness of the calling of lay people as baptized Christians. Women began to take on more and more work as volunteers either in formal societies (auxiliary to male-dominated or immediately directed by women's committees) or as adjuncts to parish or other local organizations. Brian Heeney quotes Louisa Hubbard who wrote in a chapter in Baroness Burdett-Coutts' *Woman's Mission* that ' "about half a million are occupied more or less continuously or semi-professionally" in such a fashion. Not only were these unpaid women but they did not include professed sisters or other members of religious orders.'

This in turn led to a sense of the need for such women to be given some form of training. Louise Creighton, widow of the

Bishop of London, wrote in 1901 that the new-style worker would be 'thoroughly trained and competent'. 'The first rustlings of a new women's consciousness, the first stirrings of a real desire to be professional church workers, showed themselves in a series of moves to encourage the better preparation of laywomen pastoral auxiliaries.'[5] This was another essential movement of growth leading the Church on eventually to synodical government and to recognize the possibility of ordaining women to the priesthood.

Power at that time was firmly in the hands of the bishops, at a diocesan and national level, and at a local level it lay with the squire and with the parson if he were lucky. Great reformers like Wilberforce, who with others achieved the abolition of the slave trade, or Howard who worked for Penal Reform, all functioned on the national scene through Parliament and through friends and allies. Elizabeth Fry, Josephine Butler and Florence Nightingale, also pioneers in prison reform, issues of social justice and nursing, discovered how to work in this way, became adept at it and used the existing system adroitly in their struggles for change. But for them all, their 'business' of social reform was motivated at the deepest level. Josephine Butler makes this clear: 'To the regal conception of justice, those who profess the religion of Jesus must bring into public life, and into the legislature, the stern practical social side of the real Gospel, the religion of Christ must become again what it was when He was on earth.'[6]

As the women became more active, shouldering responsibilities in Christian social work and teaching, the men began to wonder if they themselves should not be taking on some responsibility in the actual government of the Church. They did not, of course, regard the experience of the women as potentially useful in the management of church affairs, and the opportunity of enabling women at that point to exercise some power was missed; they remained in the unsatisfactory, though often effective, position of wielding influence behind the scenes. In spite of this, the women were occasionally left to themselves to direct and control voluntary work, which they did with considerable expertise. Kathleen Bliss, a twentieth-century beacon to lay women in the Church of England, wrote in 1952: 'Women have wielded influence with very great skill over the centuries and many still prefer it to any form of responsibility which brings them out into the open. But

the choice between influence and responsibility is one that women
have to make, and Churches have to make in relation to women.'[7]

The beginnings of 'church feminism'

The first expression of protest as a result of being excluded
from the official processes of decision-making happened in 1898.
Parochial Church Councils had been established in 1897, men
only being entitled to membership and voting rights. The House
of Clergy rather than the Bishops insisted that women could not
be admitted ' "because God did not intend them to have such a
role." This enraged a large number of women, and eleven
hundred of them petitioned against it.'[8] Some women were already
churchwardens and would be on PCCs *ex officio*, so the ban
created anomalies. The Dean of St Paul's, Robert Gregory, supported the women's petition, pointing out that these new bodies,
the PCCs, would be dealing with 'practical questions connected
with parish matters' — over which women were already knowledge-
able; he also said that women were often 'the most devotional
persons of the parish' who could be most helpful to the clergyman.

All the now familiar arguments were produced on the other
side: the councils would be swamped with women; women were
not made by God for public discussion; truly feminine women
would not want this anyway; and it was even said that opening
PCC membership to women would lead to 'a real danger lest
the distinction between sex and sex should be forgotten'. These
arguments won the day and, as Heeney remarks, 'By this deliberate decision of an all-male, all-clerical assembly, women were
formally excluded from election to voluntary parochial church
councils. The ban stood for sixteen years, although it was apparently sometimes overlooked.'[9] By the time equal voting rights and
limited membership was conceded in 1914 (but only to PCCs,
no other church councils), one important point had been won:
women were actually laity in the same way as men were; they
were sharing the same baptismal covenant and were heirs of
Christ's kingdom.

Learning to change gear

Before long many of these women found themselves in totally unfamiliar situations, due to the onset of the First World War. As they took up work in hospitals and factories, or enlisted in the women's services, a new world of work opened up. Heeney quotes the Church newspaper *The Guardian*[10] of 21 October 1915, which 'gave a number of reasons why the independent work of women was becoming more important, listing among other things "the experience of the real joy of work which has come to many women during the war . . . They have experienced reality, they have lived, they will not go back to golf, to bridge, to seeing the shops and listening to the band." '[11] This slightly puritanical-sounding statement reminds us of how circumscribed women's lives had been (particularly, one might add, for those who saw more of the washtub than of the band); but all those who were propelled into 'war work' must have found some new freedom as well as some new and difficult discipline.

Those women who had been active over 'Votes For Women' were already initiated into the world of public life. One of the most significant figures, first in the women's suffrage movement and then in the Church at that time, was Maude Royden (1876–1956), an Oxford graduate and an outstanding preacher. By the time women were given voting rights and membership of PCCs, she was already aged 38, and the fact that the women's movement in the Church was moving forward (though with huge difficulties placed in their path) was in no small way due to her. Sheila Fletcher in her biography *Maude Royden: A Life*[12] speaks of 'the view which Maude held more passionately than anyone else of her generation: that the women's movement stemmed from Christianity; *was* Christianity, a working-out of the Christian ideal in their own day, "the most profoundly moral movement . . . since the foundation of the Christian Church". From which it followed that the forces against it could "only be conquered by faith and prayer" since they were not based on reasoned opposition, but on prejudice and moral baseness. And against these there was no weapon but "the faith that moves mountains".' Many years later Una Kroll was filled with the same absolute conviction. She has said that at a low point in synodical processes in 1986 she became very clear that only by prayer would change come, and she later joined the contemplative community of Tymawr in Wales. We shall see that the ongoing prayer and faith of which Maude Royden speaks upheld in new ways the life of MOW and was an integral and life-giving part of the struggle to 'hurl the mountain into the sea'.[13]

Maude Royden found that among Anglican clergy most support came from the Anglo-Catholic Christian Socialists. Many of them understood that true Christian equality, in the best sense of that word, did not mean a nod to spiritual equality combined with an insistence on actual subordination. Hudson Shaw, Vicar of St Botolph's, Bishopsgate, in London, Percy Dearmer and other perceptive clergy continued to support her when the Church League for Women's Suffrage became the League of the Church Militant, which by 1925 had started actively campaigning for women's ordination.

Now we see the germinating of the seeds, planted so long ago, which in our own day have grown into a forest. The Society for the Ministry of Women in the Church (interdenominational) was founded in 1929 by Maude Royden and Canon Charles Raven, and the Anglican Group for the Ordination of Women (AGOW— specifically Anglican) in 1930. For decades both these organizations kept the cause alive, drawing in academics and senior churchmen, as well as supporting women in various forms of ministry in the churches and, with the St Ermin's Society, sustaining women with vocations to priesthood. AGOW continued to publish study guides and serious pamphlets, arranged meetings and conferences, until in 1980 it merged with the newly founded Movement for the Ordination of Women.

One of the first members of the Anglican Group (or AGOW, to use the other abbreviation) was Lady Stansgate, who remained a tireless campaigner for women's ordination to the end of her long life. In her family she did not carry this conviction alone: her husband, Lord Stansgate (formerly Sir William Benn), as Secretary of State for Air made the first appointment of a woman as a full chaplain to the RAF—the Revd Elsie Chamberlain, an experienced Congregationalist minister. This was fought at every stage by Anglicans from Archbishop Fisher onwards; but Stansgate persisted in spite of the letter which his family for ever after referred to as 'The Archbishop's Stinker'. His son Tony Benn also recounts how the *Air Force Annual* then listed Elsie Chamberlain as a welfare worker. On protesting, and being told it was too late for any changes to be made, that the printing was done, Lord Stansgate simply said 'No good telling me that. You can just pulp the whole thing and put her down as a Chaplain. Print it again.' This illustration of someone having the courage of their convictions was well received in the House of Commons during the debate in 1986 on women deacons, and Tony Benn certainly relished the telling of it.

An earlier incident in Lady Stansgate's autobiography illustrates the level of opposition in the hierarchy of the Church to any movement towards ordaining women, and the determination that this should be firmly quashed:

In 1925, I dined one evening at Nancy and Waldorf Astor's to meet Queen Marie of Romania. Among the guests . . . were Archbishop Randall Davidson of Canterbury, and Mrs Davidson. After dinner, as the ladies had coffee together, I found myself in conversation with Mrs Davidson. On an impulse I said to her: 'I wonder if I might speak to you about something I have much at heart, of which I think you probably won't approve: the ordination of women.' Although startled, she said in a most friendly way: 'You must come and talk to the Archbishop about it.'

That spring, when Anthony was just a month old, the invitation came for my husband and myself to dine at Lambeth Palace . . . After a wonderful dinner, we adjourned to the drawing room and then the real business of the evening began. Dr Randall Davidson seated himself in an imposing archiepiscopal chair and, one by one, those guests who had got to be put right were led up to sit beside him . . . I discovered that this was the Archbishop's regular way of dealing with dissidents . . .

Being very well briefed, Dr Davidson asked me in a forthright way: 'Do you want to be a priest?' I was able to say that the issue was not, at that time anyway, a personal one . . . 'Why are you interested in this movement then?' I explained: 'I have two little boys, and I want them to be brought up in a world in which the Church gives equal spiritual status to women. I believe that will make a great difference to their attitude to women, collectively and individually.'

At this the Archbishop launched into a long account of his own views. He had always been a convinced feminist and had always supported the franchise for women. Beyond that, he had always believed the professions should be open to women; but, at last homing in on the issue, he raised his voice and pronounced with an implacably dismissive emphasis: 'This is different. It cannot be. It goes against the Catholic tradition of two millennia. You must stop working for the ordination of women.' I said: 'Well, Archbishop, I do not think you can make that distinction and I shall be very sorry if the Church commits itself to that. Because I think it is right, I can't stop; and I must keep working for it.' I cannot recall that he advanced any argument. He just said that there never had been women priests and there never could be. Presently, after a few kindly personal words of advice on how to view this matter in the future, I was led away to make room for the next interviewee.

It was interesting that the Archbishop had thought it worthwhile to try and nip in the bud any such views when he came across them. Needless to say the whole incident and his words had the opposite effect. That evening I felt for the first time the full weight of the opposition ranged against the ordination of women.[14]

This one incident vividly shows how it was perfectly possible for leading churchmen to declare their support of women in the professions, even to declare themselves feminists, and yet to be totally doctrinaire in their opposition to women's full ministry in the Church. Supporters of women's ordination today are all too familiar with the problem of trying to have dialogue with people in that Janus position.

The work of education and persuasion, therefore, was particularly needed during those years from 1930 to 1970. While new developments were blossoming in patch after patch of English society, the ground in the church garden still needed patient digging over. After the decades of striking developments for women, in education, employment, in the social and political spheres and even in the Church to some extent, suddenly the Church of England began to backpedal, seeming to say 'Enough is enough'. In 1930 an approach was made to the Lambeth Conference—the ten-yearly assembly of Anglican bishops from every part of the world—for an enquiry into the alleged reasons against the ordination of women in the historic ministry. Lambeth simply reiterated the impossibility of women's ordination, and sent out confusing signals about the status of the Order of Deaconesses.

So the Anglican Group for the Ordination of Women was born in that year. Among the founder members were two women in their early twenties who were to become notable leaders in the Church: Mollie Batten, the economist, who was running a women's settlement in East London at that time, and Betty Ridley, who later became Third Church Estates Commissioner and a distinguished church administrator. In 1930 she had just married and come to live near London. Over the next 40 years they and other supporters of women's ordination saw one Report after another come out, and sat through debate after debate.

Taking refuge in reports

The Ministry of Women[15]

This Report of the Archbishops' Commission of 1935 may be regarded as the beginning of some kind of proper institutional recognition of women's ministry. But as far as the ordination of women to the priesthood is concerned, it laid the foundation for much negative thinking in the Church of England in the years between 1935 and 1970. It was set up 'To examine any theological or other relevant principles which have governed or ought to govern the Church in the development of the Ministry of Women'. They met on 24 days, heard a great number of witnesses, and considered a large number of memoranda. Among the witnesses, the religious communities were represented by the Community of St Mary the Virgin, Wantage, the missionary societies by CMS; the Regius Professors of both Oxford and Cambridge (H. L. Goudge and Charles Raven) both appeared, Raven—a founder of AGOW—sending in a Memorandum on the theological issues, which supported women's ordination to the priesthood. Many deaconesses testified, as did Evelyn Underhill and, of course, AGOW and the Society for the Ministry of Women in the Church (SMWC). The Commission itself was weighty, consisting of five bishops, the Dean of St Paul's, W. R. Matthews, three senior clergy, one lay man, three lay women and the Head Deaconess. Much of their work focused on the selection and training, pay and conditions of licensed lay workers (usually known as 'parish workers'). Also significant was their affirmation of the status of deaconesses.

> The commission saw it as an advance to have affirmed in 1930 that the deaconess was not simply the female equivalent of the deacon and

thought a new 'great Order of ministry' could channel the unused gifts and capabilities of women. They also agreed with Lambeth 1920 that ordination conferred on her a 'character', that she was dedicated to lifelong service, and that her status had the permanence of holy orders—although not parallel to any of the three orders, she should rank among the clergy. The Commission concluded: 'The Order of Deaconesses ... is a Holy Order and the one Holy Order at present open to women in the Church.'[16]

This Archbishops' Commission of 1935, therefore, supported the idea of a special holy order for women, but to be regarded as *sui generis* and not one of the three historic orders of bishops, priests and deacons. On the one hand this was a failure to grasp the nettle, keeping the ministry of women still entirely separate and by implication subordinate: the deaconesses, being not part of the three-fold ministry, were neither fish nor fowl nor good red herring. On the other hand, the Commission (perhaps simply piously hopeful) did call for the recognition of deaconesses as members of the clergy, admitted by the laying-on of hands by the bishop, and that they should have a proper liturgical function in church, leading in prayer, preaching, baptizing and in some circumstances administering the chalice. They went on to empha-size that lay women should be eligible for 'all such offices and duties in the Church as are open to lay men, including that of lay reader', and that some should be authorized to preach, and to conduct retreats. (They could hardly say less, in view of the fact that Evelyn Underhill was one of the witnesses.[17])

Reading the Report today, one is struck by the note of convic-tion and hope when they are writing about lay ministry and dea-conesses compared with the way they deal with the possibility of the ordination of women to the priesthood. There the tone becomes anxious and fearful—of breaking with tradition, of upset-ting other Churches, and so on. Dean Matthews refused to endorse that part of the Report, writing a dissenting Note which must be one of the first strong statements supporting the admis-sion of women to the priesthood in any official document of the C of E. To quote from his concluding paragraphs:

> I conclude therefore that the arguments which have been brought against the eligibility of women to the priesthood are without value ... I must go further and maintain that there is a most important theological principle

which ought to lead us to the conclusion that the opening of the full ministry of the Church is required by the Christian doctrine of human nature . . .

The Christian ministry is one of persons to persons within the Christian community. When I consider the question of the priesthood on this level and with this presupposition, it appears to me that the circumstance that some personalities are associated with masculine organisms and others with feminine is simply irrelevant, and there is no more justification for discriminating against women than there would be for discriminating against Jews or men with red hair.

The Dean made clear that he did not feel it expedient to proceed at once to admit women to the priesthood, but adds:

The ground for my acceptance of delay is quite different from that which appears to have determined their judgment. The delay in which I acquiesce would be justified by the principle that we should not use our liberty without regard to the feelings and prejudices of 'weaker brethren' . . . I . . . maintain . . . that [my view] is based upon the conviction that the Church is a living organism, which is continuous with its past but not bound by it, and that the Ministry of the Church is so high and arduous a vocation that the full resources of humanity ought to be available for its fulfilment.

This was a lone voice on the Commission. The Report might have been fruitful in areas other than priesthood if its view of the importance of women's ministry in general had been heeded. They clearly foresaw difficulties:

To carry out effectively and happily the proposals we have made will require the goodwill and hearty co-operation of all those with whom and among whom women will work in the service of the Church. It must be recognized that if our proposals are carried into effect both deaconesses and lay workers would hold a position quite different from that now accorded to them. The Commission hope that clergy and laity will unite in welcoming women to more definite status in the Church and so enable their work to attain its full and natural development.

This hope, of a distinguished body of churchpeople, was not realized. To quote Dame Betty Ridley, 'Of course nothing happened'. The official monitoring body, the Central Council for Women's Church Work, was too large and establishment-minded to act as a pressure group and the young Mrs Ridley realized on joining the Council in 1938 at the age of 29 that there would be little support for her earlier outburst to one of the leading members: 'Well, of course, all you're doing is an absolute waste of time, because none of it will be any good until women are allowed to be priests.' After that she made a conscious decision to go along with the Council's policy of gradual building up of standards of training, conditions and pay, even the contemplation of pensions for lay workers, as being the best way to provide good foundations for women priests. As the daughter of a bishop, Betty Ridley was familiar with enlightened Establishment thinking: 'I knew that I had to choose between proclaiming my views and being quietly but firmly dropped as a crank, or suppressing them, trusting that to make some useful contribution in the service of the Church would in itself serve the cause which I had at heart.' Her work led her to become the first woman to be the Third Church Estates Commissioner, from whose splendid offices she supported MOW through thick and thin.

Perhaps between the 1930s and the 1970s, those women allowed themselves to be blinkered to the reality of the opposition to any increase in women's opportunities in the Church. They were convinced of the need for a step-by-step approach, building up the conditions and salaries, and supporting the many able women who were now coming in to church work from positions of considerable responsibility; perhaps these women would have been helped by the occasional onset of leapfrog, in which some of the bishops would have joined in order to move things on. For instance, there was a huge blockage over women taking part in liturgy, and the statutory services (Mattins and Evensong) were closely guarded. One small document illustrates painfully clearly the blocks and delays which were being put in their way. This is a paper produced in 1953 by the Central Council for Women's Church Work, 'in connection with the granting of permission to qualified women to take parts of Statutory services'.[18] From it we see that God's frozen people were in no hurry.

The paper tells us that the Report of the Archbishops' Commission of 1935 led to a discussion in 1938 on the Central Council on 'the possibility of women being admitted to the Readership', followed by a letter to *The Times* in 1940 (signed by six of the Commissioners); diocesan bishops were asked to discuss the matter, but time was not found; this led to further discussions between all the bodies concerned through 1941, 1942, 1943, 1944, 1946, and 1947 when the bishops were presented with a resolution from the CCWCW:

> That this Council, whilst recognizing that men and women have their distinctive contribution to give to the Church, believes that in principle, 'lay women, provided always that they are adequately trained, should be eligible for all such offices and duties in the Church as are open to lay men'.

At this forthright suggestion the bishops drew up their skirts, considered it beyond their powers, and passed it to the Convocations (the Houses of Bishops and Clergy in the Provinces of Canterbury and York). There it met further delay, since only the northern bishops discussed it and gave general approval. Finally, in 1949, eleven years after they had set the ball rolling, the Central Council blew up and got a letter off to the Archbishop:

> The Central Council... would respectfully inform the Archbishops that the long delay and apparent reluctance of the Convocations to come to a definite decision in regard to the form of the regulations for the Ministry of Women in the churches, is causing growing concern and anxiety among many professional women and members of the Council. The Council ventures to hope that the form of the regulations may be decided this year. If they are accepted in the form approved by the Upper House, that should assist in the recruitment of workers.

Even now there was no feeling of welcome or valuing of what the women were offering: while the northern clergy approved a resolution that licensed women workers 'under certain conditions and circumstances' could take part in statutory services, i.e. Mattins and Evensong, the clergy from the Province of Canterbury rejected this; the pure air of southern churches was apparently not to be sullied by women's breath until Mattins or Evensong had been brought to a close.

This long and sorry story is a painful reminder of part at least of the background to women's ministry in the Church of England. And it is not just history. The willingness to prevaricate and delay and the long continued diminishing of women has lurked on long after sexism has been recognized as the sin it is in Church and in society. It is strange to remember that while these discussions were going on in the 1940s in Westminster, Florence Li Tim Oi's ordination of 1944 in South China, and her subsequent ministry as a priest, had lit the fuse that would flare up later when in 1971 her own Province continued the ordaining of women priests in the Anglican Communion.[19]

In the meantime, in England, the fuse was kept going by the work which the women were doing, come what may. A few were given a fairly free hand in diocesan jobs, whether in education or welfare, where they would have some autonomy. Olga Pocock was appointed Adult Education Adviser in the diocese of Lincoln in 1954 by the Chancellor, Dick Milford, a priest of wisdom and stature. This account of her work is interesting both for the feeling of pioneering commitment and for the picture it gives of parish groups at work.

> As a laywoman employed by the Church, I was given a free hand from the beginning, and embarked on a visitation, by train and meandering country buses, of most of the incumbents in the diocese. Many of them received me with courtesy, even if they did not immediately take up my offer of setting up educational activities for adults in their parishes . . . At least twice a week, my little A30 took me to remote villages where I was received with open arms by local church groups, MU in the afternoon, other groups of laypeople in the evenings wanting to learn and reflect upon their Christian tradition . . . One enterprising priest in a small country town deep in the heart of the Wolds was the moving spirit in a remarkable programme of religious education in the local G.P.'s surgery waiting-room, in which we collaborated with Hull University and the regional W.E.A. organizer. One of my most vivid memories is that of sliding my way to a Saturday conference in the Wolds in arctic weather and finding a large number of participants, gathered by this priest, who had braved the icy roads and the snowdrifts from all over the Wolds.

She also reflects on her job as compared with some of the other women:

> It is true that women educationists were more readily acceptable than those exercising a more obviously pastoral ministry. The parish workers had a much harder, more precarious time of it in the Lincoln diocese than I did. For me, this raised the question of the validity of the conventional notion that women's ministry equals parish work confined to women and children. All too many women accepted this at first, then

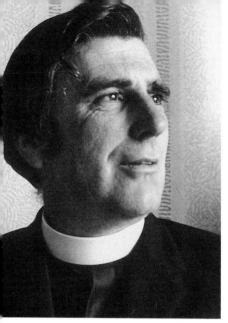

Stanley Booth-Clibborn

Monica Furlong

Diana McClatchey

Cathy Milford

Betty Ridley

Christian Howard

Una Kroll

Joyce Bennett

Mary Tanner

MOW Central Council, June 1984, outside Hartlebury Rectory.
Standing, left to right: Anne Hoad, Frances Killick, Jan Selby, Jo Stevinson, Michael Wolfe, Angela Bird, Diana McClatchey, Basil Moss, Penny Gallegos
Seated, left to right: Margaret Mascall, Christian Howard, Mary Goldsmith, Cathy Milford, Barbara Parrott, Nan Shrimpton, Margaret Webster, Margaret Orr Deas, Pamela Faull, Monica Furlong, Stephen Burnett, Nigel Harley

grew frustrated at being kept in a subservient position where their gifts were denied or not made use of.

She cites 'a few rare persons' such as Frances Moffett,[20]

who endured with great dignity the frequent slights and pettinesses she was subjected to . . . and remained in the institution, a truly Christ-like person, until she, like me, entered the world of teacher training while actively taking part in the movements which have resulted in the acceptance of the ordination of women to the priesthood by the Church of England.[21]

As there will be farmers in the Lincolnshire Wolds who are still grateful for Olga Pocock's clarity and humour, so there are countless students and women deacons who remember Frances with love, as I do. It is important to remember the far-reaching influence of these women and others like them who, more or less creating their own jobs, were able to sidestep some of the frustrations of their sisters.

Gender and Ministry[22]

At 'the centre', however, reports continued to be produced. The roll-call is depressing. *Gender and Ministry* in 1962 expressed some urgency about the conditions and deployment of parish workers and deaconesses and asked for fuller and more imaginative use of their services. John Robinson, then Bishop of Woolwich, made his maiden speech in the Church Assembly (the precursor of the General Synod, and made up of bishops, clergy *and* laity) on this subject. Robinson's clarity of vision and farsightedness are notable. He criticized the Report:

because it did not put the finger on the real deterrent to the recruitment of an adequate supply of women for the work of the Church. It hardly referred in the sociological section to the major change in their society, the almost fantastic explosion in the opportunities now open to women in the secular world, especially in responsible jobs demanding high professional qualifications and carrying equal pay. It was in this field that the Church fell so pathetically behind. The nub of the problem was their failure to give women real responsibility, with good conditions and security of employment . . . The failure to face this question of real responsibility was sterilising almost all their efforts on behalf of women and having an insidious effect on the integrity and honesty of the whole Church.[23]

The Bishop of Lincoln, Kenneth Riches, who had presented the Report, underlined these remarks in his final speech by commenting that to suggest that because it was wished that the service of men and women in the Church should reflect their changed status in the world it meant that women should ape men or be imitation men was not only offensive but also a hundred years out of date. It was rather that women were asking that the particular gifts of their own sexuality be brought to bear and used in the total service of the ministry of the Church. The result of this whole enterprise was that the Archbishops were asked to form a committee 'to make a thorough examination of the various reasons for the witholding of the ordained and representative priesthood from women'.

Women and Holy Orders[24]

Gender and Ministry, therefore, was followed in 1966 by *Women and Holy Orders* to which AGOW contributed weighty evidence. The Archbishops' Commission had deliberated for three years on this sticky question, but the Report was not actually debated and 'received' by the Assembly until 1967.

When the report came out *The Times* (17 December 1966) commented:

> The report appears to be honest . . . It finds no conclusive reasoning against ordaining women. It is other sorts of reasons that matter. Pragmatic ones . . . But how, other than with theological criteria, can a church decide whether one problem is more urgent within (or without) the Body of Christ than another?

Urgency does not seem to have been an ingredient of the process, but there was considerable interest when the Report was debated in the Church Assembly in February 1967. The reformist magazine *New Christian* carried a leading article by the editor, Trevor Beeson, who was at that time on the staff of St Martin-in-the-Fields.

> In common with many things in the Report of the Archbishops' Commission on Women and Holy Orders, the statement of Professor Gordon Dunstan that the question of the ordination of women is 'obsolescent if not obsolete' was shown by last week's Church Assembly

to be miles wide of the mark ... The Assembly Hall at Church House, Westminster, was crowded. Every seat in the public gallery was occupied. Mrs Michael Ramsey was there to see justice done and behind her was an impressive row of nuns who looked down on the proceedings with fierce interest and on one occasion broke the rules by applauding a speaker ... The Bishop of Chester [Gerald Ellison, later Bishop of London] introduced the report with the competence which comes through long experience of advocating the maintenance of the *status quo* ... In the speeches which followed, only the contribution of Mrs M. B. Ridley was notable. She held strongly that women were eligible for ordination and wondered why it had taken the Commission three years simply to set down the pros and cons. The experience of the past 30 years had convinced her that the failure of the Church to find a real ministry for women went deep down to a feeling that a woman could never be ordained. The real problem was that the Church thought of women as women and not as persons.[25]

Once again the matter was put off for further discussion at the next session. Patricia de Joux wrote in *The Times* (30 June 1967):

Valerie Pitt's resolution calling for admission of women to Holy Orders was debated with much-publicised wit, passion, erudition, and sometimes a curious illogic, then abandoned for six months without protest from even the most ardent supporters.

The debate was resumed in July 1967, and at last, in 1968 the Church Assembly was compelled by Christian Howard to see that they could make no sense of 'women's ministry' until a decision had been reached on women in holy orders and in the priesthood.

It was characteristic of Christian Howard to have propelled the Assembly into facing up to the real issue. She was already a force to be reckoned with, an astute mind and an able speaker who could think on her feet and make a telling contribution at the end of a debate. Secretary for Lay Ministry in the diocese of York, she was later made a Lay Canon of the Minster, a member of the Executive of the British Council of Churches, a Vice-Moderator of MOW and, in 1986, a Dame of the British Empire.

'If he decides ...'

Things were, of course, going on in other places which should have alerted our leaders that the status quo could not last for ever. In 1968 the Lambeth Conference moved as far as a Resolution that there were no valid theological objections to the ordination of women and asked every national or regional Church to study the question;[26] in 1969 the first woman was ordained in the Church of Scotland; and in that year the National Council of Women of Great Britain urged 'those religious denominations which do not as yet admit women to their Ministry on the same basis as men, to consider for training and ordination those women who feel called to exercise the functions of a Priest or Minister'.

The end of this long arid period came into sight in 1971. The first meeting of the Anglican Consultative Council, the newly appointed 'Standing Committee' for the Anglican Communion between the ten-yearly Lambeth Conferences, was due to meet in Limuru, Kenya. They had one decision to make which was urgent. The Bishop of Hong Kong, Gilbert Baker, had asked for guidance: his diocesan synod had approved in principle the ordination of women to the priesthood and he had two women deacons whom he was ready to ordain priest. Mindful that the last Lambeth Conference had declared that the arguments against were inconclusive and had simply asked Churches to seek advice of the ACC before taking action, the Council passed a famous Resolution. Firstly, all Churches of the Anglican Communion must give consideration to the subject of the ordination of women by 1973. More significantly, they followed that with sentences the effect of which reverberate today:

> ACC advises the Bishop of Hong Kong, acting with the approval of his Synod, and any other bishop of the Anglican Communion acting with the approval of his Province, that if he decides to ordain women to the priesthood, his action will be acceptable to this Council.

Since the Bishop of Hong Kong, Gilbert Baker, was convinced that two women in his diocese were indeed called to priesthood, and had been asking for approval to ordain, he was now able to go ahead, and in November 1971 he ordained Jane Hwang and Joyce Bennett, along with three men, to the priesthood. This courageous and far-sighted action was marked in London by a Service of Thanksgiving conducted by the Bishop of Ely, Ted Roberts, the Chairman of AGOW. The *Church Times* reported in this way:

The service was held in the Chapel of Church House and attracted a largely female congregation of about fifty. It took the form of hymns, prayers, and readings, and ended with the Te Deum said as a thanksgiving. In his address the Bishop said that he and his followers believed the ordination of women to the priesthood to be in accordance with Catholic order, and accordingly they rejoiced at the action of the Bishop of Hong Kong ... It was important that the example of Hong Kong should give the Anglican Church new impetus, so that it could bring to bear fresh qualities of insight, intuition, scholarship and spirituality. 'We hope that Hong Kong will continue to jolt us out of our complacency' said the Bishop.

On 1 December 1971, a press release was issued by the Council for Women's Ministry in the Church, from its final meeting before merging with The Advisory Council for the Church's Ministry (ACCM). The central passage makes it clear that at last, and almost unanimously, the Council were now in favour of the ordination of women:

> Although there have been strong differences of opinion in the past, the council now say, 'A very large majority of the members of this council has come to believe that the Church of England should now take steps to enable women to be admitted to the Order of Priesthood.'

It was now 40 years since the Church of England had started to backtrack on the developments in ministry that had been opening up during the previous century; 40 years in the wilderness for many women, who yet found the determination to persevere.[27] In 1971 Christian Howard, with her long experience of church government and of women's ministry, was asked by the General Synod to produce 'a survey of the present state of opinion about the ordination of women'. She produced her Consultative Document in 1972, entitled *The Ordination of Women to the Priesthood*.[28]

This magisterial survey provided background information for the Synod and remained important in the years leading up to 1975, 1978 and 1984. In those years, twice unsuccessfully and then successfully, motions were put that legislation should be prepared to permit the ordination of women to the priesthood in the Provinces of Canterbury and York. In 1975 and 1978 it failed, with many speakers asking for delay in order that the Church could make some further ecumenical progress first; in 1984 it succeeded, and the decision was made to start the process rolling.

But in 1972 they were nowhere near that point and agonizing setbacks still lay ahead before the final joyful outcome.

Notes

1   Revd R. W. Harris, addressing a women's overflow meeting at the 1902 Church Congress, quoted in Brian Heeney, *The Women's Movement in the Church of England 1850–1930* (Clarendon Press, 1988), p. 18.

2   Jocelyn Murray, *Proclaim the Good News* (Hodder & Stoughton, 1985), pp. 107–13.

3   John de Liefde, *Six Months Among the Charities of Europe* (Alexander Strachan, 1865), vol. 1, p. 171.

4   Peter F. Anson, *The Call of the Cloister* (SPCK, 1964), pp. 221–2. Anson gives a full account of the foundation, development and work of the different women's communities.

5   Brian Heeney, *The Women's Movement*, p. 79.

6   W. T. Stead, *Josephine Butler: a Life Sketch* (London, 1887), p. 91.

7   Kathleen Bliss, *The Service and Status of Women in the Churches* (SCM, 1952), p. 183.

8   Brenda Fullalove, Preface to MPhil thesis 'The Ministry of Women in the Church of England 1919–1970'.

9   Brian Heeney, *The Women's Movement*, p. 98.

10 *The Guardian* (not to be confused with the *Guardian*) was a weekly Anglican religious newspaper founded in 1846 to uphold Tractarian (High Church) principles, and to show their relevance to the best secular thought of the day. It claimed to provide independent comment upon theological, political and social issues. To the regret of many, it ceased publication in 1951.

11 Brian Heeney, *The Women's Movement*, p. 80.

12 Sheila Fletcher, *Maude Royden: A Life* (Basil Blackwell, 1989), p. 139.

13 Mark 11.23 (NEB).

14 Lady Stansgate, *My Exit Visa* (Hutchinson, 1992), pp. 199–200 and 73–4.

15 *The Ministry of Women: Report of the Archbishops' Commission* (Church House, 1935).

16 Jacqueline Field-Bibb, *Women Towards Priesthood* (CUP, 1991), p. 81.

17 Evelyn Underhill (1875–1941), spiritual director and author of *Mysticism*, was one of the most respected women in the Church.

18 Central Council for Women's Church Work: Appendix C1, Item 9, Council meeting, 3/4 March 1953.

19 Florence Li Tim Oi (1907–92) was ordained priest in the diocese of Hong Kong and South China in 1944. On her retirement in 1981 to

Canada, she became known as Florence Li. Her story is told in Chapter 6.

20 Frances Moffett was a rare spirit and fine intellect whose ministry was for many years in a parish and later in teaching, at Bishop Grosseteste College, Lincoln. On retirement she worshipped at the London University Church of Christ the King where further generations of students benefited from her faith, wisdom and good sense. She preached her first sermon at Christ the King, since, as a woman worker, she had never been allowed to preach in her parish. 'She should have been our first woman bishop', said one student, now ordained.

21 Letter from Olga Pocock to the author.

22 *Gender and Ministry: Report from the Central Advisory Council for the Ministry* (CIO, 1962).

23 Eric James, *A Life of Bishop J. A. T. Robinson* (Collins, 1987), p. 83.

24 *Women and Holy Orders: Report of the Archbishops' Commission* (CIO, 1966).

25 *New Christian* (23 February 1967).

26 *The Lambeth Conference 1968: Resolutions and Reports* (SPCK), pp. 39–40.

27 The decision to admit women as Readers was finally taken in 1969.

28 Christian Howard, *The Ordination of Women to the Priesthood: Consultative Document for the General Synod* (GS 104) (CIO, 1972).

3 *Not bread but a stone*

> I had vigilled outside beforehand, and I still had hopes . . . I remember sitting in the gallery and praying that I wouldn't have to say anything, and gradually the conviction coming that I would have to, and screwing up my courage to get on my feet, because at that moment it was extremely difficult. They had asked for quiet, so to get up and shout . . .[1]

Between 1972 and 1978 discussions continued in a desultory way. Christian Howard's background document *The Ordination of Women to the Priesthood* began to be studied and absorbed. In putting together an even-handed and lucid examination, not only of the historical background of the debate, but of the biblical evidence, tradition, theological questions, social considerations and ecumenical evidence—to name only some of the areas covered—Christian had produced a document which had to be taken seriously.

One part in particular of her Introduction echoed into the lives of many people who began to wrestle with this question during the 20 years that followed. 'In asking "Can a woman be ordained to the priesthood?" we are dealing not with a woman's question but with a church question. Our answer must be determined not primarily by what is good for women, but what is good for the Church. And consequently, "What is the will of God?" "What will further the Gospel?" '

The question that may have been in Christian's mind, though unspoken at that stage, was perhaps 'Might it not be that what is good for women could be what the Church is needing? By turning the question upside down would we not find that the right answer had crept up on us?' Perhaps there was a huge area of wrong here that needed a new approach, so that the searching for the wholeness of women in the Church would bring about a new wholeness for the Church itself.

No doubt this risky thinking was edging into churchmen's minds, and many of the questions Christian raised began to be tackled as the 1970s progressed. Her document was sent to the dioceses and found its way onto the laps of women and men who were serving on boards and committees concerned with women's ministry. In Lincoln, Chelmsford, Worcester, Norwich, Oxford and many other dioceses, meetings and conferences were now tackling the question of women's ordination to the priesthood with a certain amount of verve, even though for many of the decision-makers the question was regarded as interesting, important perhaps in the long term, but rather hot to handle now.

However the work itself was opening up, not just the debate. In 1972, in addition to the many women who were now qualified as Readers (authorized and trained to conduct services and to preach), there were nearly a thousand women professionally engaged in ministry (deaconesses, licensed lay workers, Church Army sisters and church social workers) in the Church of England. For many of them, the ordination issue was now a live question. The scope of their work had widened to include taking a proper part in liturgy, and there was beginning to be less emphasis on separate spheres of ministry for men and women.

The merging of the two central bodies concerned with men's and with women's ministry was crucial, as was the closure of Gilmore House, which had been training deaconesses since 1887. Two theological colleges were preparing to start joint training: Cranmer Hall, Durham, in 1966, and in 1970 Lincoln Theological College, known (in the words of Michael Ramsey) for Catholic worship and radical theology. Others would soon follow. Even though the immediate future of the women was still to be deaconesses, not yet 'clergy', not in holy orders as the male deacons were, still it was a creative period of living, praying and working together. The same could be said of the local ordination courses. Gradually, but only patchily, the training processes of the Church moved into the twentieth century and began to prepare women and men for a better understanding and practice of collaborative ministry.

There was, however, still a huge grey area or lack of understanding in the minds of many clergy as to what was an appropriate sharing of responsibility with 'their' deaconesses or lay
workers. Established clergy were used to women in subordinate
roles and expected to keep them there. One of the hardest things
for many a senior deaconess with years of experience was the
discounting of her abilities as one junior curate after another
arrived to be given responsibilities she could well have handled —
a situation which continued through to the 1990s. Bishops did
not as a rule have any senior woman of the diocese on their staff
meeting, and to hear a woman preaching on a major occasion was
a rarity.

At the end of her book *The Deaconess* Janet Grierson emphasized the unsatisfactory situation: 'At no time in their long history
have deaconesses in the Church of England had an assured place
in the ministry of the Church, and today when the whole question
of ministry is under discussion the future is far from clear.' She
goes on to quote Joan Diment, a former teacher and Inspector of
Schools who trained as a deaconess and came to Norwich in
1978, the first deaconess to be on the staff of a cathedral: 'In the
course of the 1977 Synod debate Joan Diment voiced the feelings
of many deaconesses: "At the present time deaconesses do not
know who they are ... and upon this uncertainty rests many an
unsatisfactory and unrewarding ministry. Upon it rests a debilitating uncertainty, wasteful of a deaconess's potential powers, and
an insecurity which can generate disillusionment and
heartbreak." ' Janet Grierson comments: 'Yet this statement
represents only one side of the picture, and it is significant that
in these recent uncertain years there have been in this country
more candidates entering the Order than at any other time in its
history.'[2]

This is part of the last paragraph of Deaconess Grierson's
book, and it is significant that she gives this position to Joan
Diment's indictment of the Church's treatment of its women
ministers. Although it is followed up by the statement about
increasing numbers, the footnote tells us that there were actually
only 285 licensed deaconesses at that time, of whom 87 were part
time.[3]

Hearing and responding

God, however, was still calling women to ministry, and in spite of the difficulties inherent in the work, and the ambivalent position it put them in, women were still hearing God's call and were often giving up interesting and fruitful careers in order to serve the Church. In a paper prepared for ACCM (The Advisory Council for the Church's Ministry), Dr Mary Tanner describes responses from women in professional accredited ministry to questions she had put in 1976 about the work they were doing and how they came to be doing it.

> What struck me most forcibly when I read the stories that came back was something I certainly hadn't been looking for. It was about vocation to ministry. What emerged from the stories was how, against all the odds of upbringing, existing role-models of male patterns of ministry, often in the face of being told to go away, think again, by the parish priest, certainly without any fostering of vocation by the bishop or the clergy, these women had become convinced of a call to minister to the Church, not always, and certainly never at first to a priestly ministry. And I was more and more struck by the fact that hardly ever was the feeling of call anything to do with a blinding flash, a Damascus Road type of experience. Rather, it was a sense of awareness that grew slowly and painfully against all that was expected, wanted, hoped for. And even more striking is the fact that so many of the stories told of the coming of the call through others. These women were aware that the community was calling forth gifts that they themselves were often not aware they had to offer. As one lay woman, later ordained as a deaconess, wrote: 'My inner convictions of a call were ratified by the way my ministry was being accepted in the parish. For me, this indicated a seal of approval, which was vividly demonstrated in the cathedral that ordination day, by over 200 people from my parish. Never have I been conscious of such love and prayerful support.'[4]

But the Holy Spirit blows through many kinds of bellows, and all round the country different sorts of pots were bubbling. Christian Action, the Christian Feminist Movement, and in particular the Christian Parity Group were all exploring the issue of 'church-womanship', the Spring 1978 issue of the *Christian Action Journal* being published under that title. Christian Parity was an inter-denominational group working to end the disparity between men and women in the Church and in society, and had already given much time to preparatory drafting of the Sex Discrimination

Act of 1975. The founding and moving spirit was Una Kroll, a professional woman who was a GP and a deaconess in the diocese of Southwark. She was a powerful inspiration to countless women and men struggling with the Church's sexism and inability to listen. One of the ways in which she pioneered new developments in the Church came out of her struggle for theological training. This account appears in the biography of John Robinson.[5]

> I first met John in 1967 when I was trying to become a theological student with the Southwark Ordination Course. It was a course for men, some of whom felt called to combine priesthood with their secular calling or profession. I felt called to the same kind of ministry, but as a woman my tentative voicings of that vocation had been greeted with laughter and scorn. Rejection had worn me down, and the appointment to see John Robinson at his home was God's last chance as well as my own, at least in my mind it was.

John Robinson did indeed recommend her to start training. Una comments:

> So began an experiment which was to pioneer a new kind of training *for women and men*. I was the first woman to do the Southwark Course in exactly the same way and under the same kind of strains as my brother students. I survived the three and a half year experiment of co-educational training that is now the norm throughout the Church and helped to prove the value of training ordinands with people who would help serve the Church in ways other than the ordained priesthood.

Many people remember the courage of Una Kroll at that time, carrying on what she has described as a struggle against stereotyping and even hatred in a more or less hostile environment. One who became part of her Christian Parity Group, Kathleen Burn, gratefully describes it as 'a circle of healthy indignant Christians'.[6] It certainly provided both a haven and a new stimulus for women such as Kath who were struggling with a vocation to priesthood combined with a high level of anger and pain at the Church's rejection of women's gifts. And sometimes Christian Parity was able to do more than provide a haven, and took initiatives with far-reaching results. The costly enterprise of supporting English-women training overseas for priesthood was one such initiative.

Kath Burn, working for USPG at that time, was unusual in being very clear that, feeling called to be a priest, it would be dishonest to train as a deaconess. She could only be accepted for training as a priest in one of those Provinces which were already ordaining women, such as Canada, the United States or New Zealand. Supported by the then Bishop of Southwark, Mervyn Stockwood, she was accepted at General Theological Seminary, New York; and in August 1979 set off 'with two suitcases and a picnic lunch' for three demanding years of training.

It was Christian Parity who took on much of her financial support at this time. One or two of the leading members of MOW had little sympathy with Kath's insistence on seeking training for priesthood abroad and tried to dissuade her—another instance of the varied viewpoints within the movement. I believe that in many ways Kath Burn's witness was heroic, and her visits home would rouse the more lethargic supporters of women's ordination. The combination of her sense of outrage that the C of E was moving so slowly, plus her sense of humour and deep love for the Church, was a welcome stimulus to the weary. She, I know, often found MOW's patient synodical approach hard to take, but that was good for us. Her pilgrimage led her back to England from her Rectory in Cleveland, Ohio, for a few months at the end of 1992. Rejoicing together at the MOW AGM a fortnight after the positive vote, it was wonderfully appropriate that Kath was able to be our celebrant and preacher.

In the late 1970s it would have been hard to believe that it would be fifteen years of solid, nation-wide slog before that moment of celebration and rejoicing would come. Christian Howard used to say 'Prepare for the long haul', a call which someone as congenitally impatient as I am did not always find easy to hear. Of course she was right; but I could only keep going on the basis that things were moving all the time and that real change was just around the corner. Perhaps some may have felt this was facile optimism; for me, it was not facile but a certain buoyancy in faith, a necessary persisting in hope.

Harsh voices

The most determined opposition at that time came from the Anglo-Catholic wing of the Church of England, spearheaded by the Church Union, a well-established organization founded in

1859. Their efforts had helped to ensure that the Anglican–
Methodist Scheme for Unity failed in 1969 to achieve the neces-
sary Anglican majority; and before that they had mounted vocifer-
ous opposition to the re-union of Christians in the Church of
South India. Later, in 1982, they were to be instrumental in the
Anglican defeat, at the final vote on General Synod, of the
Churches' Covenant for Unity. One element among many in their
opposition to all these schemes was undoubtedly the issue of
ordained women ministering in other Churches. The vista towards
Rome was infinitely more attractive.

There was an even more basic objection to women's ordination
than unity with Rome. Some maintained that it was simply impossible for a woman to be ordained priest, since this was not part of
the order of creation. Graham Leonard, Bishop of Truro and
then of London, was a leading 'impossibilist', convinced that a
woman just could not be ordained to the priesthood: it could not
happen, the ordaining ceremony would not 'take', and it was a
delusion for people to think otherwise. At the time of the Hong
Kong ordinations of Joyce Bennett and Jane Hwang in 1971, this
position was spelt out in a letter to the *Church Times* by Prebendary
Henry Cooper, Rector of St George's, Bloomsbury, and —
interestingly — Archbishop's   Adviser   on   Roman   Catholic
Relations:

> There remains the field of natural theology, so long neglected in both
> the Catholic and Protestant worlds as well as the Anglican. It is not
> mere psychology but the whole order of Creation that has to be viewed.
> At every level from the biological to the spiritual it is alleged (and not
> refuted) that, although there is equality between the sexes, a proper
> initiative rests with the male, even if it often has to be elicited by the
> female. Although normally the woman is paramount as the centre of the
> family, the man is normally the link between the family and society at
> large.
>
> For there reasons a good Creator has endowed each with the
> appropriate qualities, for families need a strong, skilful person to fend
> for them and to defend them, whilst they need a tender, protective
> person to cherish them. This is not to say that in necessity the sexes
> cannot, with difficulty, reverse their roles; but do we want *ab*-normal
> women in the ministry?

Unfortunately perhaps for Prebendary Cooper, women had long
ago discovered how to be strong and skilful, and it did not seem

abnormal to most men to be tender and cherishing. And the Church's march towards ordaining women was on.

Dissonance and resolution

In July 1975 the General Synod had two motions before it: (a) 'That this Synod considers that there are no fundamental objections to the ordination of women to the priesthood'; and (b) that legal barriers should be removed and legislation brought forward.

Both these had been debated in the dioceses; the first had passed in all three houses of 30 out of 44 diocesan synods, but the second had been carried in only 15. There was some criticism of the way the second motion had been phrased. Professor Geoffrey Lampe and other senior churchmen did their best to persuade the Synod to go ahead, the most powerful plea perhaps coming from the Bishop of Winchester, John Taylor: 'Are we once again to decide for the sake of unity and an un-rocked boat that it is inexpedient to take any action? What kind of passion for unity is this that in recent years has been so regularly invoked in support of the status quo and has so rarely inspired us to take any positive step for unity, that has justified so many refusals and so few affirmations?'

Even this prophetic call could not persuade enough people that the time was right to prepare legislation. The General Synod accordingly trod water, voting in favour of the first, 'no fundamental objections' motion, but drawing back from doing anything about it by rejecting the second. Crucial was Dame Betty Ridley's speech against moving ahead now, saying that she had always wanted to see the Church of England accepting women priests, but her conscience held her back. 'I cannot be sure that it is the will of God that our Church should be torn apart by going ahead now.' This speech may well have been determinative, and the motion failed. Deaconess Diana McClatchey, who was later to become a leading member of the General Synod and a Moderator of MOW, has described this as a 'baptism of disillusionment'. Canon Colin Craston, wise and determined, at least prevented the matter from disappearing completely, and persuaded Synod to invite the bishops 'to bring before the Synod a proposal to admit women to the priesthood' when they judged 'the time for action to be right'.

By supporters who regarded women's ordination as a matter of some urgency, the double vote represented a totally unacceptable volte-face which would make the Church a laughing-stock. Some of the dismay and anger surfaced in letters written to Betty Ridley. Elsie Baker, a much loved and respected deaconess who had already served a long parish ministry, wrote:

> For many years those of us who have known of your work for the place of women in the Church and have been proud of the honours you have received have looked to you as one whom they could rely on, one who would be unafraid to stand if necessary, with the minority ... so it was with great dismay we listened to your speech at the Synod. It is morally indefensible for a Church to pass in principle for the ordination of women and then to support the Standing Committee's recommendation 'Not Yet' and that you could publicly give your support to it is incomprehensible. You must know that opposition to women will only gradually be removed as women take their place in the ministry of the church.

Una Kroll also wrote, a longer letter:

> You had seemed to urge people like myself to 'keep quiet' on the grounds that you were fighting a delicate battle ... I do not think we shall *ever* slip this through without controversy. The controversy over the admission of Gentiles raged for 14 years or more after Peter took his courageous action, without apparently worrying unduly ... I have to say also that the leaders of the Church could do far more than they do to educate people, to get round difficulties at a practical level, to invite women ministers from other denominations to participate in services in our cathedrals and churches far more widely than they do. They could become positive not neutral ... The outside pressure groups can never do this. Only those inside the structures can invite us in to be heard and seen.

Betty's replies to both were eirenic. To Una she replied at length:

> As to whether some of us have been successful in fighting a delicate battle within the Synod and the Church Assembly, it is not for me to say. We certainly feel that we have been slogging at it for many many years and I at least hope that it may have played a small part in the voting, for I know a number of members, particularly clergy who ... over the

years have changed their attitude—and that leads me to say that I feel you had not the same anxiety I had that the first vote would be lost in the House of Clergy, and consequently not the same sense of relief and achievement that it was not.

I think this really does highlight the difference between us—for you the result was wholly disappointment that the decision to go forward was not taken, whereas I felt a real step forward had been taken in the first vote, both in the General Synod and in the dioceses, and my dismay about the other had come months ago when the results in the dioceses came in—for after that I never thought the Gen. Synod could or *should* go forward now.

... I agreed with Dean Matthews in his Memorandum in 1935 that the Church would take time after accepting the principle, to get used to the idea ... It is because of these deeply held convictions and the size of the minority who hold them ... that I felt, and still feel that it would have been quite wrong to try to go ahead. That holding as I do the view that to admit women to the priesthood is God's will for the Church, I should say that nevertheless it may not be God's will that we do so immediately.

As Betty Ridley and Una Kroll shared their very divergent views with a real effort to understand each other's position, it became clear that a division of opinion was emerging among those who were working for women's ordination. In different forms, this has continued to run through the life of the movement as a creative and fruitful tension. In 1975, those most involved with the synods hailed the passage of 'no fundamental objections' as a statement of great importance on which they could build. They were not surprised and not even unduly concerned that the second vote failed; they believed that even if it had got through General Synod at that stage, it would not have had massive support in the dioceses and would have failed at the final vote.

Others, like Una, believed—and still believe—that that was the crucial moment, and that the Church has been damaged by the long delay. Una had worked hard with other women in the Sex Discrimination and Equal Opportunities efforts, had sat on platforms in her cassock, been a church presence which was respected. 'Opinion was changing as a result of the Sex Discrimination Act, and the Church, if she had managed to ordain women in 1978, would have had more of a voice in society than I think she has now.' Una's own position in church life became hard;

she remembers being stereotyped and vilified in the years that followed, when she was almost the only woman in England who was prepared to speak openly about her desire to have her vocation to priesthood tested. 'I could see the stereotypes that were building up. I remember going to Southwark Cathedral for an Anglo-Catholic branch gathering of the Church Union, and as I came in the young priest said "Good afternoon, who are you?" and I said "I'm Una Kroll" and he said "Oh—where are your horns?" . . . He really had expected to see some kind of malevolent being, almost an unbeliever. So I think that in 1975 we missed the time.'[7]

AGOW in a higher key

The refusal of General Synod to move ahead led to some developments in the work of The Anglican Group for the Ordination of Women (AGOW). Leading figures were Mollie Batten, Principal of William Temple College, Professor Geoffrey Lampe, Margaret Roxburgh, Betty Ridley, Ruth Batten and Diana McClatchey, as well as a good number of the bishops. Throughout the decade they had been publishing literature and calling upon 'the Bishops and Councils of the Church to consider this whole matter and to take the necessary steps so that, as soon as practicable, it may be possible for women who are called by God, approved by Authority and adequately trained, to be admitted to all the orders of the historic Ministry'. After the 1975 vote, they invited Una Kroll to meetings of their Executive. Dr Daphne Hampson, already a noted feminist theologian and at that time pressing for women to be ordained, was also drawn in for consultation.

The leaders of AGOW, being among those who were encouraged by the success of the 'no fundamental objections' vote rather than dismayed by the failure to take action, began planning for the new Synod, elected in the autumn of 1975, to take things much further. In this, many of them, looking back, feel that the Church was badly let down during that time by the bishops. Instead of setting up programmes of education and discussion in the dioceses and encouraging debate, not to speak of encouraging the kind of visible presence of women which Una Kroll stressed as vital, they seemed to say 'You get on with it'. 'They grumbled away and got nothing going', as one AGOW member said.

By 1978 the General Synod was to vote again. Some dioceses had been holding conferences on women's ministry or even, greatly daring, on women and the priesthood. There had been ecumenical gatherings as well and the Society for the Ministry of Women in the Church was active in linking up women in different areas of work and in the different churches. Jack and Patricia Churchill, in East Anglia and later in Carlisle, helped to foster vocations and encourage the young. Cathedrals also tried to contribute. In Norwich in 1973, a four-day celebration of Julian's 600th anniversary brought women and men from all over the world, including many Roman Catholics. A whole day was devoted to the exploration of 'Women's Ministry in the Church of England—The Present and the Future'. Meanwhile a specifically Roman Catholic organization, St Joan's International Alliance, founded in 1911, was ploughing uphill in its own way.

Early in 1978, AGOW sent to every diocesan bishop study material with which a discussion of women's ordination to the priesthood could be opened up before the Synod debate in November. It is not easy to discover how many bishops did anything about this, but the developments in Newcastle are one example. The bishop, Ronald Bowlby, started at once to look for someone to distribute it, and when Jan Selby and Peter Selby, a Canon at the cathedral, did so and hosted an initial meeting, they found their sitting-room packed to bursting point. Having circulated PCCs and incumbents, they found people arriving from distant parts of the diocese. Many said it was the first time the issue had been raised for them, though they were conscious that they had felt quite strongly on the subject over quite a long period. Out of this grew NOW—the Newcastle group for the Ordination of Women, the first to produce a badge and the first to hand out leaflets before an ordination service.

At that time, 1978, before the national MOW network had been established, this felt quite risky, a rather un-Anglican thing to do, and even those pioneering spirits felt a little nervous. But they established a pattern of vigils in the cathedral before ordinations, and by meeting regularly kept links in place between members of the group and more distant supporters, and also with the diocesan hierarchy. Whereas AGOW had kept in touch with bishops and the Boards of Women's Work, and had never wished to function as a grassroots operation, the Newcastle group for the Ordination of Women lit the touchpaper and set off a flare in the north which was to crackle and dance for years to come.

An earlier event in Newcastle had caused a bigger, national stir. On 16 October 1977, Ian Harker, the Master of the University Church, St Thomas's, and his Church Council invited Alison Palmer, one of the four women ordained irregularly in Washington in 1975, to celebrate the Holy Communion in the church. Although these ordinations had been recognized as valid, the mechanism of the canon law of the Church of England was still only geared to permitting visiting male priests to celebrate in English churches. So Alison Palmer's presiding at a Eucharist in St Thomas's was actually illegal. National publicity resulted, and Bishop Bowlby was pressurized to condemn their action. On 29 October, he wrote to all clergy, deaconesses and lay workers in his diocese. After making it clear that he did not approve of what had happened, and that it was a serious matter, he made three important points, which should be put on record:

a) a Bishop's authority, like a priest's, is primarily spiritual or moral. The obedience we owe one another within the Church is 'in the Lord': that is, it is part of our response to the Gospel which has made us free. There must be a place for the right exercise of conscience, and we must expect that sometimes it will be exercised.

b) all of us need to remember that there is a long history of 'lawlessness' for conscience sake in the Church of England. It is also all too possible to obey the rules outwardly, yet have a very disobedient 'spirit' which can damage the Church's life and witness in many ways.

c) what I long and pray for most of all is that we now face this question: how best can we accept the deep division within our Church over the ordination of women, and so handle it in truthfulness and love that we do not tear ourselves to pieces? We have been given a Gospel of reconciliation: what does this mean in practice? Conflict there is going to be, because it is here already, and it can no more be avoided than the conflict over the Gentiles in the early Church.

Here was a bishop who was trying to hold things together but nevertheless leave some space, who was prepared to underline the claims of conscience in the Christian life and to make every effort to understand both sides of this particular question. Unlike later instances of celebrations in other kinds of settings, there was no doubt that Alison Palmer had celebrated illegally. Newcastle were fortunate to have a bishop who did not simply offer a knee-jerk reaction of hostility and condemnation, but produced a prayerful, thoughtful statement which would allow for development within the Church.

Developing theme

In London, Christian Action and Christian Parity were working in their own ways to raise consciousness. I had just moved in January 1978 from Norwich to London, where Alan, my husband, had been appointed Dean of St Paul's. Across the grass of Amen Court, the small oasis in the City where we lived, were John and Diana Collins, leaders of many campaigns—the Campaign for Nuclear Disarmament and in particular the Anti-Apartheid Movement. One day Diana phoned: Una Kroll and some others would be meeting at no. 2; would I like to come over? This was my introduction to the Christian Parity Group and led me into another stage of involvement in the struggle for women's ordination.

As well as John and Diana Collins and Una, Monica Furlong, Kath Burn and others were there, thinking about ways of influencing the forthcoming vote. Diana and the Christian Action office were working hard on a Declaration to be published before the Synod debate, signed by leading lay men and women in every walk of life. I was pulled in, and soon discovered what a lot of organization this sort of thing entails. The object was to publish a plain statement with signatures from well-known people in all areas of public life, making it clear that this was an important and urgent issue affecting not just the Church of England but the life of the nation as a whole. The promoters of the Declaration were Dame Josephine Barnes, then President-elect of the British Medical Association, Sir Robert Birley, Reith Lecturer and former Headmaster of Eton, the Earl of March, Vice-Chairman of the Archbishops' Commission on Church and State, Sir Bernard Miles, of the Mermaid Theatre, Dame Rosemary Murray, Vice-Chancellor of Cambridge University, Dame Diana Reader Harris,

President of CMS and Chairman of Christian Aid, Lord Red-
cliffe-Maud, Master of University College, Oxford—and Diana
and me. This was the Declaration we prepared:

> During this year of debate within the Anglican Communion we, Anglican
> laymen and laywomen, believe that we should affirm publicly our support,
> not only as a matter of principle, but also as a matter of urgency, for the
> ordination of women to the historic priesthood of the Church of England.

This caused something of a stir, with its surprising list of solid
supporters. Beyond the list of public figures who were signatories
were over a thousand more names, as people heard about it,
found it, copied it, and whole congregations signed up. Had we
set out to prepare a petition we might have been taken aback at
the amount of support that would have surfaced. But that was
not quite the point. In the end just the 100 signatures appeared
as planned, a weighty testimony from lay figures of all kinds,
including many from the theatre and the arts. 'Debrett For
Women Priests', the opposition called it—but we didn't care. Our
list was limited to 100, and it had its effect in the places we were
targeting.

On Wednesday, 8 November 1978, Hugh Montefiore, Bishop
of Birmingham, rose to make his speech moving 'That this Synod
asks the Standing Committee to prepare and bring forward legislation to remove the barriers to the ordination of women to the
priesthood and their consecration to the episcopate'. This time
Dame Betty spoke strongly and movingly in support. The debate
continued all day. A group which included Christian Howard,
Diana McClatchey and the Bishops of Birmingham, Liverpool
and Newcastle had been working in the background, and it
seemed likely that a simple majority would be obtained in all
three Houses. But too many of the clergy were adamant, and too
many of the laity were fearful; the motion was defeated in the
House of Clergy. This was the result: Bishops, 32 Ayes – 17
Noes; Clergy, 94 Ayes – 149 Noes; Laity, 120 Ayes – 106 Noes.
Abstentions, 3.

The motion had been killed in the House of Clergy. Into the
silence that followed the announcement of this result, Una Kroll
gave her now famous cry from the gallery: 'We asked for bread
and you gave us a stone.'[8] The shock of that moment remains:

Una standing there in the gallery with Sue Dowell standing beside her, the cry into the silence. Many people, even supporters, felt at first both shocked and hostile, but afterwards were able to acknowledge this as a protest which had to happen, and respected Una for it. Five years later that respect was shown in Una's election onto the General Synod from the diocese of Chichester.

A new movement

Shortly after the 1978 defeat the group of Synod supporters met. They were clear that the way ahead now must be to open up discussion and debate far more widely all over the country, and to establish a unified movement which would work actively for the ordination of women. By 22 November Diana Collins and I had been invited by Ronnie Bowlby, who was then Chairman of AGOW, to come to a consultation on 21 February which would bring together many of those most concerned.

Christian Howard had prepared for this meeting by writing a long and interesting letter to Una, as well as by producing a discussion paper. The letter lists the priorities as she saw them, but is also very open about the relationship between the more radical groups and a 'mainstream' organization. 'We have to find a way of keeping this as a mainstream group, relating to but not identified with the more radical groupings. My own view is that radical groups need some freedom to act without being controlled from elsewhere and that the mainstream groups do not have to bear the responsibility for what the radicals do. But that all must be kept in touch: we do not want the sort of split between the Suffragettes and the Suffragists that was so tragic for the movement for women's suffrage. (For the record my grandmother was a suffragist and had a house burnt down by the suffragettes for her pains.)'[9]

This suffragist background was an important key in Christian's thinking, as well as her acute political sense: 'I am a political animal', she would rightly say. In fact radicals from different groupings joined and remained within the Movement, often with difficulty and feeling marginalized, while the less radical wrung their hands and wished their sisters and brothers wouldn't jump up and down so much.

The February meeting turned out to be a lively gathering. Through the good offices of Betty Ridley, now Third Estates Commissioner and a DBE, it was held in the Board Room of the Church Commissioners—a spot where most of us had never set foot before, nor were likely to again. And it did assemble the kind of cross-section of opinion that has remained a hallmark of MOW ever since. About half were Synod members, the other half represented national groups such as AGOW, SMWC, Christian Parity, Christian Action, Christian Feminists and the Student Christian Movement. Perhaps for the first time, but certainly not the last, supporters with very different views on how women's ordination would best be achieved were meeting in one room to hammer out their ideas. And they did indeed lay the first plans to set up a national organization. The name was chosen—Movement for the Ordination of Women—and a 'Working Group' was appointed to prepare proposals for a bigger meeting in July at which the new movement would be launched.

The Working Group certainly lived up to its name, judging by the number of letters, memos, draft constitutions, that whizzed back and forth. I now feel contrite seeing letters beginning 'Margaret urges', 'Margaret reminds me that' . . . I wish I could remember if I was doing anything myself to help Christian, our Convenor, as she produced document after document and helped us to think out how a national organization might function effectively. The other members were Diana Collins (who wrote the exposition of the aims and work of the Movement for our first membership form, the text of which has remained virtually unchanged), Kath Burn, Dss Anne Hoad, and Ieuan Davies, chaplain at Queen Mary College, Mile End Road. It is good to see that the first letter from the Working Group came from that address—the chaplaincy which many years later was to give a home to the St Hilda Community, the group which was to explore so fruitfully and then publish non-sexist liturgies.[10] Their story is told in a later chapter.

This letter went out in March 1979, almost immediately after the formation of the Working Group. It was important to show that the issue of women's ordination was not simply going to slide into the sand. Sent to the *Church Times* and to every bishop, dean, provost and many others, it asked 'that April 29th should be regarded as a Sunday on which the ministry of women within the Church should be used as fully as possible as an affirmation of the positive value of this work'. The way the letter continues shows how much needed to be done in many areas of the Church to 'make women visible'.

In a number of Cathedrals and parishes up and down the country women have, with the co-operation of their clergy, already been asked to preach, to assist at the Eucharist, to lead the congregation in prayers, to conduct Mattins and Evensong or a special service. We hope that these examples will be widely followed, and that this may help to introduce an element of realism and of reconciliation into the ongoing debate upon the question of the ordination of women to the priesthood, and their part in ministry.

The letter was signed by the Bishop of Gloucester, John Yates, as Chairman of the 'Accredited Lay Ministry Committee', the Bishop of Newcastle, Ronnie Bowlby, the Deans of Canterbury, Westminster, St Paul's and Carlisle (Victor de Waal, Edward Carpenter, Alan Webster, Jack Churchill) and Colin Craston, Betty Ridley and Geoffrey Lampe, as well as the Working Group. Nothing over the top, nothing difficult, just an eirenic request for the concerted using of women's abilities to raise awareness and assist reconciliation. It shows what a state the Church was in that it was necessary even to make the request, and what a great need there was for the Church to experience more widely the ministry of women. It was that ministry, in all its variety, which sounded the chord which finally moved the Church to make a decision for change.

During the summer of 1979 the Working Group met frequently, joined by Diana McClatchey, Jo Garcia of Christian Feminists, and Trevor Beeson, Canon of Westminster Abbey. More memos, draft constitutions and *aide-mémoires* flew back and forth. Finally, the Movement was launched on 4 July 1979, a date engraved in my mind for ever. The setting this time was the large meeting room of USPG (United Society for the Propagation of the Gospel). Ronnie Bowlby was in the chair. It was a good feeling as people arrived to realize that they were appearing from all over the country—bishops, clergy and lay women and men. Peter Selby, coming down from Newcastle with its already active

NOW group, heard the discussion which they had already been through time and again: 'We must be gracious', and also, 'We must get on with it'; those two voices which were to be part of our lives throughout the campaign that lay ahead.

This tension never seems to have stopped our planning, however, and the Movement for the Ordination of Women was duly launched, with the Bishop of Manchester, Stanley Booth-Clibborn, as first Moderator, Christian Howard and Jo Garcia as Vice-Moderators, and a new Interim Committee.[11] In view of our task, it seemed not inappropriate that our launching meeting had taken place in the building of a famous missionary society.

Notes

1   Una Kroll, in conversation with the author, 1993.
2   Janet Grierson, *The Deaconess* (CIO, 1981), p. 116. The debate referred to took place on 11 November 1977, on *The Ministry of Deacons and Deaconesses: A Report by the Advisory Council for the Church's Ministry* (GS 344).
3   Janet Grierson, ibid, p. 132.
4   Mary Tanner, 'Towards a Theology of Vocation' (1986).
5   Eric James, *A Life of Bishop John A. T. Robinson* (Collins, 1987), pp. 186–7.
6   Kathleen Burn, *The Calling of Kath Burn* (Angel Press, 1988), p. 84.
7   Conversation with author, 1993.
8   Matthew 7.7–11 (JB): 'Ask, and it will be given to you; search, and you will find; knock, and the door will be opened to you. Everyone who asks receives; everyone who searches finds; everyone who knocks will have the door opened. Is there anyone among you who would hand his son a stone when he asked for bread? Or would hand him a snake when he asked for a fish? If you then, evil as you are, know how to give your children what is good, how much more will your Father in heaven give good things to those who ask him!'
9   The National Society for Women's Suffrage, founded in 1867 by Millicent Fawcett, was enlivened in 1903 by the Women's Social and Political Union (WSPU), founded by Emmeline Pankhurst. Described by her as 'a suffrage army in the field', they became known as 'suffragettes' and adopted a militant policy. One of the last surviving suffragettes, imprisoned in Holloway for two months, was Victoria Lidiard, who joined MOW at an early stage and remained a member until her death in October 1992 in her 103rd year.

10 St Hilda Community, *Women Included: A Book of Services and Prayers* (SPCK, 1991).
11 Members of the Interim Committee were Canon Trevor Beeson, Dss Joan Diment, Dss Anne Hoad, Dss Dr Una Kroll, Dr Myrtle Langley, Dss Diana McClatchey, Very Revd Basil Moss, Ven. Michael Perry, Margaret Webster.

4   *Learning about campaigning*

I was brought in to MOW through reading the *Church Times*. Every
Friday I would take a break from working in the University Library,
and would walk over to King's Parade and buy a copy of the CT,
I would read it and then have an attack of high blood pressure, so
in 1980 I joined MOW.[1]

There is a kind of fizz about a new movement or enterprise,
rather like opening a new building or preparing an exhibition.
MOW started five floors up, with one desk, a telephone and the
rattle of the Blackfriars trains shaking the foundations every five
minutes. This was the setting for the first MOW central office,
thanks to Christian Action who offered us a share of their eyrie
at 15 Blackfriars Lane. As I lived close by, it was suggested I
might look in from time to time to check the post. It turned out
to be rather more than that in the end.

Christian Action were our life-savers at the outset, but they
soon moved. In March 1979 we accepted another life-saving offer,
from Bill ('the best thing I ever did') Davidson, Vicar of St
Stephen's, Rochester Row, and his PCC. Thanks to them, MOW
settled in one smallish room in Napier Hall and soon filled every
space and covered every wall. The first press release from that
office states that MOW 'is growing rapidly; forty dioceses now
have active supporters engaged in prayer, study and action, membership has doubled in the past three months and support is
growing daily'. Margaret Orr Deas had joined me, her first foray
back into outside work from family life, and was showing already
that combination of energy, flair, humour and grit which was to
be so important for the development of the movement.

Study, prayer and action. A priority as the movement engaged gear was to enable the subject to be opened up, discussed, thought about. There was a huge gap between those who were really committed and the general 'church well-wisher' who in those days was quite likely to dismiss the subject. 'Well, you're certainly on a sticky wicket' was a comment I often heard at that time.

And some women in ministry were having it very hard. Their position was so painful that sometimes they could not bear to talk about it, and only discovered later the strength that MOW was offering. They were still sometimes excluded from staff meetings, and often not invited to the monthly clergy chapters; they did not regularly administer the chalice and were virtually invisible on major occasions. In fact, it was extraordinary the amount they managed to achieve under these circumstances. But even as they contended with the problems the Church put in their way, many deaconesses were quite content to watch from the sidelines. I know that I found this very difficult; it seemed to me so strange not to be able to throw your lot in with people who were working flat out on your behalf. It was, I knew, largely because of the various myths about banner-bearing strident feminists, which bore little relation to reality and yet frightened people out of their wits. I went early on to a meeting in Cardiff, to find myself being introduced by someone who said, 'Well, I've never actually joined MOW'—at least she pronounced it right to rhyme with 'go'—'because I'm not one for screaming and chaining myself to railings'. It was strange to find myself and my rather serene, thoughtful MOW friends pigeon-holed in this way. One senior woman deacon told me she had been greeted with the words 'Oh, you're the lot who let off fireworks at ordinations . . .'. And so the rather nasty game of Chinese Whispers would go on.

In so far as it frightened off women who were struggling in difficult situations, that was doubly sad, since they deprived themselves of a loving network of support which was both determined and fun. After the founding of MOW I could see, among the women who chose to involve themselves, an easing of some of the pain, as they allowed themselves to draw fresh strength from the movement and began to use their talents in some new ways.

It is hard for women who are trying to be Christians to learn to be campaigners. The very word has caused alarm among churchwomen and ribaldry among churchmen, cloaking their own form of alarm. Words like 'shrill', 'strident' and 'aggressive' were frequently on people's lips when MOW was starting up; if a woman was talking, the preface would be 'We mustn't be . . .'. It would be impossible to count the number of times that MOW speakers have been complimented at the end of an evening with 'and you haven't been at all aggressive . . .'. Sometimes one would long to be aggressive, just to make a change in the vote of thanks.

What we had to learn was our strength, and that it did not depend on anybody's permission. It was not something to be ashamed of, and people often found their strength combined with grace, wit and imagination. And humour. One reason why I think that people have stuck with MOW over so many years of struggle and snail's pace progress is that we have laughed such a lot. Countless times I have trekked out to planning meetings of one kind or another feeling that this was the last straw, and have come home totally rejuvenated. I don't know other church committees where this is the case, though there must be some. Somehow, while being deeply serious, MOW groups had an energy and sparkle that kept us going.

Looking at my 'telephone notes' I can feel again the urgency coming through from MOW contacts. Groups were 'getting joyfully off the ground', as Bristol's Elisabeth Clark put it. Membership forms were being sent out by the hundred, in temporary format before we finally designed that linked, inter-dependent, ichthus-embraced logo. After that people would look at the tiny badge with the linked letters and say 'Ministry of Women?' 'Yes'. 'Movement for the Ordination of Women?' 'Yes'. 'Men and Women?' 'Yes'. And then they would see that the letters are not only intertwined, but can be turned upside down and read the same, so neither is dominant over the other.

Stanley Booth-Clibborn, Bishop of Manchester, was our first Moderator and with blessed determination and acumen got us on the road. His agreement to help us coincided with his appointment to Manchester, where a group immediately voiced their view that this was totally inappropriate for a diocesan bishop. Stanley resisted this pressure: 'I thought about it and I prayed about it, and I came to the conclusion that I could not take that point of view. It seemed to me that bishops in the C of E were there to exercise leadership as they believed God was calling them; this was an important issue and there was no reason at all why my being a diocesan bishop should preclude me from taking a high profile stance on it.' A stand for which we have always been grateful. Many other bishops, especially as the years went on, were only too ready to give support in private but refused to declare themselves in public. But Stanley's grainy voice on the telephone was extremely reassuring, and even as an over-pressed bishop he had a wonderful capacity to respond to ideas and take them further. He remained a valuable episcopal consultant until his retirement, and many of us found that one of the best moments in Dean's Yard after the vote on 11 November was seeing Stanley standing at the top of the steps, rather white and frail after his illness, but joyfully receiving a great cheer for his courageous part in the long struggle.

St Stephen's, Rochester Row, or rather their church 'plant' Napier Hall, was an excellent place to be, within easy distance of Church House, Westminster Abbey, the London Diocesan Office, the Houses of Parliament and the Tate Gallery. We didn't set up the office with sophisticated machinery or design expertise. We had two desks, one telephone, an old duplicator, card-index boxes abandoned by Christian Action, and one big filing cabinet. This was a great surprise to overseas visitors or to the occasional television interviewer such as Edward Sturton, whose face was a picture, coming round the door and seeing our controlled chaos in such a tiny space.

Of course at first we had no money beyond the subscriptions of a few hundred members, £1,500 in pledges and just under £2,000 raised through a semi-successful private appeal to 'prime the pump'. The largest donation MOW ever received was quite late on, a gift from Florence Li of £5,000. There was no secret funding or hidden subsidy and we could not even reclaim tax from covenanted subscriptions. The Charities Commission rules that if the achievement of your objective involves a change in the law then that is 'political', and your organization cannot be a registered charity. MOW therefore did not qualify, whereas every one of the opposing groups could be classed as a charity simply because their campaign was to preserve the status quo! But the giving of MOW members and affiliated parishes continued to go up every year and the 1991–92 special appeal to raise money for printing literature and leaflets raised £20,000. By that time membership had reached 6,000, with a penumbra of 4,000 or so more loosely connected. They were consistently generous; that was what enabled such a volume of work to go ahead.

But our first *Newsletter* was a masterpiece of Do It Yourself, with the old-fashioned, splendidly generous typeface of an elderly typewriter, duplicated on a foggy machine. The next ten *Newsletters* came from different branches—Oxford, Sheffield, Newcastle, Exeter—gradually appearing in a better format. After one or two issues in which a branch's sense of humour was inadequately reflected in cartoon drawings, Monica Furlong, newly-elected Vice-Moderator, took a firm line and an elegant black and white production appeared, properly printed and with good photographs. This was the precursor of *Chrysalis*.

From then on our publications were a serious and important part of our work, taking up a great deal of time and thought. Our Moderator, Stanley Booth-Clibborn, was clear that this was an absolute priority. 'We realized from the start in MOW that we had a tremendous education job to do in the Church of England on this issue. A lot of people were not alert to its importance at all, people tend to accept what they're used to; and also there were a lot of people who felt that it was a peripheral issue. We had to show that it was fundamental to the life of the Church.'

Stephen Burnett's skilful chairing of a Literature Group over eight years, succeeded by Penny Nairne, enabled a diverse group to commission and produce a constant flow of slim but solid booklets.[2] The first of these 'Kairos booklets' came from the Bishop of Salisbury, John Austin Baker, entitled *The Right Time*. It was followed by a wide range of booklets covering the arguments and exploring new territory in a style and a format that were attractive and accessible, and which sold in their thousands. Being easily digestible by PCCs, they put the debate on the map and led people to read and think and discuss. By the end of the long process of discussion and debate, congregations and members of deanery synods had become well informed and had thought out their position quite carefully. The Kairos booklets did an important job, which was followed up in due course by a range of brief, factual leaflets, which were distributed free.

The author with the Revd Emily Odido (*left*) of Kenya and the Revd Deborah Micungwe of Uganda at Canterbury, April 1986

Handing on the light: after the consecration of Bishop Penny Jamieson (*centre*) in Dunedin, she and Bishop Barbara Harris light a miner's lamp for Cathy Milford to bring back to MOW in England

Florence Li Tim Oi in her garden in Hong Kong

Vigil on the steps of St Martin-in-the-Fields, 21 January 1984, after the Westminster Abbey service for the 40th anniversary of the priesting of Florence Li

Caroline Davis (*right*) and Jenny Standage in the MOW office

MOW launching balloons in Norwich to celebrate the enthronement of George Carey as Archbishop of Canterbury, 19 April 1991

Joy outside Church House, 11 November 1992

The house style we were developing was entirely due to the discovery of a wonderful designer–printer in Derbyshire. The Blessed Michael Gregory of West Hallam, as he became known, exerted all his skill as a designer and worked all hours to produce good-looking literature to rather testing deadlines. Leaflets poured off his presses, and in February 1986 the new MOW magazine *Chrysalis* was launched. Original in format, stimulating and informative in content, this magazine, sub-titled 'Women and Religion', blew draughts of fresh air into our lives. Under both Monica Furlong's founding editorship and that of Caroline Davis it has fulfilled an extremely important role.

Learning to work together

During the first years of the 1980s, regions and branches began the long slow business of learning to work together. The first *Newsletter* in October 1979 speaks of regional meetings—Metropolitan, and in the south-west and the north-west; by February 1980 Yorkshire, Manchester, Norwich, and Oxford were announcing diocesan meetings and consultations. Newcastle was already well established with their NOW (Newcastle for the Ordination of Women) group which had been going since 1978. It was a good moment when a letter arrived from Peter Selby saying that NOW was prepared to merge—not at all a foregone conclusion—and much insight and determination that part of the north-east has brought to the struggle ever since.

The first notable public meeting was in Church House, on 26 March 1980, when the Primate of Canada, Archbishop Ted Scott, spoke about the decision to ordain women in Canada, how it had been reached and implemented. His comment on the exceptional work of the early women pioneers, and the respect they had earned, interested us because of the way this seemed to have led to very open and sensitive discussion of the ordination issue at every level. We wondered if the opponents in this country were not aware of the hard and creative work of deaconesses and parish workers since the middle of the last century—also exceptional and often unrecognized. In Canada the first ordinations had taken place in 1976. No parish had left the Church, and only seven priests had resigned, four of whom were not in parish work.

As well as holding meetings, MOW began, diocese by diocese, to witness silently outside cathedrals before ordination services, and sometimes this would be preceded by a vigil. The first all-night vigil I took part in was in Southwark Cathedral before the Michaelmas ordination in 1980. No one who took part in it will forget that time of deep recollection and prayer, nor of spending a night in that full-of-grace cathedral, hearing the trains rattling from London Bridge to Waterloo, the traders re-opening the Southwark market when most people were asleep, and the growing rumble of the early commuters heading for the City by bus and car.

A great number of people took part in the vigil, many more than expected, and the judge who arrived at 11 p.m., taking off his bicycle clips, was as astonished at the numbers as we were pleased at his coming to join us. The following morning, Michaelmas daisies and leaflets were distributed before and after the ordination service.

I am sure it surprised nobody that the handing out of prayer cards or leaflets became a regular part of MOW activity in almost all dioceses, at least until the time when women were being ordained deacon. Knowing as we did many of the ordinands, both male and female, we felt more acutely than usual that 'joy and woe are woven fine'. This was understood and shared by very many of the men being ordained. Having trained alongside women in their theological colleges and courses, they knew how important it was to alert the congregation at an ordination that something was amiss. Not everyone coming to support a new deacon or priest was really aware of the painful position of the deaconesses who year after year watched the men being ordained into holy orders and then, twelve months later, being priested. Many of the ordinands on the other hand, were very sensitive to this. A letter arrived out of the blue in July 1981:

> I write as one of those ordained priest this Petertide in Bristol Cathedral. Far from being 'distressed' by MOW's efforts to bring to the attention of those attending the service the pain of those women who feel called to serve God as priests in the Church of England, I was extremely impressed by the sensitivity, compassion and thoughtfulness with which MOW commended them to our prayers. This 'demonstration' (if it can

be called that) did nothing to impair my enjoyment of what was, naturally, a moving occasion; if anything, it added a poignant depth to my appreciation of its significance. For as a priest (indeed, as a Christian) I am not called to a facile and selfish joy. I am also called to weep with those who weep.[3]

It was necessary to publish that because of the anxieties of those who felt that any kind of witness would 'spoil the men's special day'. And there was in fact a great deal of variation in the ways different MOW branches would choose to witness, some—like Southwark—working with the bishop to have the situation recognized during the service itself, others deciding to leave the whole area of silent witness unexplored.

Newcastle's group NOW were the first with their all-night vigil in the cathedral and leafleting of the congregation outside. Then Monica Furlong took more dramatic action, off her own bat but supported by seven others. Her silent protest inside St Paul's in July 1980 forced MOW to think out what were the best ways of witnessing on these occasions. In *Chrysalis* of January 1993, Monica looked back on their act of witness:

> Eight of us went to the Petertide ordination at St Paul's and held up banners asking for women's ordination. Despite our silence and general decorum we were thrown out of the Cathedral, and one of us was struck repeatedly by one of the wandsmen. Such happenings were so unusual that the action got into most of the newspapers, and on to radio and TV, thus giving us a chance to put our case. Robert Runcie invited us to Lambeth to put the case to him too.

Needless to say, this unexpected event focused the minds of the MOW Interim Committee, who were meeting regularly with the Bishop of Manchester, Stanley Booth-Clibborn, in the chair, and preparing for the first AGM and elected Committee. Some anxious representations had been received from MOW members who were unhappy about the publicity, and found even a silent demonstration in a church distinctly worrying. The resulting note in the September 1980 *Newsletter* conveys well MOW's own anxiety about overt 'action' while at the same time being very clear that no one part of our movement must disown another: 'Where local groups feel leafleting is appropriate, this should be carefully planned, the Bishop, Dean and Chapter being approached in good time and the ordinands informed. A vigil of prayer during the preceding night may be appropriate.'

Fairly lily-livered and tentative, perhaps, and the glaring omission is any word of support for the action in St Paul's. But at that stage it seemed impossible for the rather delicate, anxious plant which MOW was to 'own' any kind of demonstration, even a silent one, actually inside a church, and the object was to encourage branches (also, after all, rather tender and delicate at this time) to undertake an act of witness which would be right for them. Immediately members did begin to plan vigils and leafleting, handing out flowers and short statements ending with a prayer, sometimes carrying a banner. The clergy and the ordinands would now be informed in advance, which took away the shock and horror felt by clergy when something happens unexpectedly in their church. One even finds comments that 'the committee has had much help from the Bishop, Provost/Dean and Chapter in making the arrangements'.

MOW was determined to try to weave together, from the very first days, different strands of conviction under an umbrella of freedom that was hard to find within the established Church. Archdeacon Michael Perry, writing in our second *Newsletter*, of March 1980, had already made this clear: 'MOW realizes that public opinion is changed by a number of means, demonstrations as well as quiet persuasion. The Movement deliberately contains those who, though they share a common purpose, differ in their opinions as to the most effective means to that end. If it is to represent the whole church, it will need to be catholic in its membership.' And so it has been. Some have departed, probably also giving up the Church in sad despair, and a few from the more conservative end of the spectrum, but the rest of us stayed together, argued, persuaded, wept, laughed and prayed. We all changed, and learnt a good deal about trying to listen and understand.

In the process of quarrying the necessary grit and determination, women members in particular found their resolve strengthened. For the St Paul's leafletings, I always used to wear a hat for courage. On one occasion I was outside the less-used south door at the top of the steps as the Bishop, Graham Leonard, came up. 'Well, Margaret, what have you got for me today?' We were both slightly amused at ourselves, I think. But later outside that door, just as I was going inside, I found one of the young London deaconesses standing there, tears pouring down her cheeks, and trying to brace herself to go in and join the service. 'Margaret, I can't stand much more of this', she said. As I spent some time with her then, the seriousness of our task hit me afresh. Later, kneeling under the dome, I was surprised to find myself keeling over on to the black and white marble floor. It wasn't very important, and I soon revived, but it was a tiny indication of what we were all going through.

I may be accused of falling into the 'media trap' in giving all this space to our efforts at ordinations, at the expense of the year-in-year-out patient work that was going on all over the country. But there is an appropriateness in giving some emphasis to that early time of vigils and leafleting. For those who took part it *was* a test which gave a solidity to our commitment. Also, we found that the level of support from people coming to the services both surprised (at first) and encouraged us. And the process of prayerful preparation was important, as each branch worked out its statement and wrote its prayers.

Looking out and looking in

Monica Furlong's influence was enormously important as the movement was finding its identity. An established writer, Monica became Vice-Moderator of MOW in September 1981, shortly after the publication of her classic biography of Thomas Merton,[4] and a year later succeeded the Bishop of Manchester as Moderator. By now surprising events were beginning to happen which drew in new support and increased membership. The Festival of Women at St James's, Piccadilly, in 1981 was the first example, an all-day happening opened by Mary Stott with a short lecture and ending with evening worship led by Una Kroll. There was an exhibition inside the church—'The Wonder and the Woe'—and stalls on the forecourt. A very merry occasion until a spectacular cloudburst washed us all away. However, the best was yet to come: 'After Eve—A Happening', written and produced by Monica.

Anybody who came to 'After Eve' knowing its author would have been expecting a good evening's entertainment; what took people by surprise was the huge feeling of relief as the cast proceeded to dismantle so much of the edifice erected over centuries to keep women down. In this production, as in the later 'Her and Her', a powerful mix was stirred up, from some of the most misogynist sayings of the early Fathers to the familiar latter-day pronouncements. Both the cruelty and the absurdity were exposed. Above all, we relished the seasoning of wit and irreverence, and found it freeing in a very important way. To be able to laugh so much at what had seemed so threatening showed us once and for all the power of humour to take away fear. Not only that, the whole Festival of Women showed us what support there was in many different places for the women and men who were struggling with this particular issue in the Church; it was a new and huge encouragement.

Gradually the planning and the inner life of each branch, each diocesan group grew and deepened. This was without any doubt the key to the development of MOW's work. As people have recently been reflecting on what they have most valued in their association with MOW, they have emphasized the new strength they experienced in many different ways. Pamela Faull, from Chester diocese, wrote: 'The friendship and sisterhood. The encouragement to come out of the pews, and the affirming of talents and opportunities to use them. New ways of worship and spirituality. Large gatherings and celebrations. The opportunities of closeness which bridged the generation gap between my daughters and me.'

From London, understandably: 'A sense that there is breathe-able air in London diocese. Sometimes you begin to feel the whole show belongs to raving misogynists, but then you go to a MOW meeting and are reminded that this isn't so.' Another member was more specific: 'What MOW did that was so exciting was for women who had been part of the Church all their lives, who were cradle Anglicans, who had felt uncomfortable but had never really come out with that discomfort because there was no place to express it—suddenly they found that within the Church there *was* a place to express their discomfort. They had felt there was a straitjacket put on, that they couldn't move spiritually, or that the way they were moving inside wasn't right—and then here were these groups where people were expressing the same thing, and wasn't this amazing? You weren't the only person who had these deep feelings but had sat on them because there was no way of dealing with them.'

Bonds of prayer

For many women and men within MOW the on-going prayer enfolding its life was something of a revelation. The first 'Wilderness Liturgies', often held out of doors, were born out of alienation and pain but were strangely strengthening, with their sharing of milk and honey cake and strong sense of the hope and faith of an exiled community.

As each branch grew and, in diocese after diocese, developed its own ways of prayer, lovely celebrations began at times like Juliantide, the days around 8 May. This was the day newly appointed in the Church of England Calendar for the remembrance of Julian of Norwich, the fourteenth-century anchorite, mystic and first woman to write a book in English. For MOW and for hundreds of others from 1983 onwards this proved to be an occasion for joyful celebration of the work and ministry of women through the ages, as well as for meditation on the wisdom of Julian. The Dean and Chapter of St Paul's Cathedral gathered 500 members of women's religious communities, both Anglican and Roman Catholic, for a special service. 'Julian reminds us', said the Dean of St Paul's[5] in his sermon, 'that the insights of women have always enriched the Church from the time of Deborah and Ruth . . . to the women who are offering their gifts of prophecy, love and service today.' In Norwich the Julian Shrine was the centre for a pilgrimage which provided 'a still centre of prayer' to the network of events in dioceses spanning the country from Durham and York to Canterbury, from Bristol to Lincoln. In addition to these special services, many MOW members continued to draw sustenance from the broader-based Julian Meetings, groups for contemplative prayer founded by Hilary Wakeman in Norwich in 1973, which rapidly spread nation-wide.[6]

At this time MOW in the north of England rose up for celebration of Julian, Hilda of Whitby and other great and good women. Eighteen months had gone into the preparation of their gatherings: 'MAGNIFICAT' in Durham Cathedral at the end of April, and the Pilgrimage of Grace in York a week later drew people from ten northern dioceses. All these were like the first planks in a raft of prayer which was to uphold the life of the Movement for the next nine years. As well as the great national occasions which took place during those years—in Westminster Abbey, Canterbury and Coventry cathedrals, all of which were both solemn and joyous—each diocese had a particular day in the month for remembering their women deacons and all our hopes. New forms of worship were explored, new liturgies thought about, with a freshness and creativity that extended, when Catherine Milford became Moderator in 1988, to worship at a central point during Central Council meetings. After half the business was dealt with, we would have silence, movement, singing, the Bible, prayer. The bonds formed through these meetings were stronger than the controversies that were often faced.

This sense of having embarked on a new pilgrimage of spiritual growth has been expressed over and over again, both by men and by women members of MOW. Bishop Peter Selby has written:

> As I look back on that period of my life I am strongly aware of having been held in membership of a Church-on-the-way, and I can see there the foreshadowing of some kind of future model for the Church. For me the group held promise of a kind that was missing in so much of the day to day life of the official Church, whose liturgy and life claimed so much.[7]

Sometimes it would be the occasional big act of worship or other gathering which would inspire and stimulate, but somehow the regular meetings—for all the necessity to make plans or to resolve tensions—do seem to have been an extraordinary source of strength and vision. Even the conflicts could provoke new insights; for many people it was the first experience of conflict in a 'church' setting being faced out in the open, looked at, listened to, and resolved in some way without blandness, dishonesty, or disruption.

> The group, though beset by many very ordinary difficulties, found that its common life was affected deeply by the issue with which it was primarily concerned. Whether we wanted it to or not, the group had to consider how the fact that it was a group for the ordination of women would affect its style of meeting, its way of worshipping and its exercise of concern for its members. . . . The grace of mutuality seemed intrinsic to our task. So also, we found we had to find ways of combining a

strength of conviction with a gentleness of execution—qualities which elsewhere seem to pull in quite opposite directions.[8]

Monica Furlong's Moderatorship helped us to realize that the Church could discover new, genuinely creative ways of dealing with disagreement. Succeeding Stanley Booth-Clibborn, she gave endless time and thought to every aspect of the work. Her combination of deep conviction with an irreverent sense of humour brought a freshness to MOW's thinking that I wouldn't have missed for the world.

Notes

1 The Revd Dr Judith Maltby, Corpus Christi College, Oxford, in conversation with the author, 1993.

2 MOW's publication list was extensive:

Rt Revd John Austin Baker, *The Right Time*; Most Revd (then Dr) George Carey, *Women and Authority in the Church*; Janet Morley, *In God's Image?*; Rt Revd Oliver Tomkins, *A Fully Human Priesthood*; John and Gillian Muddiman, *Women, the Bible and the Priesthood*; Revd Dr Joyce Bennett, *It Happened in Xing Xing*; Alexina Murphy and Fr Philip Holdsworth, *Hoping for Women Priests: Letters from Two Roman Catholics*; Rosemary Wakelin, *Call Accepted: Reflections on Women's Ordination in the Free Churches*; Alyson Peberdy, *A Part of Life: A Study of Lay-people's Response to Women's Ministry in the Church of England*; Michael Futers, *A Legitimate Development: An Anglican Catholic Case for the Ordination of Women to the Priesthood*; Janet Morley and Hannah Ward, *Celebrating Women: A Worship Resource Book*; Janet Morley, *All Desires Known: A Collection of Prayers, Litanies, Canticles*. Earlier 'Occasional Papers' included: Lydia Speller, *Theological Objections?*; Professor Richard Norris, *The Ordination of Women and the 'Maleness' of Christ*; Christian Howard, *Women in Society and the Church*; Sr Teresa Dss CSA, *Anglican/Orthodox Relations and the Ordination of Women*; Sr Lorna Brockett RCSJ, *The Ordination of Women—A Roman Catholic Viewpoint*; Mary Michael Simpson OSH, *The Ordination of Women in the American Episcopal Church*; Rt Revd Simon Phipps, *Priesthood and Humankind*.

3 Letter from Peter Clarke, MOW *Newsletter* (July 1981), p. 21.

4 Monica Furlong, *Merton: A Biography* (Harper & Row, 1980).

5 Alan Webster, Dean of St Paul's 1978–87.

6 Julian of Norwich, *Revelations of Divine Love*, ed. Clifton Wolters (Penguin Classics, 1966). See also *Enfolded in Love: Daily Readings with Julian of Norwich*, ed. Robert Llewelyn (Darton, Longman & Todd, 1980).

7   Peter Selby, 'They make such good pastors' in *Who Needs Feminism?*, ed.
    Richard Holloway (SPCK, 1991), p. 128.
8   Peter Selby, ibid., pp. 128–9.

5   *The slow-burning fuse*

> We believe that God is using China's age-long respect for women,
> and traditional confidence in women's gifts for administration and
> counsel, to open a new chapter in the history of the Church.[1]

Early in the life of MOW more and more people began to
realize that the question of women's ordination was enormously
important not only for the Church of England but also beyond.
It deeply touched people who had little time for church matters.
It was a justice issue, and while for Christians that meant the
justice they discovered in the Gospel, for countless others it
seemed clear that they could not listen to the Church and its
sermons until this fundamental flaw in its own life had been
addressed. So we knew it was not something that was going to
go away.

At the same time, people were aware that this was not a matter
affecting the Church of England only. It was on the agenda for
the Anglican Communion, and in some parts had been dealt with
already. The Movement owed a lot, from the start, to those who
encouraged us to keep our eyes above the local and the immediate
and to remember always that when the decision to move was
achieved it would be a step forward, not just for the Church of
England but for the society in which we lived and for the family
of Anglican Churches beyond.

The story of the very first Anglican woman priest is now familiar
to many, but remains an inspiration. The letter in front of me,
its ink now fading, is dated 27 January 1944. During this time of
war, when much of China was occupied by the Japanese, Bishop

R. O. Hall of Hong Kong and South China, wrote to two friends in Britain:

> Twelve miles away from the Japanese, but not going to give myself up, so don't worry. But this is to ... give you the facts. On St Paul's Day 1944 I ordained a Chinese woman as 'a priest in the Church of God'. She works in an isolated city and came through the Japanese lines at considerable risk to meet me. For four years she has been in charge of a congregation, and both spiritually and practically she has been a most successful pastor, both to men and women. She is 35. She took the same course of study in the Theological College as all our men pastors. Before Hong Kong fell, Bishop Mok used to go to her city to celebrate Holy Communion. After Hong Kong fell it was no longer possible for him or any other priest to visit her Church. He therefore authorized her to celebrate Holy Communion. As soon as I got back I confirmed his action and have informed all my brother Bishops of the Church of Hong Kong and South China that, if it proved possible for us to meet, I should ordain her priest ... The reason in this case is 1) During war it is the only way in which nearly 100 communicants can receive the Sacrament and in peace time it means that one more congregation will receive the sacrament from its own priest; 2) She has amply proved (like Cornelius[2]) that she has the pastoral charisma; 3) Perhaps it is better ordination of women for an experimental period should come in this way out of need and out of gift than out of theoretical discussion on equality of men and women.

Bishop Hall was convinced that it was more irregular for someone not in priest's orders to celebrate than for him to ordain a woman, and repeated at the end of his letter that 'this was necessary in order that my people should have the sacraments regularly administered'.

At the same time as this was written, to William Greer and Tissington Tatlow,[3] a similar letter was dispatched to Archbishop William Temple, in which Bishop Hall spoke of having 'an amazing feeling of quiet conviction about this'. He knew, from the many refugees from Macao who spoke to him in his temporary base at Chungking, that Florence Li for about two years had been working as a priest in all but name. One person after another described to him how she was providing, with a minimum of resources, an extraordinary ministry to the sick, the dying and the destitute. This led him to the conviction that this person, doing the work of a priest, must be ordained priest.

In order to meet, both Bishop Hall and Florence had to make a long and difficult journey. They had arranged to meet at Xing-Xing, for Florence a week's journey at walking pace, through dangerous Japanese-held China to 'Free' China, a journey over mountains, and through what she has described as 'dark, wild wilderness', sometimes carried by two chair-men who carried her sedan and protected her. The Bishop travelled from Chungking, five days' journey by foot and boat. To their astonishment they arrived at the meeting-place within half an hour of each other. They then spent two days in prayer, talk and questioning before travelling to what Florence has described as a 'small, old Anglican church. It was a very beautiful place. The wider issues of the ordination of women were far from my mind as I entered the little church. I was being obedient to God's call. The notion that this step I was taking would be controversial and have worldwide repercussions was something that never occurred to me until after I had returned to Macao and the war was over.'4

Florence was able to function fully as an ordained priest for about 18 months. The news of her ordination reached the world outside through the children's page of a New Zealand missionary magazine *The Gleaner*. The *Church Times* naturally picked this up and the editor, Dr G. L. Prestige, wrote to Archbishop William Temple asking what Lambeth proposed to do. Temple's reply is important, in view of later developments: he advised taking a calm, firm line, but ended 'If we could find any shadow of theological ground for the non-ordination of women, I should be immensely comforted, but such arguments as I have heard on that line seem quite desperately futile'.5 He also wrote in his own hand to R. O., a letter which arrived after Temple's death, saying 'Whatever I may think of what you have done, it makes no difference to my affection for you'.

Temple never signed the official letter of reprimand. The question now is whether it represents his mind on this matter. His biographer, F. A. Iremonger, credits him with these words: 'Personally I want (as at present advised) to see women ordained to the priesthood.' But Geoffrey Fisher, Bishop of London, was becoming increasingly involved in this controversy because of the Archbishop's failing health. Fisher was always anxious about legalities. Did Temple actually write this letter? Had he drafted it and then, having second thoughts, decided not to send it? Or, as he was a sick man, was it drafted for him? It is curious, as was pointed out in a General Synod debate in 1975, that the official letter, legalistic in tone, does not mention the letter which Temple had himself written earlier. Fisher signed the official letter, and publicly endorsed it at the next meeting of Convocation.[6] Temple had died without having brought himself to acknowledge the Cornelius principle in R. O.'s action.[7]

Geoffrey Fisher, who succeeded Temple, did have some conversation with Bishop Hall when R. O. came home in July 1945. Fisher asked him to suspend Li Tim Oi. He pressed the point that the Anglican Communion would be 'shattered', and the ecumenical movement also endangered since 'the Orthodox would not stand for it'.[8] The appeal for post-war reconstruction in China might be endangered.

But Bishop Hall refused to suspend Florence, and wrote a long letter to Fisher, laying out the circumstances of her ordination once more and giving the reason for his refusal: 'I have only one reason. I acted in obedience to our Lord's commission. I do not believe He wishes me to undo what I have done.'[9]

Now they got at Florence. Summoned to meet her archdeacon, she was told that if she continued official priestly duties, her bishop's position was going to be made impossible. She must have entered another kind of wilderness as it was made clear to her that if she did not cease to function as a priest, Bishop Hall would have to resign. She wrote to him at once: 'I would like to keep quiet to help the church. You are an important man. I am a mere worm, a tiny little worm.' This phrase, so difficult for Western ears, came from one whose selflessness was matched by enormous courage, a tiny lion, we might prefer to say. As Joyce Bennett points out, Florence never resigned her orders as a priest: 'She recognized what the Church has called the indelible nature of Holy Orders. This spiritual gift cannot be erased. She continued in her work for her Lord whatever the Church elsewhere said about her ordination.'[10]

After Florence had offered her resignation and it had been accepted, R. O. Hall was admonished by the 'Chinese' House of Bishops, mostly Westerners. Out of ten colleagues only one voted for him and two abstained. But he remained sure he was right in

his decision to ordain. It was a decision typical of a radical
Catholic, foreshadowing some of the Hispanic liberation theologians' understanding of the Church.

The Synod of his diocese of Hong Kong and South China
meanwhile sent out a strongly worded statement:

> Members of the Church found the attitude of the Church in the West
> impossible to understand. The Reverend Li Tim Oi's ordination
> seemed to them natural and inevitable. She has shown in her life and
> work that God has given her the 'charisma' of the parish priest.
>
> It is our belief that the action taken by Bishop Mok in licensing Li
> Tim Oi to celebrate the Lord's supper, and Bishop Hall's action later in
> ordaining her to the priesthood were God inspired. We believe that God
> is using China's age-long respect for women, and traditional confidence
> in women's gifts for administration and counsel, to open a new chapter
> in the history of the Church. It is noteworthy that Chinese motherhood
> has always been more remarkable in counsel and leadership than in
> nurture of babies, i.e. essentially pastoral rather than maternal. We
> believe that the Western Churches should expect new things such as
> this to happen under God's providence, when Christianity really begins
> to take root in a civilization as mature as that of China.

After stating that 'the whole Church in South China has been
spiritually wounded and grieved in heart' they ended with the
declaration: 'We consider such discrimination against women in
the Church of Jesus Christ, unreasonable, unchristian, and
unscriptural.'

They were also responsible for the first motion sent to a General Synod asking for the possibility of women's ordination to the
priesthood; no action was taken, but Lambeth 1948 was asked to
consider the question. A negative resolution was passed and there,
as David Paton says, 'most hoped, and many supposed, was an
end of the matter'.

Florence, however, continued to work in the Chinese Christian
Church until the communists came to power, when her church
was closed and all pastors had to undertake hard manual labour.
Florence had to work in what was to all intents and purposes a
free-range chicken factory, carrying water long distances, under
threat if the chickens died. After the Cultural Revolution ended,
she took part in the new growth and building up of the Chinese

Church until she retired and joined the rest of her family in Canada in 1981.

The Tiny Lion comes to England

'Remember that the mark of a revolutionary organization is to be able to *move fast* . . . Goodbye.' David Paton's voice on the line from Gloucester. Once again the searching question, the timely reminder from this former China missionary, far-sighted radical theologian and parish priest. It was he, of course, who picked up the phone one day in 1983 to ask us if we had realized that January next year would be the 40th anniversary of the first ordination of a woman to the priesthood in the Anglican Communion.

We did move fast, wanting to prepare a fitting honouring for this brave woman, priest for 40 years, so badly treated by the hierarchy of the Anglican Communion and yet remaining so full of grace. Two services were planned, one at Westminster Abbey, on 21 January 1984, and one in Sheffield Cathedral on 28 January. An enormous amount of work went on in both places in the months before January, resulting in celebrations which mirrored the two elements in MOW—the national and international areas of our life, and the grass-roots experimental searching.

To our joy, Florence came over from Canada to be with us. A tiny figure, she processed into the Abbey with the Revd Dr Joyce Bennett OBE—the first Englishwoman to be ordained priest, also in Hong Kong, and the preacher on this occasion. Now retired, she was licensed by the Bishop of London to the Chinese community in St Martin-in-the-Fields. A thousand people filled the nave of the Abbey, pouring in as the Dean, Edward Carpenter, called for more and more extra chairs. Alan Wilson, the Director of Music at the University Church of Christ the King, was in the organ loft with 30 students, and in the quiet before the service started they sang the setting he had composed for us of words of Julian of Norwich.

Our faith is a light; By this light our Mother Christ and our good Lord the Holy Spirit lead us in this fleeting life. God did not say 'You shall not be tempest-tossed, you shall not be work-weary, you shall not be discomforted'. But God said 'You shall not be overcome'. Alleluia.

Not only the words are unforgettable, but so also was the unaccustomed sound of a single soprano voice probing the heights of the Abbey with the first lovely phrase. The anthem was a gift of Alan Wilson's to MOW, dedicated to that occasion, sung in cathedrals many times since then.

Anybody who has tried to plan a special service in a cathedral knows how the grandeur and the feeling of tradition can either enhance or reduce to nothing any attempts to produce worship which is fresh and feels different. But even in a traditional ASB (Alternative Service Book) Eucharist, which this was, it is possible for signs and signals to give people the feeling of at least some new ways ahead. The soprano voice opening the worship was one of these signals, and the next came with the processions. Processions in the past tended to emphasize hierarchy and separateness, and we did not want that; on the other hand, we needed something to mark the fact that here was a great gathering of bishops, priests, deaconesses and lay people coming together for the first time under the umbrella of MOW. So we decided that 'the procession' should be for the deaconesses, supported by bishops and overseas women priests, by the representatives of the Archbishop of New Zealand, and the 'collegiate body' of Westminster Abbey. The male clergy agreed to come in first and sit in alternate seats; as they sat near the altar waiting for the women to join them, the empty chair beside each man seemed to speak of the gaps in priestly ministry, and the men themselves said they felt this powerfully. The Dean then read the message from the Archbishop of Canterbury: 'It is with a deep sense of gratitude for your Christian witness and ministry that I send greetings to you on the 40th anniversary of your ordination to the priesthood.' Later Florence visited Robert Runcie at Lambeth.

The celebrant was Bishop Gilbert Baker of Hong Kong, successor to R. O. Hall who ordained Florence. Everyone was clear that he was the one man whom it was right to ask to preside. Gilbert was the quiet and rather conservative bishop who ordained Joyce Bennett and Jane Hwang in 1971, having obtained the appropriate permission from the Anglican Consultative Council.

This courageous act was taken out of deep conviction of the calling of these women to priesthood and the rightness of it in that situation; both were deacons and educators, and Joyce an elected member of the Hong Kong Legislative Council from 1976 till she left in 1983. This also ensured that Florence's ordination was not to be hidden away, buried, or regarded as an aberration, due to a time of emergency. It was to honour all these pioneering spirits that MOW members and countless others poured into the Abbey that January morning, to experience a joyful solidarity with other parts of the Anglican Communion which filled us with hope for the future.

The Gospel was read in Chinese by Florence and in English by Kath Burn, and three generations of women's ministry in the Church and within MOW were represented both in the offertory and in the intercessions. The administration of the sacrament by Florence and the other women priests present was profoundly moving, as more than a thousand people came up to receive Communion.

It was nearly 2 o'clock when we left the Abbey for St Martin-in-the-Fields, where Joyce Bennett's Chinese Christian congregation had prepared a steaming meal which seemed to feed hundreds. So everyone was able to mix around together and hear Florence speak to us. I have her handwritten words in front of me:

Since I am a very tiny person, a mere worm, and my influence is very small, to me a celebration of such grandeur came as a great surprise which had not been dreamed of.

How wonderful we had the successor of Bishop R. O. Hall, Bishop Gilbert Baker, to preside at the service, and the Revd Joyce Bennett gave us a splendid and inspiring sermon. It was a memorable event, and the crowded congregation was an impressive tribute. The Archbishop's personal letter to me moved me deeply. The beautiful and long procession of the clergy seemed exactly to represent the angels of Heaven. It led me to feel that I really heard the voices of countless angels . . . 'Myriads upon myriads there were, thousands upon thousands and they cried aloud: Worthy is the Lamb, the Lamb that was slain, to receive all power and wealth, wisdom and might, honour and glory and praise!'

The celebration of the 40th anniversary of my ordination has given me a chance to do an honest self-examination and to review my past

services as God's servant. In so doing, I have found that I have had
many weaknesses, and that some things I have done have fallen short
of His expectations. However, I know God is love. I know He will forgive
me for my human shortcomings and failures in some of my duties, and
will help to strengthen me and give me more wisdom so that I can serve
Him better in the days to come.

On this occasion, I have to thank God not only for preserving me, but
also for giving me new life, a new spirit and a new opportunity to help
spread His good tidings. It is my hope that I can dedicate the rest of
my life to raise high the Glorious Cross of salvation with my brothers
and sisters in Christ, and to spread widely the Holy Gospel and to win
friends for Jesus Christ. Amen.

In those moments, as Florence spoke, we experienced someone
coming to us with true humility and true authority, a tiny lion of
both sweetness and strength. There was applause, but also a need
for silence and we began withdrawing to the church for some
quiet. Later, as dusk fell, we filed out on to the steps, all being
given a torch and the service paper for our 'Liturgy of Hope' and
the torchlight vigil. Pamela Maggs, a deaconess in London, had
written this call to root our conviction in praise. 'It is the God
whom we worship who is calling women to priesthood. It is the
Christ whom we praise who is offering to his Church the gift and
the revelation of a richer priesthood.'

It was a complete and an extraordinary experience that followed.
Hundreds of us, spilling all down the steps as well as standing
among the pillars, singing, praying, almost in the midst of the
London rush-hour traffic. A huge golden banner, 'Ordain Women
Now', had been up all day, stretched across the pillars during the
morning by the indefatigable Joyce Meadows and her architect
husband. It looked wonderful. 'We think it was 32 feet long by
three or four feet deep', Joyce remembers. 'We made it by stretch-
ing it right across the floor at the back of the church. Robert did
the lettering—then we both painted it. At St Martin's we
borrowed a ladder. The banner had strings attached which we
fixed, some to the gates but most to the pillars. The verger and
I held the banner while Robert shinned up the ladder to tie the
strings.'[11]

There we all stood, singing, under this great proclamation. The
cars stopped at the lights, their drivers peered at us, hooted,

waved. We sang on. People came to join us. And then there was an amazing 'Whooosh!'—and another—and another, as six rockets shot up over Trafalgar Square, one for each Province in which women were being ordained priest—Hong Kong, the United States, Canada, New Zealand, Kenya and Uganda. Everyone was transfixed. Something about that surge of power and light into the darkness summed up how we were feeling. Only I knew that my daughter Alison had got the rockets down to the church that morning, and Nick Henderson, Vicar of St Mary's, Bow, was quietly setting them off in the providential little paved space behind the church. He chose exactly the right moment; just as the last rocket was launched, up came a policeman: 'Sorry, sir, you're not allowed to do that here.' But it was done.

The next week Florence's anniversary was celebrated again in the north, with another great service in Sheffield Cathedral. Hilary Bagshaw wrote interestingly about the contrast between the two events, making some points we needed to take on board.

> This service was smaller, more intimate, attracting virtually no interest from the national press ... The Abbey service was a grand and formal occasion. It reinforced MOW's position as a politically credible organization in the eyes of the Church of England, not to be dismissed as 'the product of a lunatic fringe'. However, one comment by Rosemary Hartill ... was that it demonstrated how little would change if women were admitted to the ordained ministry. The Sheffield service in contrast was an attempt to develop a new sort of worship where women and men, laity and priests, participated on an equal footing. Much of the service was written specially for the occasion, and was an expression of individuals' responses to God to be shared with the whole congregation ... The central lesson ... is that MOW needs to put greater emphasis on what is new and creative. We need more and diverse demonstrations of worship involving a *whole* ministry. Without this the movement will become sterile and lose its momentum.[12]

These comments were timely and foreshadowed the need an increasing number of people were to feel for fresh springs in worship and some searching exploration of questions of authority and joint ministry.

Florence died in Canada on 27 February 1992, aged 84, and along with members of the Chinese community in London, and with her family, we remembered her with joy and thanksgiving in

St Martin-in-the-Fields later in the year. I remembered her visit
to London in 1984, and travelling with her in the train to Canterbury in 1986 for the 'Joining Hands Across the Anglican Communion' celebration of women's ministries. She came again in
1988 for the Lambeth Conference and, then aged 80, joined in
the march round St Paul's, when we stopped the traffic as all the
Lambeth bishops and their wives were emerging from the service.
I remembered how she talked with everybody, holding their hand,
smiling, focused. In 1989 I saw her in Boston, USA, where she
was one of the concelebrants following the consecration of Barbara Harris as bishop. As Caroline Davis said in *Chrysalis*, 'In
her quiet patience and persistence in spite of persecution she has
been an example and a beacon of hope to us all'.[13]

Notes

1 From a statement passed unanimously by the Synod of Hong Kong and
South China in 1946.

2 The 'Cornelius Principle' refers to St Peter's unprecedented decision
to receive hospitality from and to baptize the Gentile centurion Cornelius, and only afterwards to consult the apostles at Jerusalem. At first
they protested, but after hearing St Peter's account of the gift of the
Spirit to the Gentiles, gave glory to God (Acts 10.1 – 11.18).

3 Both Tissington Tatlow and William Greer had been General Secretar-
ies of the Student Christian Movement and were close friends of R. O.
Hall. William Greer became Bishop of Manchester 1946–70.

4 Ted Harrison, *Much Beloved Daughter* (Darton, Longman & Todd,
1985), p. 45.

5 David Paton, '*R. O.*': *The Life and Times of Bishop Hall of Hong Kong*
(Diocese of Hong Kong and Macao, 1985), p. 132.

6 Jacqueline Field-Bibb, *Women Towards Priesthood: Ministerial Politics and
Feminist Praxis* (Cambridge, 1991), p. 135 and footnote 50. Canon Paton
and Mr Harrison also examine the question of the letters. See Ted
Harrison, *Much Beloved Daughter*, pp. 56–8 and David Paton, '*R. O.*',
pp. 134–8.

7 For an account of Fisher's part in censuring Bishop Hall, see Edward
Carpenter, *Archbishop Fisher, His Life and Times* (Canterbury Press,
1991), pp. 661–7.

8 David Paton, '*R. O.*', p. 135.

9 David Paton, ibid.

10 Joyce Bennett, *It Happened in Xing Xing* (MOW, 1984).

11 Joyce Meadows, letter to author, 1993.

12   Hilary Bagshaw, 'Towards a Whole Ministry', MOW *Newsletter* (June 1984).

13   *Chrysalis* (July 1992).

6 *Family and friends*

Whatever future ministry I might have as a priest, it was given to me that day to be a symbol of healing. All the strands of my life came together. Descendant of slave and of slave-owner, I had already been called poet, lawyer, teacher, and friend. Now I was empowered to minister the sacrament of One in whom there is no north nor south, no black nor white, no male or female—only the spirit of love and reconciliation drawing us all toward the goal of human wholeness.[1]

During the 1970s and 1980s the Anglican Communion began to see new threads being woven into the pattern of women's ministries. New glints were appearing, sometimes without those most concerned being aware of what was happening in other parts of the workshop. This chapter will look at ways in which different Provinces in the Anglican Communion, one after another, made the decision for women's ordination.

The story has already been told of the historic ordination of Florence Li in 1944 in South China, and of the subsequent ordinations of two women deacons in Hong Kong in 1971. The ministry of these women, Joyce Bennett and Jane Hwang, encouraged others in different parts of the world; they were living evidence that this question was not just a matter of history, an emergency action by one bishop in time of war. The decision of Bishop Gilbert Baker was significant.

By 1971 movement was getting under way in the United States. In 1970 a motion before the Episcopal Church's General Convention (the equivalent of the General Synod in England) that women be ordained to all ministerial orders immediately had been narrowly defeated. This happened again in 1973. After the second defeat, the Episcopal Women's Caucus, believing that delay and legalism could and probably would effectively outlast their vocations, began to prepare for more radical action.[2] News of the 1971 Hong Kong ordinations was encouraging, and both the United States and Canada were helped by their long history of pioneering women. It is interesting to see how differently those two countries tackled the question of getting the necessary consensus of opinion.

The women in the States took dramatic action, and were the first to break the mould decisively, to extend that hair-line crack produced in Hong Kong. The 'irregular' ordination of eleven women in Philadelphia in 1974 was crucial. But the first Anglican Province to follow the Hong Kong lead right through its synodical structures, and without too much turmoil, was Canada, where women were ordained priest in 1976. It was accomplished there with a high measure of agreement largely, it was said, because their Archbishop, Ted Scott, was committed to the ordination of women, and spent endless time talking with his clergy, listening to those who were opposed but consistently giving a lead. He did not find it necessary or desirable to be on a fence.

One ordained woman said to me that in Canada they were greatly helped in coming to a decision by the history of the pioneering women of the prairie. They were ministered to by equally adventurous and determined women: 'God's Galloping Girls', as some of them were known. And Eva Hasell, an English-woman who had experience of driving around in rough conditions in Cumberland and Westmorland, began a scheme whereby trained teachers would travel two by two in caravans along the prairie trails visiting the settlements, setting up Sunday Schools and training teachers to carry on. All her young colleagues had to be good female motor mechanics, and Miss Hasell constantly refers to the terrible state of the trails, the caravans frequently having to be pulled out of holes and mud. Not only did little girls and boys in English Sunday Schools know about all this, sending their 'Sunday Penny' to buy books and spanners for the 'Western Canada Caravan Fund', but their work was acknowledged at other levels. In 1922 the Archbishop of Rupert's Land wrote:

Only those who know the conditions which at present prevail on the prairies of North-West Canada, the isolation of the scattered settlers, and the shortage of living agents to reach them with the services of the Church, can adequately appreciate the great value of these 'travelling vans' in carrying to the children in these lonely homes some measure of Church teaching and spiritual help.

The Bishop of Carlisle, breakfasting under the crenellations of Rose Castle (permission to crenellate given in 1336), must have been pleased to receive a letter from the Bishop of Kootenay in November 1926: 'Nothing of so much importance has occurred in the history of the Diocese of Kootenay as the visit of Miss Hasell this year, and the good she has done can never be fully estimated.'[3]

The respect these women earned, and the pioneering spirit of the women they served, did not die over the years, and their successors were on the whole not denigrated in the way that became all too familiar to some of their sisters in other countries. If they met with opposition, they tackled it with an energy and persuasiveness of which Miss Hasell would have approved. So, with notable leadership from Archbishop Scott, the clergy in Canada were prepared to move ahead with little rancour or back-biting, and in 1976 the vote was passed and everybody got on with their work.

In the United States however a struggle was on, and in earnest, from 1970 onwards. A large number of theologically trained women were by that time seeking ordination to the priesthood. Many of them became convinced that their General Convention would continue arguing for years to come. Finally, in a great burst of energy and conviction, three retired or resigned bishops ordained eleven women to the priesthood, in Philadelphia on 29 July 1974. The church was packed, and great media interest was roused. This might have been even more extensive had they known that the young churchwarden carrying the cross and leading the procession was Barbara Harris, who in 1989 became the first woman to be consecrated bishop in the Anglican Communion.[4]

Nearly 2,000 people attended the Philadelphia ordination, and it caused a furore in church circles. The next General Convention (the equivalent of the English General Synod) would not be meeting for another two years. Several bishops indicated their intention to ordain women after the 1976 General Convention even if the vote went against. Four more women were 'irregularly' ordained in Washington in 1975, and in the months leading up to the Convention meeting, the Eucharist was celebrated by the women in many places. It became clear that the previously accepted wisdom (that it would be more trouble to ordain women than not to ordain them) was being reversed. The House of Deputies (Clergy and Laity), under the skilful chairmanship of John Coburn,[5] then Bishop-elect of Massachusetts, was won round, and the Convention voted that women could be ordained to all orders of ministry, including the episcopate. At the same meeting, the bishops approved measures to admit the 15 women priests without re-ordination. These decisions were met with widespread approval and relief in the Episcopal Church as a whole, which was ready and waiting for those steps to be taken. At the same time, the minority who were fervently against began to splinter off into separate groups, the process which has received disproportionate publicity in England.

One far-reaching influence of the Philadelphia ordinations came about, rather surprisingly, through the male network known as the Lambeth Conference. This ten-yearly meeting of all the bishops of the Anglican Communion included in 1978 for the first time bishops from Provinces which had officially ordained women—Hong Kong, Canada, New Zealand and now the USA as well. Ronald Bowlby, who was then Bishop of Newcastle, has spoken about the importance of this meeting in influencing some of his English colleagues. 'In terms of shifting a relatively small number of people's attitudes, but senior people and influential perhaps in the life of the Church of England and elsewhere, probably the 1978 Conference was a minor watershed. Because it actually said, by a majority, "This is OK, to go down this road—we believe this, as gathered Bishops of the Anglican Communion." . . . That was important in the sense that things had actually moved further than many people in the C of E thought they had. Any bishop who reported back faithfully here in England would have had to point out that there wasn't a great wave of opposition to this, it wasn't voted down or anything like that.'

Bowlby went on to talk about the influence of particular

bishops: 'John Coburn was influential in a behind the scenes kind of way . . . he could win converts among the more guarded English bishops. He was seen as a rather statesmanlike American bishop and therefore could be set against any idea that the American Church was just "giving way to the spirit of the times" without any kind of theological weight behind what they were doing. You couldn't say that of John. And although our vote failed in 1978, it was not lost in the House of Bishops. They thought the time had come, but they misjudged, a little, the extent of the resistance.'[6]

Visitors to England

When MOW started up in England all these overseas ordinations were in the fairly recent past. Already the history of women priests coming over to help us had begun, and we knew that one of the irregularly ordained 'Washington Four', Alison Palmer, had celebrated in two churches in 1978. This can be regarded as either a courageous or a foolhardy thing to do, according to your point of view, since ecclesiastical law (which is also the law of the land) had not been adjusted to allow visiting women as well as visiting men to celebrate in an Anglican church. So it was against the law. Alfred and Phoebe Willetts in Manchester, and Ian Harker in Newcastle, with their respective Parochial Church Councils, were the prophetic spirits behind those occasions. Later on, in the Southwark diocese, Tony Crowe and his PCC supported Elizabeth Canham—who had gone from their parish to be ordained in the United States—by inviting her to celebrate for them at the Parish Communion. Others may well have done the same.

After the Manchester occasion Phoebe Willetts wrote:

A group of very ordinary people gathered together in their Parish Church was suddenly aware that the Holy Spirit was lifting them out of their ordinariness and showing them a vision of what it was like in the Early Church. That feeling of impotence which so many feel in the underprivileged area of a big city . . . was miraculously swept away with the realization that it is God who decides and will act through anyone prepared to listen . . . It was a very simple act of faith, yet it said something which no amount of essays and books of theorizing . . . could

communicate. We acted as if we were already living in the Church which
we still have to bring into being.[7]

Because the Philadelphia ordinations were still in the air,
MOW had decisions to make about the most basic policies for
action. We recognized that the first ordination of women priests
in the Western world had been such a break with accepted tradition that it was only achieved through dramatic and independent
action. We were stirred as the Philadelphia tale was told, and we
wanted to learn from the experience of the American women as
well as listening to the Canadians. But in general the overriding
conviction was that for the Church of England it was important
to make every effort to get legislation voted through at every level
up to General Synod and Parliament. If all that failed, some of
us said, then it might be clear that only independent action could
do it. But in the meantime, our judgement was supported by
many of our sisters overseas who said 'If you can get it through
your Synod, you will have done a great thing for us'.

Women priests visiting us from overseas became a regular part
of the MOW scene; they were wonderful sounding boards, shared
our impatience and in a sometimes bewildered way followed our
instinct for validation by the Synod. They stood alongside us
when we desperately needed support and they affirmed us as our
spirituality was growing and changing. Mary Michael Simpson, a
nun, psychotherapist and Canon of the Cathedral of St John the
Divine in New York, was in April 1978 the first woman to preach
in Westminster Abbey, and became a valued friend and counsellor
to many Englishwomen; Suzanne Hiatt, one of the 'Philadelphia
Eleven', came through snow and freezing fog to preach at the
first MOW national conference in Birmingham in 1981. As we
were beginning to realize the hugeness of the task, her determination and vision and humour were exactly what we needed. She
was not, however, invited to preside at a Eucharist in the church
hall, on the grounds that this would be an embarrassment to the
vicar.

It should, I think, go on record how impressive these overseas
priests were in their willingness to put up with discrimination and
sometimes downright rudeness, as they helped people to realize
that an ordained woman did not have two horns and a tail. They

certainly brought us encouragement and clarified our vision. They seemed not to mind that we were only asking them to celebrate in private houses or common rooms, always in more or less 'underground' situations, from the basement of St Paul's Deanery to homes as far apart as Newcastle and Kent.

The glorious exception came in 1982, at the national MOW conference held at Swanwick in Derbyshire. The Revd Janet Crawford of New Zealand was the main speaker, and celebrated at the Sunday Eucharist in the chapel of the conference centre. Our former Moderator, Bishop Stanley Booth-Clibborn, was with us. The Bishop of Derby preached, characteristically making the occasion feel both strong and peaceful. Both bishops received Communion. In a central passage in his sermon Bishop Bowles said:

> So what are we doing in this service? We are, of course, declaring the truth as we see it by sharing in a celebration of the Holy Communion presided over by a priest validly, regularly and efficaciously ordained by a Bishop in the Anglican Communion. That does not make the service a public demonstration or a piece of propaganda. Every celebration of the Holy Communion is a declaration of the truth. In this service we are showing our acceptance as Anglicans of what is happening in other parts of the Anglican Communion. We are also showing courtesy to a visiting priest from another province by accepting her as our President on this occasion. This is something which has been happening to my personal knowledge for at least 45 years when men priests have been given the opportunity to preside at the Holy Communion here and at other conference centres and in parish churches using the rites of their own provinces.

In those early days, most English Anglicans had never experienced a Eucharist celebrated by a woman, and found it both uplifting and absolutely normal. Sister Rachel Hosmer, founder of the Order of St Helena, and one of the wisest, most saintly and most radical spirits who visited us, presided on one occasion when a young woman, alienated from the Church for many years, at last felt able to communicate—and there must be many more instances of the release from pain and bitterness which our visitors were able to bring through their sacramental ministry. For them, as well, it was a moving experience, more so perhaps than any of us realized at that time. The Revd Rachelle Birnbaum looks back on her visit to England in 1984 at the time of Florence Li's anniversary celebrations:

> Then I left for York to visit with Christian Howard, who invited me to celebrate the Eucharist for the family in the chapel of Castle Howard. Being a family chapel, it is not under the jurisdiction of a bishop, so the celebration would not be considered illegal; irregular perhaps but not illegal. In spite of this, I felt the excitement of one who has taken a time trip back to the first century catacombs. We knew it to be right; we knew it to be valid. We knew also that it had to be done quietly. And so in the 'intimate formality' of that chapel, we did what we knew was being done all over England that week. With words spoken by a woman, we together celebrated the mystery of the Holy Eucharist according to the rite of the 1979 American Prayer Book. And we prayed for the Church of England and the Church in the United States, and for the Church throughout the world, wherever women were not permitted to live out their individual callings, not only to ordained ministry, but to ministry in all its various forms.[8]

On two occasions only a great fuss was made. This seems now to have been precipitated more by the venues of the celebrations than anything else. In January 1982 Elizabeth Canham, an Englishwoman who had recently been ordained in the United States, was in London and was invited to celebrate, as others had done before her, in the basement of St Paul's Deanery. The fact that this appeared in the *Church Times* led to the then Bishop of London, Graham Leonard, issuing a four-page statement condemning the service and announcing that his statement was being sent to the Archbishop of Canterbury and to Elizabeth's ordaining bishop, John Spong. Spong's response was taken up in the American and Canadian church press, Archbishop Scott of Canada pointing out that the Church of England, in refusing to recognize the women priests from overseas, was raising questions about the ministry of overseas ordaining bishops, and about the authority of national Churches which had authorized such ordinations. All this was hard for Elizabeth, who by now was back in the States, and completely taken aback by the song and dance.

In England, the Bishop of Birmingham, Hugh Montefiore, made public legal advice which he had taken from the former Dean of Arches before inviting a woman to celebrate in his private chapel.[9] The advice was that a service held in private in an unconsecrated building using the liturgy of the priest's own Church was not subject to ecclesiastical ruling and that such a service could not be deemed illegal. Other legal authorities differed; nothing was ever established.

It was not until 1986 that another flurry occurred. By this time developments had taken place, and the General Synod was just about considering turning its dead march into a slow walk. But one set-back had occurred, the only time in the period since 1979 that a vote connected with the ordination of women was lost in the General Synod.

In July 1986 the legislation to permit women ordained abroad to officiate in England came up for the final vote, having been passed in deanery and diocesan synods. The Anglo-Catholic party had in 1984 delayed the decision for two years, by succeeding in a bid to require a 'special (i.e., two-thirds) majority' vote, something which is required if the matter is deemed to affect doctrine or the Ordinal. Until then the legislation had never featured as 'Article 8' business, but was seen as a simple adjustment to permit visiting women to officiate in the same way as visiting men. But 30 members (the required number) had asked that this designation be reconsidered. That night the six leaders of the Synod (the two Archbishops, the two clergy and two lay leaders of their respective Houses), meeting in private, had to make their decision. In spite of advice from the lawyers that this was *not* Article 8 business, a majority of the six leaders of the Synod had given way. So the Measure was delayed by two years while it went round the deanery and diocesan synods, where it passed in the majority.

These manoeuvrings had caused a good deal of confusion and upset. But not all supporters could see the importance of the Measure. Some voted against on the grounds that it was 'unfair to our deaconesses' or 'made too many conditions for the visiting women'. The majorities were insufficient under the new ruling. The Measure failed and women lawfully ordained in sister Churches of the Anglican Communion were still without permission to officiate in a Church of England church. I still believe that this was nothing less than a disgrace.

The sense of outrage which followed is described elsewhere in this book. The decision was perceived by supporters of women's ordination as unjust, and the political manoeuvring as unworthy.

Diana McClatchey, who had been steering the legislation through Synod, and Jean Mayland, a member of MOW's Central Council, wrote to overseas bishops expressing our shame and regret at this treatment of priests visiting England. After this, hundreds more celebrations must have taken place in college rooms, private houses, ecumenical centres, church halls; sustenance for the road was still needed and year after year these services went quietly on. In Coventry Cathedral the visiting canon would, if female, celebrate in the Chapel of Unity. On a few occasions a parish priest felt impelled in conscience to invite a woman colleague from overseas to celebrate in his church. For Englishwomen ordained abroad but living in this country, the limitation to their ministry was a grief.

Celebration at Church House

Life, therefore, continued outside the General Synod, and MOW's membership and meetings were building up. People would be quite surprised, for instance, at our Annual General Meetings, which were far from formalities, with representatives attending from virtually every diocese. They usually took place in the context of a day conference which included worship. For the 1986 AGM a room was booked in Church House, Room 301, a well-known and much used large committee room on the third floor. At the September meeting of Central Council arrangements for the day were discussed. It was unanimously decided that one of our own English women priests, Dr Joyce Bennett, should be asked to celebrate the Eucharist at midday. During the discussion Janet Crawford's celebration at Swanwick was recalled, and the support of the Bishop of Derby and the Bishop of Manchester on that occasion; it seemed fitting and right that though we were still prevented from inviting a woman priest to celebrate for us in a church, we could and would receive that ministry in Room 301.

At this time Joyce Bennett, who had retired to Buckinghamshire from a distinguished ministry in Hong Kong, was working with the Chinese community based at St Martin-in-the-Fields. There she regularly celebrated the Eucharist in Chinese with the Vicar of St Martin's or another male priest standing beside her. Joyce was happy to accept our invitation for 4 October.

Two days before that date, we were informed by Church House that a double booking had been made, and that the MOW meeting would be transferred to Bishop Partridge Hall, a finer meeting-place altogether than familiar old Room 301. We naturally accepted the rearrangement.

The meeting was attended by about 200 people from 40 dioceses. At the beginning, although no press releases had been sent out and no reporting was expected, two journalists were spotted at the back of the hall. I stopped the proceedings while they were asked to leave. When the time came for the celebration, Joyce Bennett refused to allow any photography during the service. We knew how readily MOW would be accused of 'using the Eucharist to make a point' and we were united in wishing to stick within the legal framework as we saw it. At the end of the day, the two journalists were still waiting at the bottom of the stairs, so Diana McClatchey, the Moderator and a member of General Synod, and Joyce Bennett did in the end sit down and give them the facts. And on my return home I telephoned the Secretary-General of the Synod, Derek Pattinson. His reaction was unperturbed: 'You have telephoned me at exactly the right time, Margaret.'

The short column which appeared in the *Observer* next day caused an immediate and furious reaction from those who were most opposed to women's ordination. Even the Archbishop of Canterbury, visiting Boston, Massachusetts, was reported to have commented that he was 'dismayed'. Oswald Clark, a prominent opponent on General Synod, went so far as to bring in the Monarch, insisting that Bishop Partridge Hall was under her personal jurisdiction, and appeared on television walking round Dean's Yard with a reporter and pointing out the offending site. His complaints were rounded off by a demand that the Home Secretary be approached to send a letter of apology to Her Majesty on behalf of the Church of England. Before the quill pens could be sharpened, the Dean of Westminster, Michael Mayne, stepped in to state categorically that Bishop Partridge Hall had no connection with the sovereign. Comments in the press ranged from 'First Catch Your Chalice' (*Guardian*) to 'More Supporters For Women Clergy' (*Baptist Times*) and a thoroughly sympathetic leader in *The Times*.

In all this, MOW stood firm. Throughout October letters

poured in to the MOW office. Many members were confused and anxious; the majority of letters were in support and an enormous number of new members joined. One priest from the Midlands wrote 'I would rather resign from the Church of England than apologize for that service'. But in order to reassure the bishops, the following letter was sent to them signed by Diana McClatchey, Margaret Webster and Margaret Orr Deas:

> We thought you might like to know a little more about our meeting on Saturday, October 4th, in Church House. The whole atmosphere was positive, serious and constructive . . . Plans were discussed for continuing the work of education and consciousness-raising, and four new publications were launched.
>
> The celebration by the Revd Joyce Bennett was a solemn and serious act of worship. As an Englishwoman who has had and continues to have a distinguished ministry, she is well-known as a MOW member and it seemed natural and normal that she should be invited to preside as our representative.
>
> The occasion, however, underlined the very strong feelings of sadness felt in July when the Women Ordained Abroad Measure failed to reach the two-thirds majority in two Houses, coupled with a continued sense of injustice that the special majorities were suddenly deemed necessary when the Measure was already halfway through the procedures . . .
>
> We are becoming aware of a deepening sense of shame among churchpeople that the Church of England continues to bar women ordained abroad from celebrating in churches, a growing sense of incredulity outside the Church that women who believe they are called by God to serve the Church may not even have this vocation tested. The service on Saturday was an act of healing for many of our members and a covenant with those who have waited so long.

Contrary to our expectation, the response from the bishops was largely hostile, nervous and inclined to rap us over the knuckles. We felt totally let down as their replies reached Diana. One or two, like Jim Thompson, Bishop of Stepney, made an effort to stand alongside us, and the Bishop of Manchester supported us strongly in the *Church Times*. But on the whole, for a House of Bishops who were known to be largely in favour of women's ordination, it seemed that their one concern was whether or not the service was 'legal'. It was all the more heartening, therefore, that the Bishop of Kingston, Peter Selby, who had been present, published in *The Times* on 11 October a major article entitled

'Why a Bishop Should Choose'. He described the Eucharist as a 'natural, restorative and healing event, and the promise of a better future', then, thinking of his own position, went on to examine the concept of a bishop as a 'focus of unity'. This view, Selby suggested, which allegedly prevents a bishop from allying himself clearly and firmly with a cause he would claim to support, turns him almost into a 'monarch figure'.

> During periods of agreement, such 'monarch figures' can exercise their universal pastorate with relative ease. In a fragmented society . . . the position of the 'universal person' becomes immensely precarious . . . One thing bishops could do is give up the phrase 'focus of unity'; bishops do focus the Church, but what they focus is the Church as it is. Being a focus of disunity is not therefore a sign of pastoral failure . . . Last Saturday the cruel fantasy was exposed: that you can be for women's ordination and for the Church of England's present way of doing things. The reality is that Anglican women priests are not a future hope but real people already live among us, and we all have to recognize them now or deny them now.

The Archbishop of Canterbury and the other bishops showed little understanding and Peter Selby was given a hard time. Joyce Bennett was entertained at Lambeth by the Archbishop: 'We drank tea together on his sofa. He showed me a fat file of legal opinions about the celebration at Church House, but did not open it at all. Clearly the lawyers did not agree! I would not promise never to celebrate again in England, but I did agree not to do it again in Church House.' The episcopal anxiety wafted across to the House of Commons, where William van Strauben-zee, as Chairman of the committee responsible for Church legis-lation, was working hard to prepare for the safe passage of the Measure agreed by Synod to enable women to be ordained deacon. He wrote to me on 20 October:

> What . . . this service has done is to stir up the opponents quite unnecessarily. First, it was a service conducted by stealth. Second, however you look at it, it was an illegal service, even if that is not a strictly accurate and legal definition. I regard it as quite incredibly unfortunate that very senior churchmen should have lent themselves to it. I can only tell you that a number of supporters of the Measure, myself included, are dismayed. I may say too that I know from personal contact that a number of the deaconesses share my sadness.

I felt sad to receive this letter, particularly about the last sentence. Perhaps this was the only occasion on which Bill van Straubenzee, that benign and respected parliamentarian, misjudged reaction in the House of Commons. Be that as it may, the House, voting on 28 October 1986, passed the Measure by a majority of 303 to 25, a majority which has been described as the highest ever known on any ecclesiastical matter since the Reformation.

And gradually the celebration in Church House took its place as just one of a series of occasions on which women ordained overseas presided. No legal edict was ever pronounced. During the Eucharist in York Minster before the 1987 MOW AGM, the Archbishop of York, on Diana McClatchey's invitation, attempted to 'clarify' a 'grey area'. Unlike most of his statements, this rather headmasterly address failed to carry conviction. More and more diocesan branches asked for a visit from an overseas priest, and happy and fruitful links developed. At subsequent AGMs we often had a woman celebrate during the course of the day. The question mark for some of us was how long did we have to go on being law-abiding, good little people, worshipping outside church walls with our sisters who were priests when the strictures seemed increasingly shabby. This was a question which in due course was answered in no uncertain terms by the St Hilda Community, whose story is told later in this book.

Endpiece

The failure of the Women Ordained Abroad Measure should never have happened. Perhaps it is true that it was brought to the Synod at the wrong time. But the agonizing that went on over the question of the celebrations of the Eucharist consumed a great deal of energy within MOW gatherings. This did, however, make it clear that, far from being just a 'campaign' for a cause, trying to be as efficient as possible, MOW was wrestling at a deep level with the real issues that faced us. Both those who opposed and those who longed for the presidency of a woman at our services did so because the Eucharist was central to their lives. Also, the process of working through our disagreements, exhausting though this was, taught us a good deal about handling conflict.

Certainly this issue was the one over which convictions were voiced most strongly. At one end of the spectrum were those who had decided that, wherever held, whatever rite was used, these services were illegal; they would use words like 'counterproductive'. Many of these were members of the General Synod. In the middle were the large number who found such services necessary 'food for the road' and were glad to find opportunities of being sustained in this way. They would say it was a grey area as to illegality and they saw no reason to be bound by the fears of others. The third group became increasingly frustrated with the was-it-or-wasn't-it arguments and the hush-hush atmosphere surrounding such occasions, and out of their 'despair and anger', as Monica Furlong has said, grew the conviction that the time had come to be open about celebrating the Eucharist with an overseas woman priest. The St Hilda Community met for the first time in February 1987 in the chaplaincy of Queen Mary College, Mile End Road, in east London, and, as we shall see, their witness and their publications have an important place in this long exploration. Once the ordinations began of English deaconesses to be deacons and in holy orders, a new conviction arose. Rather than always focusing on eucharistic worship, we now wanted to use more fully the gifts of the deacons. From then on, we began to create more new liturgies, exploring language and symbol and discovering some fresh springs in worship.

A very important steadying influence in all this was the work and presence of the few, much-respected English women priests ordained abroad and working in this country as deacons. Their presence here was both healing and helpful: Joyce Bennett, licensed as chaplain to the Chinese community at St Martin-in-the-Fields; Susan Cole-King, medical doctor, deacon in charge of a parish, who topped the clergy poll in the Oxford diocese in 1990 for the General Synod; Patricia Pinkerton in the Gloucester diocese, also having to work as a deacon. All these women in their different ways ministered as they could, and did their best to respond to the demands that were placed upon them.

Lambeth 1988: 'Our mission is impaired'

Before the Lambeth Conference meeting of bishops of the Anglican Communion in 1988, a press release was issued by the Bishops of Bristol, Manchester and Southwark[10] with news that 144 bishops had signed a Pentecost message in support of the ordination of women. The signatories were from Australia, Brazil, Burundi, Rwanda and Zaïre, Canada, Central Africa, England, the Middle East, New Zealand, Scotland, Spain, Sudan, Uganda, USA, West Africa. This was in response to a message from 47 bishops opposed. Part of it ran:

> We believe that the Ordination of women to all three orders of Bishop, Priest and Deacon, is vital to the mission of the Church. The full ministry of women and men claims that there are no Barriers of race, economic status or gender. Without women in the ministry of the Church, we do not represent the wholeness of the Church and our mission is impaired.

This strong statement in the middle of a long message helped to prepare the bishops coming to Lambeth for the atmosphere of support for women's ordination which they were going to find at Canterbury, even though it was still deeply flawed through the absence of any women members. And a number of North American bishops sent out another statement later declaring that since some of their priests were not accepted in England, they themselves were not prepared to celebrate Communion during their visit other than during the Conference itself. Many of the family and friends of the Church of England had been finding their loyalty severely tested by the continued ban on their women priests.

When the Lambeth Conference met at Canterbury in July 1988, MOW set up a presence in the Canterbury Centre, a converted church, installed an excellent exhibition, 'Women of God', and so were able to offer a pleasant place to meet. MOW members travelled at their own expense to Canterbury to staff the Centre. It was hoped that our bishops would come in. In the event, it was more used as a meeting-place for overseas bishops, for our own bishops' wives, and for many women from overseas. Among them was Dr Pat Brennan[11] of Sydney who was at that time in the midst of the hard, but in the end successful, struggle in Australia.

At the Conference itself impressive presentations were made by Elizabeth Templeton of the Church of Scotland, by Mary Tanner and Sarah Coakley, and by the Revd Nan Peete of the Episcopal Church of the United States. Women visitors were about and making their presence felt, women consultants were consulted. The 'alternative' conference of the bishops' wives was demanding and lively, and much of it was said to be a great deal more interesting than the episcopal deliberations. But the Lambeth Conference still had no woman present with a right to vote.

Most people were sure that by 1998 this would be a thing of the past. The Episcopal Church was poised for the election of a woman bishop, and many members of the Lambeth Conference were glad to think that at their next meeting women bishops would be present in their own right. At the end of the meeting, the Conference resolved that every Province should be free to ordain women to all orders of the ordained ministry, and rejected by a significant majority a resolution restraining Provinces from consecrating women as bishops.

And so the process continued to go ahead in the Anglican Communion. Mercifully, the Church of England's rulings did not affect the development of a whole ministry in other countries. Just as in 1986 bishops in Puerto Rico, Brazil, Hong Kong, Kenya, Uganda, as well as those in Canada, New Zealand and the USA and the Church of South India had respected and cared enough about their women priests to fund their travel to the Canterbury gathering of thanksgiving for women's ministry, so the process of recognition and valuing was still going on. Preparing to ordain three women priests in his cathedral at Mityana, Bishop Mutebi of Uganda said to Charmion Mann, visiting from the twinned diocese of Bristol, 'I am very elated!' The decisions of these Churches have been of great significance for us, and from these women called to ordination we have much to learn.

On 21 October 1990 another 'first' of real significance took place, the ordination of the first Anglican woman to be ordained priest in the United Kingdom. The Church of Ireland, which covers both Northern Ireland and Eire, had voted in favour and saw no need for delay. Christ Church Cathedral, Dublin, was packed, and senior Roman Catholic clergy actively participated in this ordination, the priesting of a woman deacon, Virginia Kennerley. Many other Roman Catholic clergy or lay people who had known or worked with Virginia were present. As Diana McClatchey commented in *Chrysalis*, that Catholic presence seemed to be giving a signal to the Anglican world.

By the time General Synod came to the historic vote on 11 November 1992, the list of Anglican Churches which were ordaining women, or had just taken the decision to ordain, was just over half the member Churches: Canada, the Episcopal Church in the USA, the Churches of the Provinces of New Zealand, Kenya, Burundi, West Africa and Southern Africa, the Philippine Episcopal Church, the Episcopal Churches of Brazil and Cuba, the Churches of Ireland and Uganda, the Extra Provincial Dioceses of Puerto Rico and Hong Hong and the Anglican Church of Australia. For some, it had come relatively easily, for others like Australia it had been a hard fought battle. With the English vote, the rift which had been a source of division and sadness within the family had at last been healed.

Notes

1   Pauli Murray, the first African-American woman ordained to the priesthood, writing of her first celebration of the Eucharist in the North Carolina chapel where her grandmother had been baptized as a slave child. Quoted in *Episcopal Women: Gender, Spirituality and Commitment in an American Mainline Denomination*, ed. Catherine M. Prelinger (Oxford, 1992), p. 232.

2   The Episcopal Women's Caucus was formed in 1971, after the American bishops had called for another study of the issue of women's ordination. A letter was sent in response, from a meeting of women church workers and seminarians, informing the bishops that they would not serve on another study commission, and that they were forming the Episcopal Women's Caucus, to promote actively the ordination of women.

3   'Eva Hasell', paper, author unknown.

4   Barbara Harris was consecrated bishop in the diocese of Massachusetts on 11 February 1989 in Boston, by the Presiding Bishop. 54 bishops were present and 1,400 priests of the Anglican world, including Florence Li herself.

5   John Coburn, before becoming Bishop of Massachusetts 1976–86, was

Chairman of the House of Deputies during the period following the Philadelphia ordinations in 1974 and saw the vote through the Convention in 1976.

6   Interview, June 1993.

7   *ONE for Christian Renewal* (Spring 1978).

8   Letter to the author, 1993.

9   Bishop Montefiore wrote to the *Church Times*: 'I have in my possession a copy of an Opinion of the former Dean of Arches in which it is clearly stated that, since the practice of religion in this country is free, a priest or minister (of either sex) of any non-established Church may celebrate the Holy Communion in accordance with the liturgy and regulations of his or her own Church, providing that this does not take place in a consecrated building and providing that (in the case of an Anglican priest) he has not been given the Archbishop's permission to officiate under the 1967 Measure. (Naturally it must be made clear that any such person is not acting as a minister authorized by the Church of England.)' (*Church Times*, 12 February 1982). Alan Webster, Dean of St Paul's, continued to maintain that in this country people did still have freedom to worship in their own homes. In spite of this exchange, and although some anxiety was caused among a good number of MOW members by the Bishop of London's attack, nevertheless the ministry of women priests was still sought out and valued year after year

10   Barry Rogerson, Stanley Booth-Clibborn, Ronald Bowlby.

11   Pat Brennan was in 1983 made a Member of the Order of Australia, an official and public acknowledgement of her unflinching leadership of the Movement for the Ordination of Women in that country.

CANTERBURY CATHEDRAL

Invitation

April 19 1986

EUCHARIST

and Thanksgiving for the Ministry of women
in the Church of England
and in the Anglican Communion

As responses to the large white invitation card began to come in, we realized that we had set something rather big in motion. The service was to be set in the context of a pilgrimage to Canterbury, from all parts of England and many parts of the world. The central act would be the Eucharist but that would be part of a weekend 'Joining Hands Across the Anglican Communion'. We hoped to gather ordained and lay women from all over the Anglican Communion as well as our own members. It was planned as a great act of affirmation of all the Christian ministries that women undertake.

Central to the planning had been the invitation to the Archbishop of Canterbury, Robert Runcie, to preside at this service, to be the celebrant. It was obvious to us that a great assembly with such a high proportion of overseas Anglicans was exactly the occasion to which the Archbishop should be invited, so we were delighted when he accepted the invitation extended by Monica Furlong, then Moderator of the Movement: 'I welcome the service at Canterbury Cathedral in 1986. I hope very much that I can be celebrant at such a gathering. It would be a great help to me as I see it in my Anglican Communion responsibilities.'

With great joy we set about the arrangements. Discussions continued with the Dean, Victor de Waal, canons were brought in, thinking about the worship went ahead and Christ Church College, Canterbury was booked.

For two years we prepared, planned, drafted, telephoned, corresponded. The first publicity went ahead, the MOW *Newsletter* of February 1985 stating that 'The Archbishop of Canterbury hopes to be present as the Celebrant on this occasion'. The tiny office at Napier Hall became an amazing sight as files grew and lists expanded. At that time we had no computer or word processor, so we were covering an immense amount of work with minimal resources; Margaret Orr Deas and I had to keep our heads very clear. As responses to our invitation began to come in from all over the Anglican Communion, Caroline Davis in Lincoln became involved and took all the work on lists and registrations off our shoulders. We had a happy and fruitful threesome arrangement, conferring on the telephone every day.

In all the preparations during those two years, only one problem proved impossible to resolve, the Archbishop of Canterbury's cold feet. Out of the blue, at the end of March 1985, a letter arrived at St Paul's Deanery, addressed to Alan Webster, indicating that the Archbishop was having misgivings about the service. Rather surprisingly, instead of contacting for clarification Monica Furlong or Diana McClatchey the Vice-Moderator, both of whom he knew well, he entrusted to Alan the information that

> There are a number of factors which have since arisen which convince me that it would be wiser for me not to preside at this service. I have weighed very carefully my responsibilities in the Anglican Communion, and it is quite clear that this is to be (and I am not objecting to such an event) a celebration for those who rejoice in the ordination of women and wish to see it developed as soon as possible throughout the Anglican Communion. I am sure you are aware that it still is a minority fact in the Anglican Communion, and put somewhat out of balance by the very considerable number of women priests from the Episcopal Church of the United States.

The Archbishop then explained that he was in correspondence with various international church leaders, mentioned 'these great sensitivities' and then produced the anxiety which presumably had been bothering him all along: 'Furthermore, at no stage has it been made entirely clear the nature of my presence in this service. In a recent publication it was stated that I would be *a* celebrant.'

Alan, somewhat taken aback by this approach, at once consulted Monica. None of us knew of any MOW publication that used the phrase 'a celebrant'. So Alan described once more the nature of the event: 'It had always been envisaged as, to use your words, "a straightforward canonical celebration of Holy Communion" . . . I cannot believe that you want to distance yourself from such a service. Your presence as Celebrant would be a recognition of the work of ministry being exercised by women in our Church.' He ended by suggesting that he might come with a small group of three or four of those concerned so that the service might be carefully considered.

The Archbishop's reply is revealing: 'I recognize the force of the points you make about a canonical celebration at Canterbury in the course of the conference at Christ Church College. *The fact is that many of those who advise and inform me of what is happening have somewhat different perceptions of this occasion* [my italics] and they are likely to be shared by ecumenical partners with whom I am in regular correspondence in order to maintain our relationships.' He agreed to meet a small group after returning from a forthcoming visit to Australia, and on 24 May Diana McClatchey wrote as the convenor of the group planning the service:

> Before any detailed plans can be made I do need to understand from you the role which you believe would be appropriate for you to assume on this occasion. Certainly the women who are coming from overseas, with some of their supportive Bishops, look on you as head of the Anglican Communion, and coming to the Mother Church will naturally expect to find you as the President of their Eucharist. If, as I have been told, you have reservations about that role, and have been advised of the dangers of 'misunderstanding' it would be so helpful . . . to know your own wishes.

The Archbishop replied on 10 June, apologizing for holding things up but

it has hardly been possible for me to consult with those people to whom I owe a conversation before I meet with you ... I have taken some soundings with bishops most of whom are in favour of the ordination of women to be implemented in this country ... They are very uncertain as to whether I should associate myself so visibly with an event which is planned by a single issue campaign. On the other hand I still have a desire to do what I can to be a pastor in a changing situation and for the sake of the women who are realizing that it is a tough road to get their proper standing in the life and witness of the Church. I have thought of ways in which this might be done through the introduction of varieties of ministry including the women's orders, and there would be an opportunity for me to preach as well as to preside in this situation.

He ended the letter with a further comment on how unsure he was as to the best line to take, and invited Diana on her own, not with a group, to come and talk with him about it.

Diana duly went to Lambeth from Worcestershire (and remembers that, the train being inordinately delayed, she actually got a message phoned to Lambeth from a signal box at the side of the line!). She wrote on her return, saying the conversation had been 'frank and helpful'.

As I understand the conclusion of our conversation it is that you hope to be able to preside and give a keynote address of welcome at the commencement of the service ... This is on the understanding that the Service is so designed and conducted as to emphasize both thanksgiving for the varied forms of ministry exercised by women in the U.K. and throughout the Anglican Communion, and commitment to the ongoing pilgrimage.

At this point it is important to remind ourselves that all this was taking place in 1985, before women in the Church of England had been made deacons. Deaconesses are lay women, not in holy orders, and one of the things lay women could do, and were doing with distinction, was to preach. It had seemed very clear to us from the start that a woman preacher was essential, and by this time Dr Mary Tanner had been invited. A well-known lay theologian and teacher, and Vice-Moderator of the Faith and Order Commission of the World Council of Churches, she seemed an inspired choice and we were delighted that she accepted. Diana explained this to the Archbishop and came home thinking that a compromise had been reached. It seemed to have been agreed that he would give a 'keynote address of welcome' which would give him the opportunity to make specific points, and that Mary Tanner would still be the preacher.

However, the reply from Lambeth to Diana's letter after the visit still hedged:

> I am grateful for the way in which you understand the difficulty about making any clear decision at the present time. However if after discussions with the Archdeacon of Canterbury and certain assurances about the balance of the congregation and the service I can come to preside and give an address I would be ready to do so . . . I am not yet entirely convinced that my address should not be the address of the service and not simply a welcome with another preacher . . . Now that I have thought about it I have some reservations.

Again Diana had to reply with reassurances, and laid out very clearly the reasons why, even though Mary Tanner had now offered to withdraw, it was crucially important for us to have a woman preacher.

> We had wanted a woman preacher on this occasion for the obvious reason that preaching is an important ministry for which the Church does make use of women. We had considered, and decided *against* inviting an ordained woman . . . I hope, in your opening Address, you would allow yourself sufficient time and space to clarify the situation and make it abundantly clear to everyone exactly what your presence meant, and what it did not mean.

By this time I was beginning to wonder what kind of a message the Archbishop would be able to give if he came to the service so full of doubts, uncertainties and, in particular, anxieties about his own position. Had we bent over backwards so far that our vision was going to be impaired? Three weeks after Diana's letter, the Archbishop replied:

> As you know, I am strongly of the opinion that if I were to attend, I should both preside and preach. On the other hand, I now take your point that a woman preacher would be an important witness to a ministry which is already widely exercised and greatly appreciated . . . I now think there is only one way out of this with integrity for both of us and that is that I should not be present.

Diana's sad note to me, 'He is pulling out', set many emotions in train. Feelings of failure (of course) that we couldn't even persuade our own Archbishop, whom many of us had known for 30 years, to come and preside in his own cathedral at a gathering of his own people from all over the world. Useless anger in the knowledge that he had been advised against participation by people who had never consulted us, had no idea of our thinking and probably cared less. And the horrible familiar realization that once again the proper concerns of women in the Church had been put to the bottom of the pile because of the 'sensitivities' of other church leaders. Just once, I felt like yelling, couldn't some sign be given, some gesture of encouragement that might actually involve some cost, some sacrifice? The interminable machinations of ecclesiastical politics, as practised by the (all-male) leaders of Roman Catholic and Orthodox Churches, the everlasting diplomacy, seemed a million miles away from the struggles I knew so many women were having in their parishes, their chaplaincies, in so many areas where women were hanging on with patience and grace while the Church awarded them absolutely no priority.

We decided not to give up the struggle. An Emergency Meeting of MOW's Central Council was called. This was extremely difficult; I was on holiday without a telephone, and my chief memory of the first week is of spending hours in baking telephone boxes ringing every single Council member to tell them what was happening. The meeting of Council and of others most concerned took place and a difficult decision was taken. In the letter sent on 14 July from this meeting, we tried once more to clarify our hopes and to offer another opening.

> We hoped we had reassured you on a number of points and find it hard to understand that you now wish to distance yourself from this Service of Thanksgiving for the ministry of women in the Church of England and the Anglican Communion. It is not really clear to us how the situation has changed since you said in November 1984 and again in July 1985 that you 'hoped to be present and to celebrate'.

The letter went on to describe the first responses we were receiving from overseas, that Archbishop Ted Scott had set up a group to select women from various ministries in the Anglican Church of Canada, that New Zealand was sending representatives of the Association of Anglican Women, and that many other Anglican Churches were already preparing to send representatives. And in this country support was widespread: 'Part of the importance of this service is to demonstrate the work being done by women within the ministry of the Church, so we are encouraged by the warm support of the Mothers' Union, the Church Missionary Society, and the YWCA, and by the fact that the following religious orders are sending representatives . . .'[1] The letter reassured the Archbishop that

> we are not expecting, and do not wish, particular positions on the
> ordination of women—either pro or con— to be featured in any
> address. The Bishops of Manchester and Liverpool have suggested that
> two separate addresses are not impossible. We would seriously ask you
> to consider this and that our Officers may come and talk with you . . .
> on your return from abroad. Of course we accept that you may be
> approached in a similar way by other organisations of opposing views.
> Nevertheless, this Meeting fervently hopes that you will still find it possible
> to endorse your original response.

This time the reply to Diana came quickly:

> I am sure you know that I am very sorry to disappoint MOW, and that
> there has been some misunderstanding between us arising from my earlier
> hope that I would have been able to participate in the Service. My
> decision has, however, now been made . . . Be sure of my prayers for
> you; and remember me in yours.

It had all become too difficult. The Archbishop seemed unable or unwilling to trust us. Perhaps his advisers had invented their own nightmare that he would be hijacked at the altar and find women priests from overseas standing beside him and concelebrating. It would have been helpful to have met these advisers; who were they anyway? Perhaps he guessed from the beginning that it would be made impossible for him to come, but genuinely wanted to help us along part of the way. Who knows what convoluted thinking accompanied the misunderstanding and misrepresentation. By the end it was a clear choice for us: either give up on having a woman preach, prepare for more possible provisos from Lambeth as the months would go on, but realize our original wish to have the Archbishop there with us; or cut

our losses, accept his good wishes and go on from there with
integrity to make the worship, the movement and music, the
readings and the prayers the very best possible for a celebration
of women's ministry in all its aspects. And that I believe we did.
It was symptomatic of the situation in the Church of England that
we felt we were offering the Archbishop some lovely moments of
grace and joy, and that this was being distorted and put beyond
his reach.

'Joining Hands Across the Anglican Communion'

To arrive at Canterbury after months of negotiation and preparation, travelling with Florence Li Tim Oi (or Florence Li as
she was now called), was to liberate our spirit. We began in the
foundations.

'*We stand before you as penitents.*'

The priests standing before us in the crypt of Canterbury
Cathedral, cassocked, serious, had just come to the end of a vigil
of penitence and prayer. Priests for Women's Ordination had
asked its members to undertake this as part of the weekend of
Thanksgiving for the Ministry of Women. Together they
expressed, in a simple litany, their sense of shame that over many
centuries the Church had so mistreated women. It was a moving
prelude to the days ahead, which were to be searching, painful,
joyful and affirming in ways that none of us, for all the planning,
could have imagined.

'Joining Hands Across the Anglican Communion' was the title
for a gathering of people from all over the world, coming together
to give thanks for the ministries of women. 18–20 April 1986
proved to be an extraordinary weekend, a powerful experience of
solidarity and hope, and for most of the participants unlike anything they had taken part in before.

We began with a late-night Liturgy of Hope in Canterbury
Cathedral. Friday evening, people are apprehensive, hopeful,
travel-weary. Women priests are with us from Brazil, Canada,
Hong Kong, Kenya, New Zealand, Puerto Rico, Uganda and the
United States; and from the Church of South India we have a
woman presbyter. Hannah Ward and I, who have had a large

share in devising this service over months, are anxious about the logistics; we have planned a liturgy on the move, groups moving from one part of the cathedral to another, praying and singing in different places. Far more people turn up than we expect, but the arrangements for their 'shepherding' round the dusky cathedral work well. The groups move in different directions, remembering modern martyrs, praying for justice, and in the cloisters remembering 'women of all centuries and all countries who have served the Lord in Christian ministry'. Women who have nurtured, taught, inspired, loved us; their names float into the darkness as we stand together on the grass. For us, their successors, it is a profound moment of recollection.

One of the US visitors, Eleanor Smith, of the Episcopal Church Women, wrote about it afterwards:

> The Liturgy began in the Crypt, womb of the Cathedral, a place where the cold and the prayers and footfalls have accumulated to become a part of the stones. Far beyond the heads of those people quietly assembled there, a diffused golden light shone to mark where the altar was, where priests, having ended their prayer vigil, stood to say 'Lord, give us courage to change' . . . We moved into greater darkness, climbing with care the ancient worn steps. The shadows we cast seemed to increase our numbers; the light flickered upward to become lost in the great fanning arches overhead.
>
> Voices were disembodied; 'Behold now, praise the Lord: all ye servants of the Lord; Ye that by night stand in the house of the Lord.' 'For the darkness of waiting, of not knowing what is to come, of staying ready and quiet and attentive, We praise you, O God.' Curiously there were no echoes. These great reaching windows were black but seemingly filled with watching angels, with the eyes of God looking in.
>
> We wound to Thomas à Becket's shrine, moved carefully around the stone markers in the Cloisters where we prayed into a still black night—aware of distant pilgrims, appearing and disappearing, surely pilgrims from other ages.
>
> Far away came in Alleluia, the Taizé setting, lifting, so right for female voices, and it was taken up in haunting responses, over and over again. We moved, singing, into the choir where the first group were already seated, transformed by the light of their candles into ranks where one would not be surprised to see the face of one's father, one's ancestor, an abbess, a monk.
>
> In the Crypt the tapers, now extinguished, were collected. Voices were

hushed. The night no longer felt cold. In the one Spirit we were all baptized into one body.[2]

Eleanor's words about the final stages of that liturgy touch me especially. I hope I never forget sitting in the choir in the near-darkness as the apparently endless number made their way round and up the steps to take their places; always when one thought 'That must be all', more would appear, and more. There was a sense during that evening of renewing—of vows made for us or by us at baptism, of commitment, of determination, of faith. Then Diana McClatchey, our Moderator, led us in a meditation on the Lord's Prayer. And because we were all gathered together at that place, traditionally the men's place, the place for only-male singers and clergy, there was a sense too of claiming a share in that space, that there should be no more exclusion.

The 'Joining Hands' weekend was deliberately designed to allow time for unorganized meeting and talking; Monica Furlong, who was planning the conference, had wanted to avoid the usual rigid timetable and sense of rush. After all, when would these women priests from all over the world meet again? They were all staying in Christ Church College, and on the Saturday morning they made a fine sight as they began to assemble for the service of thanksgiving which was the central event of these days.

2,500 people converged on Canterbury Cathedral for this cele-bration. Among them were 16 bishops, 100 clergy, 150 deacon-esses, lay workers, Readers, members of religious orders and 40 women priests and deacons from the eight Anglican Provinces which by then were ordaining women to the priesthood, as well as Padmasina, a South Indian and a leading presbyter in that Church. Ordinands and staff came from General Theological Seminary, New York, with former students of that college, now priests, who had come to Westminster in 1984 for the celebration of Florence Li's 40th anniversary. Later we understood some-thing of the financial effort that lay behind all these journeys, and also the commitment of overseas bishops and college principals; just then we were only conscious of links being forged or renewed.

There was a tremendous sense of 'crowd' and of expectation. The nave of the cathedral seemed to have shrunk. Chairs had been almost entirely cleared from the nave, so except for elderly or disabled people, the congregation sat on the floor. Outside, the procession of the women gathered; the English deaconesses in blue cassocks, the overseas priests in white robes and coloured stoles. One Canadian woman, Evelyn Voyageur from British Columbia, wore a splendid headdress on top of her vestments. They walked across the half-mile from Christ Church, stopping the traffic, to join the banner-bearers—women and men from all the English dioceses, and from some beyond, bearing banners for a procession of 'Women of Faith'.

I was standing hovering, when the procession started coming in through the great west door. First the banners, a holding up of the names of faith-women past and present: Hilda of Whitby, Julian of Norwich, Josephine Butler, Elizabeth Fry, Florence Nightingale, Mary Sumner.

They were followed by the male clergy who, as at the service in Westminster Abbey two years earlier, processed in to wait in alternate seats for the women priests. Alan Wilson's Julian anthem was sung, then a long silence brooded over the congregation. Outside in the cold wind, everyone else was waiting, the women's procession joined now by our bishops, shepherded by former Archbishop Donald Coggan. A hierarchical procession, we were well aware, coming in, but not—as we shall see—going out.

The Readers passed, in their surplices and scarves; I reflected how many of them must have been the first woman to preach in this or that church. I remembered the years of waiting for permission to speak in church, and how much women Readers had done to prepare the way for the ministry of other women. Somewhere in the procession there was a group of overseas visitors, one of them carrying her baby on her back. Then came 150 deaconesses, rather dignified and even apprehensive at this point. Looking at Elsie Baker's white hair, I thought 'How long do these women have to wait, *how long?*'

Then an unprecedented thing happened. After the welcome on behalf of the Cathedral, the Secretary General of the Anglican Consultative Council, Dr Sam van Culin, stepped forward and not only thanked the cathedral on behalf of the Anglican Communion but actually thanked the Movement for the Ordination of

Women for the work it was doing. That public affirmation took us wonderfully by surprise; it was a new experience, a sudden encouragement.

There was a freshness about that service; and Canterbury Cathedral seemed entirely appropriate for the blend of tradition and innovation which Diana McClatchey and others had tried so hard to achieve: the psalm of praise led by a woman cantor, and the Peace brought not only from Scotland, Ireland, Wales, but also by Anglicans from Australia, Belgium, Brazil, Canada, Ghana, Hong Kong, India, Kenya, Liberia, Mozambique, Namibia, New Zealand, Sri Lanka, Uganda, Zambia, speaking one after the other in her own language. That was an extraordinary few minutes, bringing home to us a new sense of the family of churches. Michael Brown of the *Yorkshire Post*, in his report of the service, described 'Dame Christian Howard announcing in the great church: "I bring peace from the province of York." And suddenly it became in Canterbury Cathedral like the first Pentecost as women from . . . 16 countries in all brought, each in her own tongue, daughterly greetings to their doddering old Mum, the C of E, as she continues dithering and asking herself: "Shall I or shan't I?" '[3]

Two visual symbols stuck in many minds long after the detail of the service was forgotten: the reading of the first lesson by a young mother with her small son nestled into the curve of her neck; and then, quite unplanned, one of those happy accidents which must have made the angels laugh. When the moment came for the congregation to sit, the bishops realized that there were not enough chairs for the women priests—so many deaconesses and English clergy had turned up unexpectedly that the count beforehand had been almost useless. One creative bishop, Stephen Verney, simply led his brothers to sit on the chancel steps, and there they remained, looking gnomish and happy.

Mary Tanner, preaching on 'You did not choose me: I chose you. I appointed you to go on and bear fruit, fruit that shall last', ended her sermon with words both sombre and joyful:

Our rejoicing today is only worth anything if we know in the depths of our being that to respond to God's choice, to co-operate with God's grace, is to make ourselves vulnerable, to be open to the possibility of

ministering in the way Christ ministered . . . Many here know what it
is to ache for the wholeness of women in priesthood to be lived out in
this place and also for the unity of the broken body of Christ, and who
are told the two are incompatible. Whenever there is a collision of values
in the Christian community there is uncertainty, confusion, pain. But
when we respond with understanding and care for those who see things
differently, we testify to the possibility of greater wholeness, greater
holiness: the vision of the end and the way to that end belong together . . .
As we look forward in hope to greater wholeness, greater holiness, we
give thanks that women have always exercised the ministry of Christ and
have and do find in their ministry joy and fulfilment: they do bring to
birth and bear fruit.

The celebrant was Canon John de Sausmarez, gentle and rever-
ent. There was a sense of awe as this great gathering of women
and men moved slowly up to receive the sacrament, administered
at twelve points by women priests and deacons from every Province represented. Finally it was over, the bishops and the Chapter
'withdrew' and the deaconesses and the men and women clergy
made their way out, through the great crowd filling the nave. Joan
Unwin, who had travelled down from Newcastle, reflected on it
later:

For me, the Celebration of Women's Ministry at Canterbury was
unquestionably a watershed. One of the most powerful experiences I've
ever had. And it was of the women and men together walking out of the
service, and applause starting, and you didn't even know it was applause,
it was as if something funny was happening somewhere in the building,
and then you realized people were clapping somewhere . . . and then
everyone started to clap . . . and it was the faces of the women—who
had never expected to be clapped. There was a particular face, of a
nun, who looked round to see what this noise was, and then she smiled,
and that was for me just the most moving experience. For the first time
in my life I had a glimpse of those women as God saw them, and they
were beautiful and beloved in a way I had never seen women before.

For Susan Cole-King, a medical doctor and an Englishwoman,
ordained priest in the States and at that time Rector of an inner-
city parish in New York, the service was a key moment in her
life: 'The Canterbury celebration made me realize that England
was where I needed to be, this was what I needed to do, to be
part of the struggle. I felt such a sense of identity with the other
women, and a vocation to be back among all that was going on.'

Everybody poured out into sunshine and a cold wind, 2,500 people, groups forming and re-forming as photographs were taken of deaconess mothers and daughters, of the overseas priests, of MOW members with their bishop. A picnic was provided in the cloisters; friendships were made or renewed; some sunned themselves against the ancient stone, others made energetic plans. Our first big international act of thanksgiving and hope was over.

The conference

Gradually some of the crowd drifted off, home to the four corners of England. Others stayed on as the 'Joining Hands' conference took up again later in the day. In a memorable session, to an audience that filled two halls, ten women, ordained and lay, told their story. Florence Li, speaking of faith and prayer, followed by a young priest from Kenya, describing the problems of training in a male-dominated college; a Canadian priest ministering to a remote community after a period when there was no priest at all. The effects of this on her Sunday School became evident when they received a parcel of books from a Sunday School elsewhere. Seeing a picture of a priest consecrating the sacrament one child exclaimed 'Oh! He's a man!' 'Yes', she replied, 'Some priests are men.'[4] Penny Nairne from Oxford remembers that evening well: 'For me, the climax to the whole Canterbury experience was listening to the overseas women talking about the oppression and the acute difficulties they were suffering. That made me feel this was all far more important than I'd realized. I began to feel that I had to be much more committed than I had been up to now.'

At the end of the telling of tales there was a turbulent meeting discussing MOW's decision that the next day's (Sunday's) Eucharist should be celebrated in the college chapel by Christopher Hall, rather than in an unconsecrated part of the college (or in the open air) by a woman priest. The ban on overseas women celebrating in English churches was, we thought, about to be lifted: the dioceses had voted to permit such celebrations and the General Synod would be making the final decision in July. Central Council had decided (not without heart-searching) to make the difficult decision to be meticulous, that in spite of the presence of all these women priests from overseas, it would be appropriate, fitting and acceptable to use the beautiful college chapel and invite a male priest to celebrate. Christopher Hall, son of R. O. Hall, the bishop who had ordained Florence Li all those years ago, was invited and, with sensitivity, accepted. *Chrysalis* later spelt out the anguish this caused:

> It was clear that many of our Anglican sisters were disappointed in the slow progress of the Church of England and the conciliatory attitude of MOW. It was clear, too, that within MOW the old division between the conservative and radical elements is still very strong, with some members feeling that too much of women's power and self-esteem is lost in attempts to be somehow 'acceptable' to Synod and to the hierarchies of the Church ... It was therefore both painful and fitting that on Sunday morning when MOW, trying to obey canonical requirements, asked a male priest to celebrate (though so many women priests were present), many women felt unable to stay throughout the service. Some lit tapers and stood outside throughout—others left at the offertory.
>
> Canterbury, therefore, despite all the joy, ended in tears—fitting tears, since women are intolerably stressed and torn by a Church that gives them so many contradictory messages that they are no longer sure where loyalty lies. MOW's immediate task is to rethink the answer to that difficult question.[5]

What this account does not tell us is that at the Peace, as we joined in a huge circle, we were suddenly unable to bear being separated from sisters and brothers, and hands were extended through the door to those holding candles outside. As I turned to the Canadian woman priest standing next to me in the circle inside, both of us with tears streaming down our faces, we knew that our sharing in this Eucharist was for us a sharing in Christ's brokenness as much as for those others their separation was a commitment to the Christ of radical change. And as Christopher Hall said the words of consecration, we were aware that dozens of voices were quietly joining in.

Ruth Hook, who had done so much to facilitate all the arrangements in Canterbury, wrote to me afterwards: 'Everyone will cherish their own highlights. To me the most moving thing was—against all expectations—the Sunday morning Eucharist. The walk-out was not to me disruptive, but a sorrowing within the framework of the Sacrifice: not an angry action of divisiveness, but taking its place within the loving process.'

Una Kroll also wrote: 'It *was* a great gathering, yes tinged with anger and frustration and spilling over sorrows, but such a meeting would have been inconceivable even ten years ago, as I well know ... I could wish we have an event where the women and men priests together refrain from the exercise of their priestly ministries in solidarity with those here who cannot do certain things and yet who mediate Christ to others. We focus too much, I believe, on what is exclusive to priests ... We need now to proclaim Resurrection and live it out.'

It was good to hear from them, and sacks of other letters came in. We all certainly hoped that this would be the last occasion on which we would have to be so careful. We felt sure that the Measure lifting the ban against women ordained abroad would be passed by the Synod at the July meeting in three months' time. After that our sisters would be able to celebrate the Eucharist in our churches. They had been patient, and so—rightly or wrongly—had we. As it was, we left Canterbury knowing full well the meaning of William Blake's line 'Joy and woe are woven fine'— but enriched, and stirred.

Links made that April still hold firm: bishops present at that service perceived a new future for the Church and have not wavered; women across the Anglican Communion continue to weave their own delicate, strong network. In the years since Canterbury all this has deepened and strengthened. Especially during the Lambeth Conference in 1988, or when any of our Provinces have approached a decisive moment, the strength and support of Anglican sisters across the world has been beyond price.

Notes

1   The religious orders who were preparing to send representatives were: Community of St Peter, Woking; Community of St Mary the Virgin, Wantage; Community of the Sisters of the Church, Ham Common; Order of the Holy Paraclete, Whitby; Society of St Margaret, East Grinstead and Hackney; Deaconess Community of St Andrew, Westbourne Park; Society of St John the Evangelist, Westminster; Society of the Sacred Mission, Durham; Society of St Francis, Scunthorpe.

2 Eleanor Smith, 'A Pilgrimage to Canterbury' in *Joining Hands at Canterbury* (MOW, 1986).
3 *Yorkshire Post* (21 April 1986).
4 From 'Telling Tales', private paper by Mary Fewster, Norwich.
5 *Chrysalis* (June 1986).

8   *Synod's stately dance*

Well, let me tell you, Dad, the Church of England, as far as I can
see, has the power and engine of a lawnmower but the brakes of
a juggernaut...[1]

The vision of the Canterbury worship with pilgrims from every
continent was light years away from the intricacies and legalities
of the synodical system of the Church of England, a system
derived at point after point from the parliamentary procedures of
the Palace of Westminster.

On the General Synod it is a question of a few steps forward,
one step back. This particular dance which we are watching has
been in progress for a long long time, yet some of the participants
seem surprised that it is going on at all. Others glare from the
edges of the room and try to interrupt the music. Outside there
seems to be a crowd of people trying to get a message through.
Finally they manage to hand over a parcel, carefully wrapped. It
is delivered straight to the kitchen where certain guests proceed
to carve it up, arguing loudly as they do so. From time to time
the crowd outside hear some of this, and feel worried.

Maybe a dream sequence is as good a way as any other to
describe the workings of the General Synod, and the preparation
and subsequent carving up of legislation. But when that system
of government was adopted for the Church of England, it wasn't
meant to be that kind of nightmare. A synod is a 'coming
together', a church council, and at its best it is a democratic
process which is based in the grassroots of church membership,
and tries to hold itself open to the Holy Spirit. The General
Synod debates major issues on behalf of the Church and is often

loosely described as 'the Church's Parliament'. It operates on behalf of the community of the Church of England.

The church community sends its representatives up to London in all shapes and sizes. The average age is falling, and in 1990 the proportion of women elected to the House of Laity was 49%. Another development was the setting up of a crèche in 1985. One small daughter, Anna, from Blackburn shared the first crèche with Rebecca and Ben—her grandmother in the background while mothers did their stint in the debates downstairs. At the other end of the spectrum was Christian (now Dame Christian) Howard, whose 25 years (1960–85) on the Church Assembly and then the General Synod were so productive and enlivening. Her humour, combined with her acute political sense and clarity of mind, made her an influential and respected speaker. Deaconess Diana McClatchey was another leading figure on Synod from 1975 to 1990, closely involved, as we shall see later, with all the Measures concerning women priests. Of course there were also notable opponents of women's ordination, like Oswald Clark, who was a member of the Church Assembly and then of the General Synod from 1948 to 1990. Grave, lined, effective speaker and politician, Chairman of the House of Laity from 1979, he was a tireless opponent of the ordination of women. Another opponent who left no strategy unexplored was Margaret Hewitt, President of Women Against the Ordination of Women. When she died in 1992 the Synod lost a sharp mind, a witty speaker, and a unique presence dedicated to appearing in a variety of remarkable hats.

Perhaps it is important to look at the way the Church's synods come into being and what 'synodical government' means.

General Synod members are elected by means of a system which stretches right down to the parishes. The members of each parish who support the church put themselves on an electoral roll; from this the Parochial Church Council (PCC) is elected, and also the parish's representatives, to the next stage up, the deanery synod. The deanery is a geographical grouping of parishes and its synod will consist of anything from 30 to 70 lay representatives, who are elected every three years, plus the clergy of the deanery. All kinds of church business are sent to them for discussion and for voting; the lay members not only elect representatives onto their own diocesan synod, but they also directly elect lay members to go from that diocese to the General Synod. Clergy vote separately to elect their diocesan and General Synod representatives. The House of Bishops consists of all the 44 diocesan bishops by right; the suffragan bishops elect nine representatives from their own number. Cathedral Deans and Provosts are elected in the same way. In addition, both the Houses of Clergy and Laity have a few places for members representing special categories. This results in a Synod of 566 members of whom 267 are laity.

Major items involving change in ecclesiastical law have to be drafted in the form of a Measure, to be presented to Parliament. Because the Church of England is an 'established Church', these decisions become part of the law of the land. A Measure must be debated in deanery synods, debated and passed in the majority of diocesan synods and then go through the General Synod with a two-thirds majority in each of its three Houses. The Measure is discussed by the Ecclesiastical Committee, 30 members drawn from the Lords and Commons, who decide whether it is 'expedient'. If expedient, it is presented to the Commons and the Lords, who can pass or reject, but not amend. The Measure finally, like other legislation, needs the Royal Assent, the Queen's signature.

Just occasionally, all this discussion and debate attracts considerable public attention, and before the final debate on women priests there was no lack of media coverage. Some reporters had no idea of the background, and seemed to think that the proposals might have come forward through a sudden inspiration of one or two Synod members. They sometimes found it hard to believe that proposals such as the Measure enabling women to be ordained priest would have to go through a process of discussion, debate and voting right through the church system as far as deanery synods and even Parochial Church Councils, and back again.

But this kind of debate certainly happened. People turned out on stormy nights, picking their way to steamy Nissen huts or chilly church halls, to hear points for and against. The issue would be discussed in groups and in the full meeting, the main speakers would respond, and a vote would be taken. Deanery synods are therefore a real attempt by the Church of England to have parishes and their representatives involved in discussion of and voting on major issues of faith and order in as informed a way as possible. In the case of the women's ordination Measure, there would often be a preparatory meeting with literature available for study; members would consult with their PCCs before coming back to deanery synod for the discussion and vote required of them by General Synod.

A new start—November 1984

The earlier history of discussion and debate on this issue has already been outlined elsewhere in this book. By 1984 a real conviction had at last taken hold that the time was now right and that the Church must not delay any longer. Parishes had begun to write to their bishops, deanery synods were sending up motions to their diocesan synods asking that the matter be raised there and sent forward to General Synod for action. The first Resolution came from Wheathampstead, in the diocese of St Albans, as early as 21 February 1981. But it was not until 15 November 1984 that the motion was put to the General Synod, proposed by Ronald Bowlby, then Bishop of Southwark:

> That this Synod asks the Standing Committee of General Synod to bring forward legislation to permit the ordination of women to the Priesthood in the Provinces of Canterbury and York.

It was significant that eight other dioceses from different parts of the country had already sent up similar motions: St Albans, Ely, Chelmsford, Rochester, Canterbury, Carlisle, Derby, Worcester and Liverpool. The movement for change, therefore, came to General Synod from a wide spectrum of churchpeople and not as the pipe dream of a few enthusiasts.

This vote would only be for the first stage, the setting-in-motion of change. But it was the first real testing of the water since MOW's foundation: six years since the Synod had last debated the issue, five years since the foundation of MOW, four years since members of this Synod had been elected or re-elected. They had been years of intensive work, all over the country. The initiative of David Driscoll and Chris Bard, two priests in the diocese of Chelmsford, in setting up 'Priests for Women's

Ordination' had been very important for the encouragement of the clergy; Women in Theology (WIT) was active, and the Catholic Women's Network was encouraging us from the sidelines. 1984 had been a good year for MOW, beginning with the great service in Westminster Abbey to celebrate the 40th anniversary of Florence Li's ordination to the priesthood. We knew that, for one reason or another, there was widespread support on this Synod. On the other hand, groups of opponents were becoming active, and the Church Union and other bodies with names like Ecclesia were bitterly opposing any legislation for women priests, or even for women deacons.

As soon as Church House opened that November day in 1984, queues formed for seats in the public gallery, winding up the wide circular stone staircase. Officials picked their way through the waiting young and old: deaconesses of many years' standing, anxious that the legislation be put in place before it was too late for them; theological students sounding a note of hope. Eventually we all squeezed into seats and had time to observe the debating chamber. As it began to fill up, friends greeted and sat down beside each other, bishops mostly sat together on the front three rows of the circle. Everyone stood for the opening prayers, then the Bishop of Southwark began.

Early on in his speech, he tackled the objection that this was a 'divisive' issue that should be left till later:

> The fact that it is a divisive issue does not in my judgment constitute an argument for indefinite delay. William Wilberforce presented to Parliament his motion for the abolition of the slave trade annually from 1791 to 1799 and again in 1804 and 1805. He was constantly asked to desist on a variety of grounds, many of them to do with the alleged unpreparedness of both planters and slaves in the West Indies; but he did not give up, believing the issue too important to be laid to one side.

Bishop Bowlby spoke of the growing experience of women's ministry, of the increase in the number of women ordained priest in the Anglican Communion, of the importance of women's experience now: 'Many women in all walks of life share a common perception of changes that they welcome or would like to see.'

The central passage of his speech was profoundly theological, and was listened to with close attention:

> I want to argue that the only way to safeguard the doctrine of God in its fullness is to ordain women as well as men. Why? Because the tradition, grounded in scripture, is precisely that mankind, male and female, is made in the image of God and because, when Christ died and rose again from the dead, he redeemed all who believe in him, women as well as men, and incorporates them in his body, the Church, by baptism. This is the new royal priesthood, and it is made up of men and women, the new humanity.

The Archbishop of Canterbury, Robert Runcie, spoke recommending a policy of 'gradualism' and ended by saying that he did not believe we could yet move with integrity to the stage of legislating for the ordination of women and that he would be voting against the motion. Deaconess Diana McClatchey then moved the whole debate out of the realm of anxious diplomacy and in a spirited speech looked beyond the Church and into the future with hope:

> Talk to a group of educated young women, your own daughters and granddaughters . . . In the world of thought we shall never succeed in putting the clock back and it is the Christian feminists who are committing themselves to bridging a growing gap, affirming insights, affirming much that the Spirit seems to be revealing through secular feminism, testing and judging other ideas by the canon of scripture and reclaiming much of feminism as within the Christian tradition . . . If you want a Church which retains the atmosphere of an exclusive men's club on ladies' night, you will have little sympathy either with Christian feminists or with this motion . . . Do not be surprised, however, if in ten years time you then find even fewer young women in the parish church and even more in the feminist house groups.

In a setting where there is a high level of predictability, this was the most unexpected speech of the day, and carried weight accordingly. Christian Howard also moved things along by quoting Archbishop Anthony Bloom, of the Orthodox Church, saying to her 'Although the Church of England should listen to what other churches have to say, to find out what they are witnessing to, it should not spend its time calculating its moves on what others will do. What matters is what is right, what is doctrine, not what is expedient.' That also provided a little gust of fresh air.

So it went on. Monica Furlong and I sat side by side in the gallery all day. Gradually we sensed the mood of the Synod. At some point in the afternoon Monica turned to me: 'It's going to go through.'

This first vote to start the process of preparing legislation was passed in all three Houses: Bishops 87%, Clergy 57%, Laity 63%. An overall vote of 307 to 183 in favour. At this stage only a 51% majority was needed. After the defeats of 1975 and 1978 seasoned Synod members in particular were full of thankfulness; there was a long road still to travel, but the necessary two-thirds majority in each House at the final vote seemed a realistic hope.

After the vote there was an enormous feeling of relief. At last synodical work could start on preparing the legislation. We knew it would grind on slowly (Christian's 'long haul') but as MOW and Synod members made their way back to the MOW office in the early evening we were sure that what had started that day could not now be stopped. We celebrated in a huge shared supper of spaghetti and red wine cooked in the tiny, steamed-up kitchen opposite the MOW office and ate it in the little sitting-room alongside. It seemed a far cry from the days when that was the sitting-room for the many bachelor curates of that parish, as we munched, talked, laughed and even, from sheer exhaustion, went to sleep on each other's shoulders. We were more than ever grateful to St Stephen's, Rochester Row, for giving us a home in their Napier Hall.

York, July 1986: Three decisions on women's ministry

Once a year the General Synod has a residential meeting at York University. Those sessions have a different feel about them: between the meetings people walk about the campus, sit at the edge of the lake, have unexpected conversations. The crèche is managed by the local Mothers' Union and feels easier. No struggling with the Underground; members actually get to know one another over a shared meal or a drink, rather than round a committee table or manipulating the mike in the debating chamber.

That group of sessions at the York Synod in July 1986 felt like a watershed for the movement towards women priests. There were three important decisions to be taken on matters relating to women's ordination, two of them involving major debates.

(1) Women ordained abroad

First was the Final Approval, we hoped, of the Women Ordained Abroad Measure. This was to permit visiting women ordained abroad to celebrate the Eucharist in churches in this country, a Measure hedged about with provisos but which would extend to women—in particular circumstances—the normal courtesy extended to male visiting priests.

By the time this Measure reached the stage of Final Approval, it was surrounded by a high degree of tension. To those opposing women priests it was critical that women, even if they were already priests, should not celebrate Communion in English churches. They realized that once people had the opportunity to experience a woman presiding, even occasionally, much of the prejudice would melt away. We were equally anxious that the permission should be extended.

As we know, it had been expected to go through earlier, simply as an adjustment to an existing arrangement. However, those who were opposing women priests in any shape or form had achieved delay and referral to the dioceses. Many Synod members had been surprised, even angry, and regretted what they had seen as an extraordinary reluctance on the part of the Archbishops to show firm leadership. This background was not forgotten now, as the Measure came back for Final Approval, duly approved by the majority of deanery and diocesan synods.[2]

Deaconess Diana McClatchey, who presented the motion, has said that by this time the Women Ordained Abroad Measure had ceased to be a minor decision extending a courtesy to visitors; it had become for many a vote on the principle of women priests. Added to that, a significant number of supporters were unhappy about the legislation, on the grounds that the special permissions required only for women, not for men from abroad, were insulting. Other supporters felt it was coming up at the wrong time, that it was unfair to our own deaconesses, that the cart was being put before the horse. For all these reasons and in spite of the Archbishop of Canterbury's plea—'It is a step which will build up our Communion and thereby in the long run assist our all-round effort for Christian unity both international and national'—the two-thirds majority was not achieved.

One of the most difficult things about that day for us was the very public popping of corks in the bar before lunch. It was a dark day for those who cared about the ordination of women and many tried to find ways of expressing solidarity with their sisters overseas. A letter from Helen Wickham, a Manchester MOW member and the wife of the Bishop of Middleton, describes a courageous act of witness the following Sunday:

Dear Margaret, I feel I should let you know about my one-woman demo in Manchester Cathedral last Sunday. First I must say that I am not really a demonstrator, going on marches for this and that is not in my life-style. I am also not a feminist; I believe that in all callings and professions and work in the community we need to see women and men working together. However the Synod's decision last Saturday to refuse Anglican women priests the same rights as their male counterparts from abroad seemed to me an affront to the dignity and stature of women that was too much to bear.

The Laity are allowed to read the OT Lesson in Manchester Cathedral at the Sunday morning Eucharist. It was my turn this last Sunday, July 6th. I read well, even though I say so, and I had the congregation's full attention. So at the end of the reading, still at the lectern, and instead of saying 'This is the word of the Lord' which would have given the cue for the organ to start the psalm, I said 'Ladies and Gentlemen, as a demonstration of my sympathy with the Anglican women priests ordained abroad, who the Church of England said yesterday cannot celebrate Communion in Britain, I leave this service with great sadness.'

From the lectern I then walked right out of the Cathedral and went home.

Anne Booth-Clibborn was in the congregation. She phoned me later to say that my action had electrified the service. She said if she had been quicker on the uptake she would have walked out too (I did not tell anyone in advance, as I was afraid I might not have the courage to do this in the end) and a number of other women said the same to me afterwards. One man told her that he suddenly saw the ordination of women in quite a different light.[3]

For many people such a gesture would simply not have been possible. Coming from Helen Wickham, a loved and respected

older member of the Christian community, it stiffened the backbone and gave fresh heart. But the cathedral responded by re-
moving her from the list of readers, and she has never been
reinstated.

(2) Women into holy orders as deacons

Going back to the Synod at York, the defeat of the Women
Ordained Abroad Measure was not the end of the affair. One
small step had to be taken to finalize a much more far-reaching
change. The Measure to enable women to be ordained deacon
and, like the men, to be in holy orders had to come back to
Synod for a final minor adjustment (Parliament's Ecclesiastical
Committee had, sensibly, sent it back for a small technical
change). It had received massive support in the dioceses and now,
having been grinding round all these processes for five solid years,
it was back for a (second) Final Approval. Some leading Anglo-
Catholics, Graham Leonard in particular, had consistently supported women deacons; he, most honourably, never wavered in
this, even though he must have known that the blocking of women
priests would be that much harder once women were deacons.
Others remained fiercely against; even at this last minute, determined opposition was mounted and long speeches made in spite
of pleas from the chairman. This irritated and wearied people, as
Laurence Spicer points out later in this chapter, and the Measure
went through again with the 'thumping majorities' Christian
Howard had asked for. The passage of this Deacons Measure to
Parliament was one of the most crucial votes in a decade of
debate. The Church of England in six months' time would be
able to welcome women among its clergy.

(3) Women priests—bishops to the rescue

At the same group of sessions in York, the Synod were expecting
to hear from Professor David McClean, Chairman of the House
of Laity. A more liberal mind than Oswald Clark, in whose place
he was elected, it fell to McClean, Professor of Law and Pro-
Vice-Chancellor of Sheffield University, to chair a group set up
to explore 'The Scope of the Legislation'. This was an unusual,

additional stage to enable Synod to express its mind before legislation was drafted. A human academic, his integrity and acumen
won respect from Synod members of very divergent views. But
the first Report—he was insistent that 'These are *not* Proposals'—
consisted of such a large number of provisos and safeguards, put
forward by the opposing members of his committee and others,
that the majority of Synod members were appalled. David
McClean delicately conveyed to Synod some of the problems he
had encountered: 'Unlike the more usual group [of this sort] we
did not have a built-in majority favouring the legislation under
discussion . . . we have concentrated . . . on the needs of those
who cannot accept the principle.'

Synod heard, therefore, of meetings that had been treading
stony and unproductive ground. Their disappointment surfaced
in plea after plea that proposals should be made which would
enable the Church to move forward together; many of them
echoed Sister Carol: 'We are in travail together . . . There can be
no truthful opting out. The task of this Synod is to find the
creative, Spirit-led way . . .'

Nobody (least of all, perhaps, David McClean) saw the Green
Report as introducing a path down which the Church could
possibly go. An amendment was carried unanimously handing the
matter over to the House of Bishops, who agreed to report in six
months' time, preparing the way for legislation. The feeling of
relief was almost tangible.

But for many there was also a feeling of anger at the continued
delays. They felt that the meetings of the Working Group had
been wrecked, and had also taken up months, apparently to no
purpose. Some others saw this as the lancing of a boil, and
a necessary exploration of much pain and bitterness. Professor
McClean's judgement was that there was a marginal advantage in
playing it slow. Opinion was all the time moving in favour as
Synod members found the tactics of those opposing the legislation
increasingly irritating. The Movement for the Ordination of
Women put out a press statement welcoming the fact that

for the first time the Bishops of the Church of England have taken
responsibility for planning the next step towards the ordination of
women . . . This followed a debate on the [Green] Report whose

proposals were demolished by speaker after speaker. In this debate it was noticeable that the ordination of women was approached not as a problem to be solved, but as an opportunity to release new energy and creativity in the Church for the sake of the Kingdom.

A view from the press gallery

Laurence Spicer, a well-informed London journalist, has written perceptively about these votes, seeing July 1986 as a watershed for MOW:

The proposal to enable women to be ordained deacon was reasonably assured of going through. Many of those opposed to the priesting of women, including Graham Leonard, Bishop of London, were very much in support of women deacons. However, the issue of the overseas women was a very different kettle of fish. To those in opposition to the women's cause this was the thin edge of the wedge and, in any case, to them, a woman could not be a priest wherever she had been ordained. Therefore, the proposed measure had to be fought with ferocity.

By the time of this Synod the support for women priests had, in all three houses crept past the 50% mark and the general view was that it was growing steadily. The important votes were those in the Synod who actually had no objection to women priests but who felt, for various reasons, that the time wasn't ripe. Some were worried by the effect that a positive vote would have on reunification with the Roman Church (and a letter from Cardinal Willebrands to the Archbishop of Canterbury on the subject had underlined this); others were more concerned about the strife that the decision would cause in the church should women be ordained. My own estimate was that those in the latter camp were very much in the majority.

Those in charge of the Synod were very concerned about the dangers to a residential Synod of a fiercely fought, bad tempered and thoroughly divisive debate. Whether they liked it or not the protagonists would be cheek by jowl at the dinner table after the debate. It was also pretty obvious that the 'Women Abroad' measure had little chance of getting through. So the thinking was to debate that measure first, get an agreement from the victors that their jubilation would be muted and, also, an agreement from them that their battle against the Women Deacons (reckoned a certainty) would be quiet and generous.

The debate on the women priests from abroad was as vicious and nasty as had been expected, and the motion was defeated. As the battered Synod emerged from the hall the Bishop of London called a Press Conference at which he appeared to be sticking to the unwritten agreement and declared his support for women Deacons. However, there were others in the winning army who were not prepared to let go of the initiative. Peter Geldard, pithily and belligerently, announced that his followers would be opposing any change in the existing orders of women. His belligerence and, subsequently, the belligerence of others of like mind, was stunning. Far from there being a gentle period of wound binding and finding common ground the battle erupted anew and the atmosphere of the remainder of that meeting was irretrievably soured.

Spicer continues:

As I watched and listened and talked there were two major consequences of this. Firstly, the majorities in favour of women deacons were rather larger than expected. Secondly, there was a perceptible and immediate shift from the 'Yes, but not yet' camp into the 'Yes' one. Amongst those who still remained in that camp there was also a move from the certainty of opposition into a rethink. Thus, in my belief, were the first moves begun that would bring victory to the women . . .

The reason why I felt so certain over the next years that the measure would succeed was based on three things. First, the tone of the opposition's campaign changed from the strident to the plain nasty. Those opposed took the Geldard line and even the late Margaret Hewitt, who behaved in a friendly and comfortable manner, could not bring a little lightness into their campaign. Second, the opposers could not conceive that they could possibly lose, even when the writing was on the wall in ten foot high letters. Thirdly, the success of MOW in responding positively, answering invective with fact. This policy was enhanced by choosing the politically right moment to strike with the often repeated and unarguable sentence 'It won't go away'.[4]

This is an interesting comment from a long-established observer of the synodical and church scene. Certainly, the defeat of the Women Ordained Abroad Measure galvanized supporters in many ways. This seems to have been the time when most people felt most depressed, not only Synod members but supporters all over the country. But the strength of the opposition was realized at last, and also the effect of their persistent and successful lobbying; in spite of the majority support in the dioceses, the Synod was persuaded against extending hospitality, even in limited circumstances, with graciousness and recognition to visiting priests of our own Communion.

Even so, my view at the time of that group of meetings was rather different from Laurence's. Although we were wrestling with our shame and regret over the Synod's discourtesy to visiting ordained women, the real news was the final vote on Women Deacons. Although a hardening of the opposition had been signalled which, according to Spicer, was to lose them allies, we knew that afternoon that we could rejoice. Parliament would soon be voting on the Measure which would bring our own women into holy orders, a far more fundamental change.

By the last day, when the Working Group's Report on the Ordination of Women to the Priesthood was debated, the Synod did seem to me to have changed. The whole of Sunday had been given over to a prolonged and at times moving discussion of the Bishops' Report on *The Nature of Christian Belief.* The Monday morning was given over to South Africa and the Report *Prisoners of Hope*. This was an important and serious debate, at the end of which a majority of 394 to 21 supported the Report, and a message was sent to Archbishop Tutu.

By the Tuesday morning they may have felt they had been through fire and water. They had been thinking about faith and they had been thinking about justice. The Synod turned to the bishops for some fresh guidance on how the Church should proceed over its own most burning issue of justice in the light of its understanding of Christian belief. This brought to a significant and cheering end a group of sessions that the most seasoned Synod members had found exhausting in the extreme.

From stately dance to slow march

Six months later, in February 1987, Robert Runcie presented to Synod the bishops' First Report on the Ordination of Women to the Priesthood. The bishops had kept to the time-scale promised and had produced a three-part Report which was unanimous. They sought to identify the main theological issues involved, they set out the principles on which legislation should be based, and finally they set out a more detailed framework for the legislation and for the 'safeguards'. Archbishop Runcie did now call for legislation to be prepared, and after a morning's debate the process of preparing a Measure was restarted, with an overall majority of 317–145 in favour (Bishops 80%, Clergy 65.9%, Laity 69%). David McClean burnished up his very considerable skills of chairmanship, and the members of his committee and others who had now been added to it prepared themselves for lengthy negotiation, if not downright battle.

It would still be argued over every step of the way. An article I wrote for the *Observer* after that Synod meeting reminds me of the kind of thing we had to listen to year after year:

> On occasions like this, the gallery is full to overflowing. People seem intent and rather serious, though we are not supposed to huff and puff, let alone wave a fist or a flag, while sometimes things which are unbelievably offensive to women are being said below. Could we have heard an elderly clergyman correctly, saying that if this came about it would be of the Devil? We may find it difficult to bear that the ordination of women is approached with such anxiety.
>
> The escalation of the 'Bogey Time' campaign of the past few months has had the rest of our society watching open-mouthed, wondering how they can take seriously a body of men and women who still continue to argue over this issue. They find it strange that the protection of some clergy from encountering a female priest should be such a central concern. 'They will be in the bloodstream' said one speaker nervously, as if women were measles. But in the bloodstream of the Church is precisely where women ought to be, and indeed already are.[5]

So the struggle was still going on even as the legislation began to take shape. But it was already a rearguard action. That article appeared just two days after the first ordination of women deacons. Parliament had passed the Women Deacons Measure by a huge majority, and Synod had made the necessary 'promulgation'.[6] The first steps of the synodical pavane were completed.

Robert Runcie ordained 14 Canterbury deaconesses into holy orders in his cathedral on Friday 27 February; this was followed by special services in all cathedrals, including St Paul's, where Graham Leonard ordained 71 women who were already serving in all parts of his diocese. London parishes turned up in force to support their deaconess, making this an unforgettable occasion. As women all over the country joined the male clergy, bringing their own skills and theological insights, so people discovered how good it was to have them conduct a marriage or a funeral. But they still could not celebrate the Holy Communion, and a woman in charge of a parish would still have to bring in a male priest to say the words of consecration. Pressure continued from the parishes that this should be put right.

Synod gives 'General Approval'

By July 1988 the work of the Legislative Committee was nearing completion. The proposed legislation consisted of two Measures: the first enabling women to be ordained to the office of a priest, together with the controversial 'safeguards'. These would enable a bishop, cathedral or parish to make a declaration distancing themselves from the ordination or ministry of women priests.

The second part of the package concerned the financial provision that should be made to clergy who would resign from the Church of England if women were ordained priest. These and the 'safeguards' had caused both anger and anguish as supporters wrestled with proposals that were discriminatory and insulting. How could they vote for this? On the other hand, generosity was a Christian virtue. And Parliament needed to know that minorities were protected.

The Synod first of all discussed for half a day a theological Report, the Second Report prepared by the bishops, which was presented by Archbishop Runcie. He declared himself again in favour of the principle but indicated doubts about the actual legislation: 'It would be less than candid of me not to remind the Synod that there is a distinction between being theologically in favour and believing that the ordination of women in the Church of England opportune.' Some might have been excused for believing they had entered a 13-year time-warp back to the famous 'double debate' of 1975, when the principle was approved but the motion to implement it was defeated. Some, of course, were delighted to hear this permission to vote against. Other bishops were more positive. Una Kroll's testimony to the receiving of the ministry of women priests was both moving and important; Jean Mayland brought some present-day reality into the ecumenical discussion:

In my ecumenical work I do not find the polarization which I sometimes find in my own Church. What I do find is that the Churches throughout the world, on a whole mass of issues, are stretched out in a long line . . .

of love and concern as well as difference of opinion . . . Many of us
know that below the surface of the Roman Catholic Church there is an
absolute ferment of opinion. In huge areas of Latin America ministry
to people, especially to the very poor, is carried on at the moment only
by nuns . . . It is a burning question in those countries as to how soon
those nuns can be ordained priest so that they can take the fullness of
ministry to those people.

When I re-read those debates of July 1988 the whole thing
comes alive for me: I can hear the tone of voice, see the speaker,
feel again the anxiety and the relief. The first day opened the
subject at a deep level; on the second day the question for the
observer was, will Synod at last give general approval? John Sentamu, quoting his daughter Grace, delighted the Synod, and it
was generally hoped that her perception and turn of phrase would
be fully used in the Church before too long. At the same time
many wondered how the juggernaut could be de-activated while
the lawnmower went to work.

That whole day meeting was chaired with sensitivity and skill
by Canon Ivor Smith-Cameron of Southwark. It was a long day.
Robert Runcie announced, as expected, that he would be voting
against the legislation. But the lawnmower was feeling nippy, and
the brakes of the juggernaut didn't quite engage. David Edwards,
Provost of Southwark, spoke for many:

Let us not nail our colours to the fence for ever. Let us not make fudge
our permanent and single diet. We are Anglican because we inherit
the correct decision that the Bishop of Rome has no jurisdiction over
us. With all due respect to him and his office, he has no more right to
stop us having women priests than to stop us having married priests . . .
We are Anglicans: let us do it.

To this speech the Synod responded with quite un-Anglican
enthusiasm and prolonged applause. Many more men than women
were called to speak. Perhaps the Bishop of Norwich was as
influential as anyone; briefly but forcibly he pointed out that,
recognizing the dilemma many people were feeling about the
timing, the only way to make a judgement was to test the mind
of the Church and vote for the legislation to proceed to the next
steps. At the end of this long day, Synod did indeed so vote.

Processes of revision

The next steps involved a lengthy and detailed revision of the
legislation to prepare the package that would go to the dioceses
for acceptance or refusal. This took another 15 months. David
McClean steered the Legislative Committee through the detail
without losing his vision of the objective. One clause would be
dropped, another inserted, as the bargaining went on. In November 1989 Synod spent two whole days, first in another general
debate and then dealing with amendment after amendment. It
was tense and concentrated; Robert Runcie spoke of 'two
unusually taxing days of debate—the most taxing in terms of
attention to detail and emotional investment that I have known in
nineteen years as a bishop here'.

After these two days the legislation had been hammered into
its final form to be referred to the dioceses. It was sent on its
way with large majorities voting in favour. Once again the people
of the Church of England were to consider and vote on this issue.

The Synod's stately dance had turned into a purposeful if slow
march. It was moving out of the ballroom, through the hall and
out the front door to the people waiting beyond.[7]

Notes

1   Grace Sentamu, quoted by her father, Dr John Sentamu, during General
    Synod, 5 July 1988.
2   See Chapter 6.
3   Helen Wickham, letter to author, 1986.
4   Laurence Spicer, letter to author, 1993.
5   *Observer* (1 March 1987). Contemplating schism in the Church of
    England, the speaker, the Ven. Eric Evans (later Dean of St Paul's), said:
    'There will be such a very large rent and it will take a long time to
    recover from it. And the only winner of course will be the Devil.' I find
    it rather amusing that I was writing the article quoted looking down on
    Amen Court from the top of the house he would later be living in.
6   To promulge—to make known publicly, to declare, in this case that the
    canon is passed.
7   The verbatim report of every Group of Sessions of the General Synod,
    Report of Proceedings, is published by The General Synod, Church House,
    Westminster, London SW1.

9　*The moving landscape*

> The New Testament does not encourage Christians to think that
> nothing should be done for the first time.
>
> Lambeth Conference 1968[1]

We have to pause at this point and try to discern what were the
influences, who were the people who in the Church's recent
history opened up the possibility of women's ordination and led
others on to contemplating a scene change.

This chapter will look at the background and some of the
processes that were going on as the Church of England opened
its eyes, if only slowly its arms, to the women who were doing
some of the finest work in ministry, though often hidden and
unsung. Change takes time: attitudes have to be shifted, arguments won, hearts turned. To some of us even the recent time
required for the Church of England to discuss and move on
women's ordination has felt like several lifespans; but we should
try to catch the mood of those earlier decades when the question
'What's your view about women priests?' was still regarded as
surprising.

The turmoil of the 1960s was in many ways a freeing experience
for the Church; it was a time when dreams were dreamed, some
reforms were prepared, some notable reforms actually went ahead.
A great deal of energy was put into the revision of the Prayer
Book, into preparing for synodical government, into plans for a
more sensible deployment of clergy, and into the scheme for
Anglican–Methodist unity. Adrian Hastings summarizes:

'We need urgently, all of us whether Anglicans or non-Anglicans, new
beginnings. I say deliberately *beginnings*': so wrote Donald MacKinnon

in 1962 [D. MacKinnon, 'Intercommunion: A Comment', *Theology* (February 1962), p. 56.] People were calling for this 'New Reformation' upon every side. One had anyway to keep up with Rome. A new beginning could be made in many ways. There was first the theological, and *Honest to God* would soon be followed across the Atlantic by the still more radical 'Death of God' theologians; secondly, the pastoral, ministerial and liturgical—the attempt to look afresh at the Church's own daily life and organization; thirdly, the ecumenical—a suddenly surfacing impatience with the stale, often seemingly trivial separation between denominations; fourthly the turning to the secular: the conviction that religious life should be far less concerned with the Church itself, far more with 'the World' and particularly with the struggle to overcome misery and injustice.[2]

In spite of all these stirrings, the question of ordaining women seems to have remained underground, though enough molehills were thrown up to indicate that something was going on. At that time there was a great gap between those church leaders who saw it as an important issue for the future health of the Church, such as Bishop Leslie Hunter of Sheffield[3] and others, and the majority of churchpeople for whom it was hardly on the agenda.

One example of this myopia can be seen in the organization Parish and People. It campaigned for 25 years for liturgical renewal in the Church of England, an objective which was achieved with the publication of the Alternative Service Book in 1980 and the more general use by the Church of the Sunday Parish Communion as the main service. But in their thinking the place of women's ministry, let alone inclusive language, did not noticeably figure. To quote Trevor Beeson, former editor of the journal *Parish and People* and now Dean of Winchester: 'Parish and People did not have women's ordination on its agenda. Individuals may have cared about it, but it wasn't an issue on the programme. *It didn't seem important enough to go on a reformer's agenda*' [my italics]. Trevor himself, looking back, thought this was surprising and, as if to explain, added: 'Parish and People was mainly a liturgical movement—all over the country, but heavily "clergy".' In the end, some observers felt that the local groups were not really committed to renewal, and that the interest in liturgy took the form of discussions about the time of Evensong or how to do the offertory procession. Any radical woman's voice would have to be heard elsewhere.

John Robinson, Bishop of Woolwich, whose *Honest to God*[4] was published in 1963, tried to stimulate new approaches about ministry, both from the point of view of including women, but even more perhaps in the hope of equipping and affirming lay people. He lectured on 'Taking the Lid off the Church's Ministry' at the launching conference for Parish and People, and, stirred up by a visit to Sweden, wrote an article in *Prism*[5] in April 1964 in which he made clear his conviction that this was not an isolated and secondary issue of ecclesiastical controversy.

More effective than words was the work which was actually going on. One towering figure was Mollie Batten, Principal of William Temple College from 1950 to 1966. A scientist and economist with degrees from Liverpool, London School of Economics, and St Anne's College, Oxford, Mollie Batten had worked in settlements in London's East End and in Birmingham before starting her career in the civil service. This was to lead to her appointment as the first Principal of William Temple College, a small but influential college founded by the Bishop of Sheffield. For 16 years Mollie Batten was the driving force in training Christian men and women to work with academic rigour towards understanding the Church's role in society. Her authority was unquestioned: she has been described as 'the first woman bishop in the Church of England'. The combination of her scholarship and experience of the world was compelling, in the same irresistible way as her habit of smoking a pipe was endearing.

Mollie Batten had a profound influence in many spheres; but for the women whom she trained she was a model unlike any other, her ability acknowledged, her credentials respected. Just as the then Bishop of Sheffield created opportunities for women to undertake hard and interesting work, so Mollie Batten gave them the intellectual and spiritual backbone to see it through.

Freda Matchett, a former student of Mollie Batten's at William Temple College, went to join Margaret Kane,[6] a member of the Industrial Mission team, to work in the mining parish of Maltby, in the diocese of Sheffield. 'My work was in the parish's newest district, the Cliff Hills estate, where we worshipped at first in a disused ambulance garage and later in the primary school, and where I experienced, as Margaret had done, the joys and frustrations of leading a community in everything except its central act of worship.' One of the churchwardens has written about their work at this time:

> We had experience of them in every function which a lay person in the church can fulfil. We saw them as organisers and teachers, as fund raisers, as ministers to the sick. They chaired our meetings, inspired us with new effort, restored our flagging zeal. They prayed with us, sang with us, and were unfailing in their encouragement and comfort to the bereaved or suffering. In time we came to look askance at the organizational arrangements which stood in the way to their fulfilling a completely priestly function ... We have never found women exercising such a complete ministry anywhere else since. Bishop Leslie Hunter was very much in advance of his time.[7]

Other remarkable work was going on in other places — of course — and right across the decades the Church has seen examples of women going either to open up or to resurrect areas where male clergy have scarcely survived. Sometimes the cost to the women has been very high; but these ministries form one of the strong threads in this weaving. They were the predecessors of the many deaconesses and women deacons who have had charge of a parish, been known as 'The Vicar' and who — 40 years later — were still having to arrange for a clergyman to come in and take over the central part of the parish Eucharist.

Patterns of change: women's movement, Church's rumination

In the 1970s, as the question of women's ordination to the priesthood began to move nearer to the top of the Church's agenda, most people who observed the Church of England from outside found the ban on women incomprehensible. 'I can't understand what all the fuss is about' was a perennial comment. Members of the Free Churches, most of which had been ordaining women for some years, watched with some concern as their sister Church appeared to be tying herself into knots. Between the late 1970s and the 1990s, there was considerable movement of opinion in the Roman Catholic Church. From being a question that was hardly considered, it crept gradually into at least informal discussions, as every stage of development was reported in the Roman Catholic press. A gap began to widen between official pronouncements from the hierarchy and the views of many Roman Catholics, both ordained and lay.

As far as the C of E was concerned, MOW rather expected, when it began its work in 1979, to find hardened opposition everywhere. With some relief we realized that, though this certainly existed, it was not widespread. Uncertainty and a gut-feeling of apprehension were much more common. This is highlighted by Dr Rupert Davies, formerly Principal of Wesley College, Bristol, and a past President of the Methodist Conference, in the chapter entitled 'The Low Standing of Women' in his perceptive book *The Church of England Observed*.

> Evidence for an attitude of mind is, no doubt, difficult to collect and assess, since few people nowadays are willing to confess openly to a belief in the inferiority of women, and the many Anglicans who hold this belief try to conceal it with such phrases as: 'I am a great believer in the equality of the sexes, but . . .' But they do not conceal it successfully. It comes out in insufferably patronising remarks made to women and about women (of which I heard many in meetings of clergy in which it has been my duty, and very often my pleasure, to be present), in the quiet sidetracking of projects in which women would bear an equal responsibility with men, pained comments about certain 'militant women', and a multiplicity of snide jokes (the most offensive being reserved for all-male assemblies and private conversations), such as the recent remark of a diocesan bishop in a diocesan synod, on the subject of the 'Movement for the Ordination of Women', to the effect that he would find it difficult to be associated with an organisation the initials of whose title rhymed with 'cow'.[8]

I am not in the least surprised to hear of that last remark, only that it was made on such a public occasion. The subject of women's ordination needed to be opened up so that people could be enabled to look at their feelings and prejudices, not only to grasp the issues more firmly and clarify their minds. Our task was to set a process going whereby this could happen in the Church of England and beyond.

Part of that task was already being done for us through the air we breathed. People cannot live and worship oblivious of the changes in the world around them, and God through the prophets has shown us the interdependence in which we live. We know we are bound up together and must listen to each other. Between the 1960s and the 1990s a new deep-down understanding began to take hold of very different kinds of people, about women, their gifts and what it was that they were offering to the Church and to society. Many, both women and men, could not endure to wait and watch while the Church went through its minuets and pavanes, and it will never be known, I suppose, how many despaired and went elsewhere. They made no fuss, but their comments linger in the minds of parents and friends. 'I could never have been ordained into a church that does not ordain women', said one young man, now a Buddhist, to his father, an Anglican priest. And a senior woman deacon wrote: 'I felt angry many times: whenever a man (especially a priest or even more a bishop) threatened to leave the Church the word schism was used—compared with the deafening silence when the many women I've known have left (something I've had experience of for thirty years).'

Over these years women began to speak out with a new strength, as they recognized the sin of sexism in society and in the Church, and set about ways of overcoming it. Slowly, painfully, legislation was introduced and the Sex Discrimination Act made radical alterations in employment opportunities. It excluded, however, from its provisos 'employment for purposes of an organized religion', along with (at that time) midwifery and mineworking. Certain provisos were also made for dramatic performance, some aspects of police work, and the care of lavatories. But in general the Act was of great importance. The old-boy network was still in existence, and is still effective even today, but unable to operate in quite the same way. It was inevitable that first attempts to enforce equal opportunities should change official thinking.

Two processes for change can be seen to be taking shape. Two patterns were forming which moved sometimes independently, sometimes together, becoming more or less dominant at different times. These were on the one hand the pattern of ecclesiastical reform and on the other the pattern of what Brian Heeney calls 'Church feminism'.[9]

Heeney uses this phrase of Maude Royden and other early leaders. The two words do need to be put together. Long before the present explosion of books and articles exploring every aspect of Christianity and feminism, women were struggling to reconcile their experience of being diminished or unheard in the Church with the loyalty and love they still felt. The Movement for the Ordination of Women helped to hold such women in the Church, acknowledging their suffering, encouraging them to clarify their perception of the Church's need for change, and giving them confidence. As encounters took place in small groups, often with a task in hand, a new consciousness was raised among church-women who would not at first call themselves 'feminist'. Although they dreaded being labelled, and perhaps had a distorted view of what feminism stood for, they were in fact being feminists through the work they had done in helping to lead other women out of the ecclesiastical wilderness. Ursula King, now Professor of Theology and Religious Studies at Bristol University, in the 1984 Cardinal Heenan Memorial Lecture defined the new conscious-ness:

> If we adopt an inclusive definition of feminism, then every person who recognizes the subordination of women and aims to overcome it, is a feminist, whether woman or man. Feminism is a unitary, but diverse, movement, not without its internal contradictions and tensions. Yet over the last twenty years women have spoken out with ever increasing strength and entered into new dialogue. They have discovered themselves and each other; they have learnt to perceive and criticize the deep injustices done to them; and they have also developed an amazing ability to envisage alternatives.[10]

Groups with this kind of vision—the Christian Women's Infor-mation and Resource Group, the Feminist Theology Group and Women in Theology (WIT)—were full of energy and creativity, and from 1980 onwards they published, arranged conferences, kept women theologians talking and thinking together. New lan-guage and liturgies were explored, and as women discovered their voice, groups would take root in other places. There women's experience was valued, not trivialized, and the non-hierarchical setting was a new experience for many.

Dr Mary Tanner in a lecture 'Christian Feminism: A Challenge to the Churches' assesses its importance:

> To dismiss Christian feminism on the grounds that its origins lie outside the Church is to misunderstand one of the fundamental beliefs of Christianity. The God of the Christian religion is a God who created all things, who sustains all things and who is at work outside the Church

as well as within the Church ... Christian feminism cannot be 'put down' merely by the accusation that it is slavishly imitating 'the secular assumptions of a passing age'. Christian feminists do confidently and thankfully acknowledge that they in fact owe their early inspiration to secular feminism ... However the growth in confidence and the rapid spread of Christian feminism today no longer feeds upon external sources, but finds its inspiration in the depths of the Christian tradition.

She goes on:

What is new in feminist theology is that for the first time in the history of Christianity, women in significant numbers are using their 'women's experience' to interpret the tradition. It is precisely that experience which has been shut out of theological reflection, and out of the ordering and structuring of the Church's life. The use of 'women's experience' explodes as a critical force, exposing classical theology as for the most part based upon male experience, western, academic, male experience at that, rather than a universal human experience. By bringing 'women's experience' to bear on the Christian tradition women are breaking into the closed circle of men who have formed the majority of those who have written, guarded and interpreted the Christian story.[11]

This breaking of women into the community of interpretation has been a source of life and inspiration to very many who were working for the ordination of women. Dimly we began to perceive that our sisters who called themselves Christian feminists had an enormous amount to offer, and that from their gentle exploring of language and experience, their careful examination of biblical texts, would come a bubbling-up of energy and creativity for the Church.

In 1991, Monica Furlong looked back at the development of feminist theology in Britain and the specific question of women's ordination:

For those of us bent on confronting the Church with the issue, it was not a matter of an idle whim, still less an attempt to treat ordination as simply one more hurdle women had to vault, like the law or medicine, on their way to full human stature—although the justice issue *is* one very important strand in the whole matter, and one on which the Church is properly judged by many outsiders, including women.

Our point was that women's sense of calling, their spiritual and pastoral and moral gifts, their devotion to Christian beliefs, were being wasted in frustration and disappointment. Many women longed to be priests, others, both women and men, liked the idea of women priests, and of women as Christian leaders and role models . . .

Only as we pushed for change did the hidden agenda of centuries become clear to us—the sense of women as inferior, as beings who needed to be carefully controlled and subordinated. And behind that was another and more secret taboo, of woman as Eve, or Flesh, the culpable inspirer of lust, of women as somehow dirty and unclean, or as representative of troublesome Nature herself.

After making some gentle fun of Dr William Oddie,[12] a great describer, with others, of the horrors of feminism and the axes feminists were sharpening in order to lay waste Christian belief, the Church, and civilization as we know it, Monica continues:

Their claim is that we are out to wipe out God, and replace him with earth goddesses, to destroy the Church, and replace it with, if I read them aright, dancing in sacred groves and celebrating Beltane. When you remember that, to date, women have never even exercised voting rights at the Lambeth Conference, it seems a rather curious attribution of power to suggest we can annihilate God: I cannot say that I, for one, feel equal to it, or even attracted by the idea . . .

The revolution I at least have in mind is a very different one, in which the Church might genuinely treat women as equals, listening to their insights and experience, appreciating their qualities, using their astonishing gifts and talents to the best advantage; in which old ideas of domination, whether of women, the earth, animals, native peoples, Nature, might give way to a more tender nurturing from both men and women . . . In which the old-boy network of the Church of England might yield, generously, to a man-and-woman network which cared about proper opportunities for everyone. It may seem a far cry from these ends to insist that a woman be allowed to stand at an altar and hold the Body and Blood of Christ in her hands, but only by such an action, some of us believe, can ancient taboos be changed.[13]

It seems sad that this eirenic approach was frequently perceived in negative terms. Churchpeople were as ready as anyone else to polish up their stereotypes, and in addition often had and voiced the feeling that if a change was taking place in society, it must for that very reason be mistrusted or denied in the life of the Church.

But there were churchmen and women who could see the hand of God in this surging movement. Expressing itself in so many different ways, it seemed to be offering the Church glimpses of a better way ahead. The idea of God's moment, the God-created opportunity, the *kairos*, is examined by John Austin Baker, then Bishop of Salisbury, in his lecture 'The Right Time':

> The Bible does not see these *kairoi*, these critical junctures, simply as openings that occur in the evolutionary march of history and which some people are ready to exploit. It is a matter of God creating the pregnant or opportune situation.

Looking at how these moments are brought about, Baker explores further:

> The development of what we call 'secular' thought or culture is not to be dismissed as no part either of God's preparation of a *kairos* or of the interpretation that divine love and wisdom want us to put upon it. The Bible will not allow us to draw any such pious conclusion . . . It would, in my judgment be quite impossible, on biblical grounds, to argue that because 'equality for women' or 'the liberation of women' (or whatever label for the sexual revolution is least misleading) is a fashionable cause in secular circles it is something which Christians should either deeply suspect or even avoid on principle. On the contrary, its presence in the secular world could well, on biblical precedent, be a creative factor preparing a divine *kairos* . . . It is not reasonable nor biblical to say, 'We will not take this step *just because* it would be very like current developments in the world'.[14]

As the task of education and information developed, MOW published new booklets at regular intervals which were rapidly dispersed to a variety of meetings and bookstalls in every diocese. George Carey, then Principal of Trinity College, Bristol, wrote the second one, *Women and Authority in the Church*.[15] In this he took the specific arguments based on biblical texts which are most commonly used against women's ordination, and dealt with them one by one. Writing 'to help people who are trapped between their loyalty to the teaching of scripture and their instinct that it seems to be unjust and wrong', the present Archbishop of Canterbury helped many Evangelicals to think their way through to a new position about certain texts.

As far as voting on the General Synod was concerned, it was among the clergy that the pattern of change most needed to be woven: in the 1978 vote, both the bishops and the laity had voted in favour. Why were the clergy for so long, more than any other section of the Church, reluctant to welcome women into full ministry? For the moment I will look at the objections as they were presented, though I believe that, as Monica Furlong suggested in the article quoted, there were many other unspoken factors at work behind the statements that were made.

The strands of argument

1. Impossible? We have already seen that the most basic statement against women's ordination was that it was quite simply impossible for a woman to be ordained priest. Ronald Bowlby remembers: 'When pressed, Graham Leonard and others used to argue in terms of masculinity equalling the "initiating" activity of God, of which Jesus is the supreme example.' This statement kept on appearing, in different forms, some more offensive than others. Some Roman Catholics joined the fray. Joanna Bogle, a Roman Catholic lay woman who came to interview my husband and me in St Paul's Deanery during a series of six 'Conversations'[16] she was preparing for television actually said during the interview that you could 'no more ordain a woman than you could ordain a poodle'.

2. Man the head of the woman In this kind of biological/biblical fundamentalism Anglo-Catholics who opposed women's ordination were joined by allies from the opposite wing of the Church of England. For most Evangelicals a woman celebrating the Holy Communion was not a problem; they did not share the other Anglo-Catholic argument about a priest being the icon of Christ and therefore necessarily male (to paraphrase Dean Matthews' attack on this argument, being white, fat or bald did not seem to matter). But some Evangelicals opposed women's ordination as priests (or presbyters, their preferred word) on the basis of their understanding of the man–woman relationship which emphasized the divinely intended dominance of the male. This was their interpretation of the story of Adam and Eve, coupled with their reading of certain New Testament texts.

Groping for allies, the two extreme wings of the Church of England described above met to found, in August 1985, the

Association for the Apostolic Ministry (AAM). An unholy alliance, many people thought, observing that the one link between these uneasy bedfellows was their opposition to the ordination of women. William Temple's comment in his *Readings in St John's Gospel* seemed as apt now as when it was made: 'It is sad to reflect that when the extreme wings of ecclesiastical opinion are found united, it is usually in resistance to some movement which is afterwards seen to be blessed.'

3. *'The Doctrine of the Unripe Time'* A wider band of Anglo-Catholics and others were moved by the argument about unity with Rome. They held that ordaining women now would jeopardize relations with the Roman Catholic Church. Later, when the Anglican–Roman Catholic International Commission (ARCIC) came to a standstill, those arguments changed to an insistence that the Church of England had no right to ordain women without the Roman Catholic and, they now added, the Orthodox Church being in agreement. The leaders of the organization WAOW (Women Against the Ordination of Women) fell largely into this camp, as well as some of the clergy group Cost of Conscience. These were arguments that had been advanced over many years, and were a notable element in what we began to call 'The Doctrine of the Unripe Time'.

Rome and the Church of England

In all its dealings with the Church of England, Rome had insisted that it alone was the Church. Pope Leo XIII in 1896 condemned Anglican orders as null and void and Pope Pius XI forbade Roman Catholics to take part in conferences with other Christians. In England, even in wartime, many Roman Catholic priests would not say the Lord's Prayer with Anglican clergy.

John XXIII became Pope in 1958 and changes began to happen. In 1959 he greeted non-Catholics as 'separated brethren and sons', set up the Secretariat for Christian Unity and received Archbishop Fisher in 1960. Paul VI met Archbishop Michael Ramsey in 1967 and arrangements were made to begin theological discussions between the Churches. In 1982 John Paul II went to worship with the Archbishop of Canterbury in that cathedral though they did not receive Communion together.

During those 20 years, therefore, some discernible progress towards unity seemed to be taking place; the longing felt by many Anglicans for closer links with Rome appeared to have some prospect of reality. In all the debates on women's ordination, the possible effect this would have on closer unity with Rome was emphasized. The bishops in particular took the Anglican–Roman Catholic International Commission (ARCIC) seriously, as developments would be discussed regularly at their Bishops' Meetings. They probably cared more about these developments than did the majority of English Anglicans. The supporters of women's ordination became aware that for some bishops it was easier to be concerned about the cousins in Rome than about the sister at your palace gate.

Then the whole process of conversation with Rome stalled. The Vatican kept their response to ARCIC II (the second series of meetings of the Commission) under wraps for years and, when it came, it was a huge disappointment. Many Catholic-minded Anglicans saw that their hopes for unity with Rome could no longer be given priority over everything else and began to rethink their views about women priests in the Church of England.

From 1989 onwards a new breath of air could be felt gusting in on the Church. It was called Affirming Catholicism, and it did indeed affirm those who were being excluded from the old Anglo-Catholic club. It also tried to support other Anglican Catholics who were beginning to wonder if they ought to 'go to Rome'. The Archdeacon of Middlesex, Timothy Raphael, captured some of the background to these dilemmas in his letter to the Middlesex clergy, *Middlesex Roundabout*, of Rogationtide 1993. Under the heading 'Roman Auction', he describes the Anglo-Catholic scene of some 30 years ago:

> Rome exercised a fascination for the young catholic ordinand. It gave us the permission to be different, the glamour of the Avengers and the mystery of the 'mole'. We talked about authority and sniffed at our own bishops. We avoided evening communion with a well-bred disdain and suddenly became enthusiastic for it when Rome changed its mind. A tiny number 'poped' and some of them bounced back. Most of us were

too involved in real life to fantasise much about Auntie (Mother Church's unmarried sister). Anyway Rome tried a bit of overdue reform and destroyed the last of the day-dream. The last thing we wanted was low church services in the vernacular.

For many of us Rome failed by never really taking its ecumenical role seriously. Vatican II tried hard to say the right things but it could never accept its place as one church among others. Until and unless we treat other groups of Christians as Churches in their own right no ecumenical progress is possible. We should know, we did it to the Methodists a few years ago and lost much credibility . . .

The hopes placed on ARCIC seem to have been dashed by their response to the latest report. For most of us Rome has not changed since our youth and we cannot understand why some of our colleagues can go back in time and feel happy about it. As for the extraordinary reason that the C. of E. had no right to make its own decision—was it us who unilaterally proclaimed Papal Infallibility or the Assumption or rejected Anglican orders? Why is it wrong when we do it? For me Roy Strong said it all when Lord Rees-Mogg was being patronising about mere Anglicans. 'British society has survived because its institutions have on the whole known when to change and move on. We are just at such a moment.'

Tim Raphael's light touch catches the atmosphere of the old Anglo-Catholic ethos, something that can perhaps only be properly understood by one who has been part of it. But beyond the note of sadness is the conviction that there is no going back, that Catholic Anglicans must find a new strength in working with change. Though a minority were devastated by Rome's lack of response, others—encouraged by open-minded Roman Catholic friends—came to the conclusion that it was not tenable to hold up change any longer for the sake of what was appearing more and more like a mirage.

The texture of ministry

While all these arguments had been going on and while the rest of society had been bringing the gifts of women to the attention of the Church of England, one factor was constant, steady, and impressive. This was the ministry that was actually going on month after month, year after year, which could not be denied and which resisted all efforts to minimize or degrade it. I see this ministry in three parts, which together wove the texture of the changing Church: first, the ministry of the women of the Free Churches, going back over many years; second, the developing ministry of the Anglican women; and third, the ministry of prayer that was such an important part of the life of MOW.

Sisters in the Free Churches[17]

The women in the Free Churches who encouraged us most were not always ordained themselves, but their belief in a whole ministry of women and men, ordained and lay, was clear and articulate. One of their strengths was the inner confidence that came from the fact that Free Church women had from the very beginning had an important part in leadership. The pastoral, teaching and preaching work of women was part of the rock of their reforming tradition. The influence of Susannah, a classical scholar, and mother of John and Charles Wesley, is well known; within our own memory, or that of our parents, is Elsie Chamberlain, ordained into the Congregational Church in 1941, and known to millions through her radio broadcasts. She was a pioneer as 'a Reverend lady in public office'.

Equally significant was Pauline Webb's work in the BBC World Service over the past 30 years, complemented by her work in Methodism and in the World Council of Churches. She played a crucial part in pushing the ordination of women in the Methodist Church on to a new stage in 1966. At that time the Methodist Church was going through the same contortions with regard to negotiations with the Church of England as their Anglican cousins suffered over the Anglican–Roman Catholic relations. Pauline Webb cut through a tangle of careful statements which balanced the theological affirmation of the reasons for ordaining women with an anxiety about the possible effect on Anglican–Methodist relations; characteristically, her amendment was clear and forceful. She pointed to the wider ecumenical context, where more and more Churches were ordaining women, and added that the cause of unity would not be furthered by Methodists refusing to have any convictions of their own. The amendment was carried by an overwhelming majority.

This side of the ecumenical debate is important, and it is absurd that the concern about unity should have been hijacked in the C of E to mean, apparently, relations with Rome. To our shame, although the Methodist Conference voted in 1967 by 77.4% in favour of the Anglican–Methodist scheme for unity, they were let down by the Church of England, since the Convocations (Houses of Bishops and Clergy), meeting two years later, did not reach the special majority of 75%. In 1973 Conference took the final decision to admit women as ministers, after which, in 1974, 17 women were ordained.

Another more comprehensive attempt to move towards unity with the Free Churches was the Covenant for Unity, to which the Methodist and the United Reformed Churches and the Baptists had pledged themselves. Just as Archbishop Ramsey had wholeheartedly supported the earlier scheme, so now Robert Runcie, with the majority of the bishops, supported the Covenant. But the spectre of allying with Churches who ordained women ensured the implacable opposition of Anglo-Catholics, whatever their bishops might say. The General Synod failed to achieve the 75% majority necessary in all three Houses.

This time many Anglicans hardly knew how to face their Free Church friends. It was very clear that, in spite of reasonable majorities in the Church of England as a whole, expressed through votes on synods, the Anglo-Catholic influence could at that time ensure the defeat of any scheme which did not lean towards Rome or which incorporated ordained women. This defeat of the Covenant in 1982 was important for MOW: awareness was heightened of the kind of struggle that was on hand and of the power of the Anglo-Catholic groupings. Large numbers of people joined MOW at this point, especially clergy, and many Anglicans discovered a new humility as they surveyed a Church where the tail appeared to be wagging the dog.

I think myself that this is one of the reasons why MOW, in its central planning, was strangely backward in asking for help from our Free Church sisters. I think that for some years those of us who were committed to the ecumenical movement could hardly face them, turning away from contact with those whom we had bruised. But their ministry, sometimes in ecumenical teams, or simply as neighbouring clergy was important. People became conscious of Rosemary Wakelin's skill as a broadcaster, of Janet Wootton's new hymns, and of the fact that in 1991 and 1992 the United Reformed and the Methodist Church had elected women as Moderator and President of Conference respectively.[18] North of the Border, the Queen appointed for the first time in 1992 a woman among her Chaplains. This was Mary Levison who in 1963 petitioned the General Assembly of the Church of Scotland that she be admitted to the ordained ministry of word and sacrament. The Church of Scotland gave an example to other Churches of how to combine theological *gravitas* with some sense of urgency, by agreeing after just five years of deliberations.

The work and witness of these women and many like them has been, and continues to be, a living statement that women in our country have been ordained for many years, are ministering also as lay people, and continue to be an encouragement on many levels. In case this should be forgotten, Janet Wootton's fierce reminders are salutory:

> How dare the women who are currently undergoing the struggle deny the ordination of those for whom the same struggle is almost a century in the past? [She adds on a positive note:] There is an ideal, then: for women and men in many denominations to work together, sharing the vision of a whole ministry of women and men for the health of Christ's Church. Where women are already a full part of that ministry, and perhaps especially where this has been the case for several generations, there is a wealth of experience to share. Where the front-line action is still being fought, fresh insights and new challenges are constantly arising. If the vast machinery of establishment within the Churches of England and Rome has succeeded in cutting off from the debate the only people who have practical experience of the matter under debate, then half the argument will never be heard.[19]

Women deacons, their own best argument

The second element in this texture of ministry that was all the time supporting the arguments is the work of the women deacons themselves. Here is a story I was told by the woman concerned. She was invited, when a deaconess, to preach at the neighbouring parish church. After she had finished preaching (not about women's ordination, of course) the Vicar swept out from his stall and, addressing the congregation, said 'Well, *didn't she do well?*' and compounded this by adding 'And doesn't she deserve a *nice kiss?*' Result: deaconess put in an impossible position, feeling both patronized and embarrassed and unable to think of any suitable riposte; while no doubt the Vicar was wondering what on earth was wrong.

But of course they *were* doing very well. And, especially from the time the women were ordained deacon, their ministry was as powerful a persuader as any argument. The passage of the Women Deacons Measure and the first ordinations in 1987 made a huge difference to opinion both within the Church and outside it. The ordination services received much publicity and the anomalous situation of the women was generally understood for the first time. They could see there was something very wrong in the situation: in parishes the deacons-in-charge[20] were able to do almost everything a priest could do, but still could not consecrate the bread and wine at the Eucharist; they had to stand aside, having arranged for a male priest to come in and take over at that point. Not surprisingly, parishes began to rise up and write to their bishops. When the final General Synod vote was approaching, its members were left in no doubt as to how strongly people felt (on both sides of the question). This letter, written to General Synod members from 28 churchwardens in the diocese of Norwich, all of whom were working alongside a woman deacon, testifies to a clear perception of the rightness of women priests. This began to be experienced all over the country as a result of the work the women were doing.

> We write to you as Churchwardens in a parish served by a woman deacon. Much of our diocese is rural and it is one which might be considered conservative. Nevertheless we would like you to know that lay opinion here is strongly in favour of proceeding with the legislation to ordain women priests. This is reflected in our diocesan voting: 71% in favour in deanery synods, 73% in Diocesan Synod. We are therefore looking forward with joyful anticipation to the time when those whose ministry we greatly value will find that ministry extended into priesthood. Since it is now generally agreed that the matter will not simply go away, we view with dismay any possibility that our Church might be condemned to further years of divisive debate. It

is vital for the mission of the Church, not least in our parishes, that the issue is resolved now.

Hearing the reports from General Synod, we realise that some hesitate to support the legislation because of their interpretation of Biblical texts on headship and authority. We can only say that we have experienced the exercise of authority by a woman in a way which is consistent with Scripture and guided by the Holy Spirit.

Over and over again this is what people have said. And the deacons themselves tell of the recognition of their ministry in what, for some parishioners, was almost a conversion experience. 'I'd noticed that this woman always moved over to the other line in order not to receive the sacrament from me. I knew she felt quite strongly about women being ordained. Then she had to go into hospital and I visited her, and after some time together she asked me to visit her neighbour in the next bed. I didn't do anything special at all, just did what I could, but that woman in our congregation has totally changed. She's home now and receives from me like everyone else, and seems to support my ministry.'[21]

Because of this growing support for women deacons who were by now known and loved as persons, not just as a good idea, another factor crept in to move opinion. Many people began to be heartily sick of all the argumentation and also the protests of the opponents, with claims for special safeguards against ordained women and financial provision if they left the Church. This was reflected in the deanery and diocesan synod voting. The two-thirds majorities that were achieved across the board resulted partly, also, from the opponents' arguments which were constantly shifting and therefore were regarded with some suspicion; and because people were now able to confirm what their head had been telling them with that true conviction which also comes from the heart.[22]

The raft of prayer

The third element in the texture of ministry is the prayer which went on over all those years. Even as we joined in some specially written liturgy, we might reflect on how the women, newly priested, would uphold the sacramental life of the Church. Their ministry would be both in bringing freshness and life to worship which had hardened and grown stale, and also in maintaining the regular celebration of the Holy Communion week by week.

Something of the prayer and celebration within the life of MOW has already been described. It is not surprising that through the struggle our prayer became more, not less, important. For many the experience of prayer grew and changed. For everyone these things are different, but what is clear is that the exploration of new forms of prayer, of inclusive language, of fresh symbols and imagery stirred people deeply and brought new energy. This would be true of those who might regard themselves as conservative in their church-going, who have specifically spoken of the value of the big services at Canterbury and Westminster and Coventry, and who may also be the most committed in keeping going the regular prayer of a MOW branch.

Many different groups now feed into the life of the Church a renewed understanding of language and liturgy. The St Hilda Community, whose story is told in Chapter 10, has been influential (and their book of prayers and services *Women Included* has gone to record-breaking heights). But far beyond St Hilda's, from the celebrating of Julian and the other women mystics, to the creation of services for Pentecost or Advent, or through the keeping of a regular day of prayer, diocese by diocese, MOW members discovered depths they did not know they had. Sometimes we would be working with opponents of women's ordination, to produce a vigil together, sometimes the new life would come through a special liturgy group.

One event might feed another, or it might have to be unique. One such was a service early in 1987 to celebrate women's entering into holy orders as deacons. The church where it was held, St Mary-le-Bow, in the City of London, has a chapel at the east end which is behind an iron grille and is lockable. After people had assembled and were in silence, the deacons came in at the east end and sat in the chapel waiting. There was a Litany of Penitence which Janet Morley had written for the occasion. Then a group of six walked up the aisle to the chapel: the former Archbishop of Central Africa, Donald Arden, two priests, Victor Stock and Suzanne Fageol, a retired lay worker, Frances Moffett (in her eighties), supported by a lay woman, Pat Schleger, mother of one of the deacons, and finally a lay man and Member of Parliament, Frank Field. In the silence the grille of the chapel was unlocked and the women, led by Anne Gurney, Head Deaconess of the Diocese of London, came through and took their places in the church as we said Janet's 'Litany of Blessing for Women Taking Authority'[23] and sang the Magnificat. For all who were present that was indeed a moment of thanksgiving and of looking ahead.

These special services whether national or diocesan, and these prayer groups, continued right through MOW's life. Twice a Novena of Prayer united all members, as we prepared for the Synod vote in 1984 and the final vote in 1992. Thousands of copies were sent out from the MOW office and were used by groups and individuals all over the country. On Day Nine of the Novena, the reading and the prayer committed our hopes and fears to God in faith:

> When our vision is clear, we can see the first steps we need to take. We cannot necessarily see how the ultimate transformation will take place. No evolution takes place as predicted, for change on the grand scale is a mystery, impossible to completely know or control. To open ourselves to that mystery should not make us passive, but eager to move forward, curious to see how events will unfold. We move on as far as we can see the road; and from that vantage point a new horizon is revealed.[24]

The raft of prayer was not exactly a safe place but on it we got through the rapids, and on through a moving, changing landscape.

Notes

1 'Women and the Priesthood', *The Lambeth Conference 1968: Resolutions and Reports*, p. 106.

2 Adrian Hastings, *A History of English Christianity 1920–85* (Collins, 1986), p. 538.

3 Leslie Hunter was Bishop of Sheffield from 1939 to 1962.

4 J. A. T. Robinson, *Honest to God* (SCM, 1963).

5 *Prism*, the radical Anglican monthly journal, edited by Timothy (now Lord) Beaumont. It was succeeded by the ecumenical *New Christian*, edited by Trevor Beeson.

6 A description of some of Margaret Kane's work appears in a footnote by Ian Ramsey (Bishop of Durham 1966–72) to her lecture *Secular Experience and Theological Thinking*: 'Margaret Kane is my theological

consultant in industrial and social affairs and is working ecumenically throughout an area that goes beyond the Diocese to cover both sides of the Tyne and Tees. Her task is to help provide a background of theological thinking that can support the churches' attempts to present the gospel in a way that speaks to the specific needs of the North East and its people.' See also Margaret Kane, *Gospel in Industrial Society* (SCM, 1980).

7   Freda Matchett, 'The Ministry of Women' in *Strategist for the Spirit: Leslie Hunter, Bishop of Sheffield*, ed. Gordon Hewitt (Becket Publications, 1985), p. 191.

8   Rupert E. Davies, *The Church of England Observed* (SCM, 1984), p. 36.

9   Brian Heeney, *The Women's Movement in the Church of England 1850–1930* (Clarendon Press, 1988), pp. 96ff.

10   Ursula King, 'Women in Dialogue: A New Vision of Ecumenism' (Cardinal Heenan Memorial Lecture, November 1984), *Heythrop Journal* no. 26.

11   Mary Tanner, *Christian Feminism: A Challenge to the Churches* (Loughborough University Chaplaincy Annual Lecture 1986), pp. 2, 5.

12   William Oddie, *What Will Happen to God?* (SPCK, 1984).

13   'Faith and Reason', *The Independent* (22 June 1991).

14   John Austin Baker, *The Right Time* (MOW Kairos Booklet No. 1).

15   George Carey, *Women and Authority in the Church* (MOW Kairos Booklet No. 2). For a full list of MOW publications see Notes at the end of Chapter 4, p. 65.

16   These were in fact reduced to one programme in which a number of people appeared.

17   The Congregational Church admitted women to the full ministry of word and sacrament in 1917, the Baptist Union in 1918, and the Presbyterian Church of England in 1956.

18   Ruth Clarke was elected Moderator of the United Reformed Church in 1991; Kathleen Richardson was elected President of Conference (Methodist) in 1992; Janet Wootton was President of the Congregational Federation 1990–91.

19   Janet Wootton, 'Oh, You're One of These New Women Deacons!' in *Women Experiencing Church*, ed. Dorothea McEwan (Gracewing, 1991), pp. 175, 178.

20   This was the official title for most of the women in charge of parishes; almost invariably the parish simply called them 'The Vicar'.

21   The Revd Jill Robson, in conversation with the author, July 1993.

22   This process took roughly two years. The results show majorities of two-thirds in favour of the legislation whether counted by Houses or by overall figures. See Appendix of voting figures, p. 212.

23 Both these litanies can be found in Janet Morley, *All Desires Known* (SPCK, 1992), pp. 60–2.
24 Starhawk, *Truth or Dare: Encounters with Power, Authority and Mystery* (HarperCollins, 1987).

IO *Every vote counts*

The longer we avoid the moment of decision, hoping that the
consensus will grow—it *will* grow but only in the process of
decision-making and theological discussion—the more polarized we
become . . . It is only when we have committed ourselves to action
that the work of healing, bridge-building and real mutual respect
can begin.[1]

At last, in 1990, the legislation was squarely before the Church,
to be presented to deanery and diocesan synods. The substantive
clause was there, clear and strong: 'It shall be lawful for the
General Synod to make provision by Canon for enabling a woman
to be ordained to the office of a priest if she otherwise satisfies
the requirements of Canon Law as to the persons who may be
ordained as priests.' But many people could hardly believe their
eyes when they read what followed; they found it impossible to
be enthusiastic about the rest of the package, with all its provisos
and safeguards. It leaned over backwards to accommodate the
opponents: a number of Declarations had been worked out which
could be made by a bishop, a cathedral, or a parish, effectively
distancing them from contact with a woman priest. An opposing
bishop could refuse to have any woman ordained priest in his
diocese, or any woman licensed as a vicar, or even refuse to have
any woman licensed to officiate in any way as a priest within the
diocese. A parish could pass a Declaration refusing to have a
woman celebrate the Holy Communion or to be incumbent or
priest-in-charge. A cathedral could make a similar Declaration
against having a woman to preside at Communion or as Dean.

These were the 'safeguards' which had been hammered out in
deference to those who were most opposed to women priests.

They were a response to a sustained campaign threatening mass resignations of clergy, defections to other Churches and, broadly speaking, the break-up of the Church of England. This campaign did not slacken as the issue went under debate in the dioceses, and the air continued to be thick with threats right up to and beyond, the final vote.

It was, therefore, a fairly dreadful set of propositions. If the word 'Scot' or 'left-hander' were inserted to replace 'woman' the legislation would be seen as totally discriminatory and impossible, e.g. 'That this Parochial Church Council would not accept a Scot as the incumbent or priest-in-charge of the benefice', or 'That the administrative body would not accept a left-hander as the Dean of this cathedral church'. And beyond the discriminatory words could be sensed the distaste with which women in the sanctuary were sometimes viewed, the unease at the prospect of a male–female collaborative ministry. All that was a part of the protest which had led to the provision of these 'safeguards'.

There were in addition financial provisions for any clergy who decided to leave the Church of England if it went ahead with ordaining women priests. This also raised problems: in principle, was this right? and even if it were right, could the Church of England afford it?

For two years the synods wrestled with these questions. Some decided quite quickly to support the proposals, saying 'We are a Christian body, we know a minority feels strongly about this issue, and some may be prepared to give up their job and their home rather than go along with this change. It is right to be generous, especially since many clergy live in a tied house and do not own a home of their own.' It was also thought that few Declarations would be made, since this would be a serious business; those people would have to call special meetings, and send copies of their Declaration to the Queen, the Duke of Cornwall, the Lord Chancellor, the Archbishop, and maybe a few others. Not a very likely scenario, it was said.

Members of Parliament constantly have to vote for legislation they do not feel very happy about, but it was a new experience for voters on deanery and diocesan synods. MOW members had a difficult time persuading themselves that this was the only way ahead, that it was this legislation, provisos and all, or possibly nothing. The main point of the legislation, it was pointed out, was to enable women to be ordained priest; the absolute priority was to achieve that. So in the end MOW members threw their lot in with the great effort to get the legislation passed with good majorities in synods up and down the country.

Sea-change

From 1987 it seemed that MOW began to go through a sea-change. Some members felt quite strongly that since the House of Bishops had produced their own Report, and the legislation was about to go to the dioceses, the waters were calming down and the energetic breaststrokes were scarcely necessary any longer. Or rather, that the swimming could now be confined to a smaller area, and not too much splashing please. Other MOW members saw this as certain death, that cramps would ensue, the whole Movement would seize up and sink to the bottom. Energetic signals were still vitally necessary, we said, to make clear we were waving, not drowning.

Everyone, however, was agreed on the importance of the synods at every level. Rosemary Tucker of Oxford has described this as a very profound time, this going out and speaking at deanery meetings. MOW members and their opposite numbers often cemented some way of connecting with each other. 'I remember thinking "Here's this woman and me with very very strongly different views, and yet there's lots of things on which we do agree. And the Church expects us to get ourselves to the meeting, and that we'll still be able to communicate . . .", and that was fine, that did happen.' For her, the work of MOW at that point was more about contact at a deep level, trying to understand the other and yet not go down on her own principles: 'I really don't find it possible to understand anyone's anti view, but I do find it possible to understand how they got to that position.'

Those who undertook most in the way of speaking were supported by their MOW branch. In some dioceses opponents and proponents were asked to produce a leaflet or broadsheet giving pros and cons; in others, there was some working together in the context of a vigil liturgy. Because those concerned cared very much about the Church, a kind of reaching-out could happen, leading to a new respect. In other places, however, the bishop would simply throw together a number of people who were diametrically opposed and expect them to come to some sort of understanding. With no facilitator, such groups usually ground to a halt, with everybody feeling miserable and angry. Unproductive encounters like that, or even, early on, downright refusals to enter into dialogue, seemed to confront MOW with an implacable brick wall. The London diocese in particular was in many ways a world apart from the rest of the C of E, with the rulings of some churches against women, even a woman deacon, entering the sanctuary and the encouragement, in the Edmonton Area, of the Roman Mass as the main Sunday Eucharist. These un-Anglican developments were not amenable to the kind of patient outreach and effort towards mutual understanding that could operate in Oxford and elsewhere. The pressure on women working in some London churches was nearly intolerable, and MOW members often felt outcasts.

So MOW had to continue the struggle, in every possible way. In 1987 the decision had been taken to enlarge Central Council in order to enable every diocese to send a member (previously dioceses had been paired). Diana McClatchey (Moderator from 1985 to 1988) felt that it had become too London-based, and not sufficiently representative, and the change had been welcomed by the Movement as a whole as it gave each diocese direct contact with central networks.

At this time there was quite a strong feeling among the radicals that they were being marginalized. The Radical Group took shape in 1987 to discuss issues and plan forms of action; they did not want MOW's emphasis on synodical matters to lead to a quietist policy which would be unproductive. They believed that if MOW's voice were not heard at this stage, much ground would be lost as the stridency of the opposition battered at the minds and spirits of the bishops and the hierarchy in general. They were concerned at the disparaging tone in which women were discussed in church circles, and also that women's working experience in the Church was not, in many cases, a very happy one. This view, shared by both older and younger MOW members, continued to make itself heard on Central Council. Out of this group grew the St Hilda Community.[2]

Diana McClatchey retired as Moderator in 1988. She had piloted MOW through the years in which the General Synod was girding itself to legislate for women priests. Although Diana's Measure on Women Ordained Abroad had been defeated in 1986, a bitter blow after years of patient negotiation, she continued to try to get Synod to move forward, as she also tried to persuade bishops individually to be a little more courageous.

In July 1988, during the General Approval debate, Diana made a prophetic speech calling on Synod to face up to conflict. Part of it is quoted at the head of this chapter. She challenged members: 'From somewhere this Synod, this Church, must find the courage to take this risk, knowing it to be a risk, knowing that we stand in need of judgement, knowing that the pain and the divisiveness will come and, I believe, knowing that this is the necessary precursor to new life.'

When Cathy Milford succeeded Diana as Moderator, the legislation had been passed with General Approval by the Synod and was undergoing revision before, it was hoped, going to the dioceses. Another crucial stage was about to begin. Cathy saw the enlarged Central Council as necessary for synodical reasons: 'Now that the legislation was to be debated in every deanery and diocese, and all the voting registered, then MOW in every diocese had to be firing on all cylinders. The direct input from Central Council became essential; one of its main tasks came to be that of *feeding* the dioceses—politically, theologically, liturgically, spiritually.'

The majority of Central Council was now firmly focused on synodical persuasion. Barry Rogerson, Bishop of Bristol and one of our Vice-Moderators, set up planning for extensive discussions in his diocese at parish and deanery level, and encouraged his fellow bishops in the way. Chris Bard, Communications Officer for the Diocese of Chelmsford, and an invaluable adviser to MOW right up to the final vote, insisted that MOW's prime task was to help people to 'feel good' about voting for women priests, to regard this as clearly the right thing to do. This was an important new thrust in MOW's policy. Members continued, therefore, to emphasize the need for MOW to have a high profile, whether through 'prayer and parties' as one diocese decided, or through the encouragement of various kinds of publicity including the 'Ready and Waiting' placards outside General Synod.

Choppy water

When it was clear that the legislation was likely to be referred to the Church of England's elected synods, those organizing opposition decided that once again it was 'Bogey Time', time to put on the frighteners. Never allowed to grow rusty from disuse, the frighteners on this occasion consisted of a list which caused the *Mail on Sunday* to carry, on 11 December 1988, front-page headlines 1½ inches high: 'CHURCH IN TURMOIL'. This was on the basis of a list of names of more than 1,000 clergy who had signed up their opposition to women priests. Words like 'schism' flew about. When keen MOW members began to examine the names carefully, the number of retired clergy on the list was noticed, as well as some deceased and some whose link with the working ministry was tenuous.

But the effect of the list was potentially serious; the claims might be exaggerated, but the newspapers loved it. Their emphasis on the possibility of a split in the Church continued to influence members of General Synod, and the last vote before the final one showed only 61% of the Laity supporting the legislation. The day of that July vote in York is one which most of us will probably remember as long as we live. MOW had organized a big rally to coincide with the Synod meeting; we all arrived in pouring rain to hear the surprising and depressing Laity result. Never had we felt more cast down. But somehow the crowded MOW meeting took off, thanks largely to Cathy Milford's opening announcement, 'MOW will continue in existence until women are ordained priest in the Provinces of Canterbury and York . . . !', and to Christian Howard's managing to make some of the history and the Reports actually very funny, and to the presence and wisdom of Martha Grey-Stack, a priest of the Church of Ireland. People who went into the hall dripping wet and dejected emerged with hope.

It was translated immediately into a vigil of prayer, a kind of extension of the 'Waiting' witness, which by then was beginning to matter more and more. It may have made some Synod members uncomfortable, but as Cathy Milford said, it reminded them that their decisions were about real people. That night at York University, as Synod members emerged from supper and made their way to the assembly hall, over 100 of us stood on the other side of a small stretch of water, with candles. 'There's cloud-cuckoo land', a Synod member was heard to say. But as we sang the meditative Taizé prayers, on and on, the dusk falling and the little candle lights glimmering round the edge of the lake, it seemed to me that the prayer deepened and the silence and the singing took on more and more meaning. 'The sight and sound of you all standing on the other side of the lake was very moving, very beautiful', one Synod member wrote afterwards. 'And the singing going on after we'd gone inside, was lovely too. Thank you all so very much.' 'Gifts for the Church—Ready and Waiting' ran some of the placards; this was not just a cerebral matter for discussion and argument.

Cathy Milford was the first Moderator to chair the meetings of the much enlarged Central Council, and her skills were immediately visible. She brought to the Moderatorship experience as a teacher at Budo College, Uganda, as a deacon in a big Bradford parish, including managing a year's interregnum, and as Adult Education Adviser in the Diocese of Winchester, her current job. The meetings were lively, thoughtful, decisive, as she enabled Central Council to move about, to get to know one another, to disagree, to resolve the dissonances, and to carry on planning. From 1988 onwards her main objective was to help every branch to work for good majorities in deanery and diocesan synods as the legislation came to be discussed. We knew there was real support among churchpeople in general, but only if this was expressed in the synods would that carry weight at the final vote. Even at this stage, every vote would count. At Central Council members began to get a clearer picture of opinion throughout the country, and what the different bishops were doing, or not doing. All this was rooted in a central act of worship lasting at least half an hour during every Council meeting, bang in the middle of the proceedings. An experience very far removed from the vicar's 'Shall we just . . . ?' approach with which many of us had grown up; often this was the first opportunity members had had of sharing in worship which used inclusive language and explored fresh images. These meetings continued to be demanding, enjoyable and strengthening at a deep level.

Of course dissonances resolved themselves in different ways. In 1991 Margaret Orr Deas felt she had had enough. Over ten years she had developed MOW's relations with the media, and alongside a mass of other work had discovered her own considerable skills in that area. Margaret and Caroline Davis had shown that a job-share can work well, fast and efficiently; but now Margaret was clear that she had done what she could as a joint Executive Secretary and resigned, though she continued her involvement with MOW in the London diocese. Caroline continued with Jenny Standage as her assistant. Those two bore the pressure in the office of those final years, the immediate run-up to 1992 and its aftermath, dealing with a volume of work in a week which would defeat most people in a fortnight.

Pressing for change

One of the crucial elements in this work, and one which had been there from the beginning, was our relationship with the press and media. At first only the religious press was willing to give the issue any coverage; the secular press and media regarded it as a rather boring church matter. A church service such as the 40th anniversary celebration of Florence Li Tim Oi's ordination, although held in Westminster Abbey, only roused limited interest, and even the banner across St Martin's portico and the candlelit vigil on the steps found most of the photographers passing by on the other side. Later in 1984, when the General Synod passed the first vote to move ahead and prepare legislation for ordaining women, there was a real flurry of interest. One did sometimes feel that the journalists could have been better informed than they were. Late at night, on the day of that vote, reserves of cool had to be summoned to deal with the millionth enquiry, which included the question 'So is the Roman Catholic Church under the wing of the C of E?' Apart from certain Religious Correspondents who wrote thoughtful pieces over the decades, it was only gradually that the secular press woke up to the importance of this issue. After 1986, and especially after the women were ordained deacon, they began to understand what was involved.

Around that time MOW was given an extraordinary bonus. Pure serendipity, it was. I had given up after seven years as MOW's Executive Secretary, but was still in London and had been asked to speak at a lunch-time meeting of an organization called the City Women's Network. I prepared something for a gathering of women many of whom, I thought, might be nearing retirement and for whom this lunch was a haven. Arriving early, I saw the church hall filling up with highly competent-looking younger women who, as it turned out, were in mid-career in banking, accountancy, computing, the Stock Exchange. I scrapped my prepared talk.

At the end of the session, I was wandering round meeting people. One woman asked if we ever needed help with publicity, her firm might like to help us, free of charge. This was Kitty O'Hagan, Director of GGK,[3] one of the top firms in advertising. Caroline Davis was able to take this further and worked with them for the next four years. Not everyone found it easy to swallow the idea of MOW being helped by a real live advertising agency, a view which was compounded when the first advert and leaflet appeared using the word 'sexual'. It may have been one of the best things MOW ever did, but it was never reprinted. The slogan 'Sexual Discrimination Is Legal In England' was too much for some digestions. Other adverts had a longer life as leaflets, or appeared in *The Times*, always with an approach very different from what might be expected from church advertising. When the new Archbishop of Canterbury was due to be appointed, the picture of the mitre was simply captioned 'It's a Boy!'—which really said it all. GGK continued to offer us hours of creative work free of charge throughout the campaign, and were never paid a penny.

St Hilda Community

Another development, nurtured by MOW members but not directly under the MOW umbrella, was the formation of the St Hilda Community. This arose directly out of General Synod's failure in July 1986 to make it possible for visiting women priests to celebrate the Holy Communion, even under limited circumstances, in Anglican churches. Monica Furlong has described the disillusionment and frustration:

> For many of us that anti-vote made it clear that the Church was not keeping faith with women. We had submitted to the interminable legal processes and determined delaying tactics with monumental patience. We had listened to all the arguments and had fondly imagined we were being listened to in return. Now it became clear that ... women were a long way down the Church's list of priorities ... Our trust and patience were exhausted. We believed in the validity of women's orders and wished to see them exercised.[4]

A group began to meet and soon decided that, for many people, the time was past for the quiet 'irregular' Eucharists celebrated by a woman priest which had taken place up till then in people's homes. 'Now we decided that we would hold eucharists openly, to be celebrated by women priests and, not to be underhand, we would advertise them. We wanted men, as well as women, to be an integral part of the Community ... we wanted a Community that worked by consensus and not by hierarchy ... and we wanted to share—gifts, leadership, vision and perhaps sometimes possessions and money.'[5] In February 1987 the Community met for the first time. Thanks to the vision and determination of Peter Francis, the chaplain of Queen Mary College, the Community's worship started off in the ecumenical chapel, circular, domed and beautiful. Later it was decided that, even though a Methodist woman minister could have celebrated in that chapel, it would be prudent to hold the services in the adjoining unconsecrated Common Room. Caroline Davis has commented: 'It was astonishing how week by week people would make a huge effort to get there, sometimes from quite far away. Almost always, for example, there was a group from Cuddesdon; and others, if they were passing through London, would make sure they were there, or if coming up on Monday, would come early in order to be at St Hilda's on Sunday evening.'

I remember best the services at Easter and Pentecost. It was an extraordinary experience, sitting on the floor in that Common Room, in a circle of 70 or 80 women and men who had come to the East End of London from many other parts of the country. The altar was a table placed in front of the door through to the chapel. As we sat in prayer and recollection before the service began, we were very conscious of that space from which we were excluded, the chapel beyond, with just one candle of hope burning in the dark. Suzanne Fageol, an American priest studying in England, bravely took on the privilege of celebrating for and with the Community.

After 18 months an article in the *Sunday Times* brought these celebrations to the attention of the Bishop of London, Graham Leonard. Although Queen Mary College was sympathetic to the Community, the chapel itself belonged to the diocese of London. The bishop decided to ask the diocesan solicitors to write threatening to charge the Community with trespass. The days at St Benet's were limited, but the Community was not going to be evicted without a struggle. On the last Sunday there was a final celebration of the Holy Eucharist, but not in the chapel or even the Common Room, but in the car park, the open air being, presumably, not open to the attentions of Winckworth and Pemberton, the diocese's solicitors. Since the bishop's tough line had been the cause of much public discussion for weeks, the press and television braved the bitter cold and stood around, astonished at the whole situation. Suzanne celebrated with a kind of strong reverence, supported by a woman deacon on either side, and a congregation of about 100.

This caused a full-blown sensation. People quite outside the Church glimpsed the importance of having a woman preside at the Eucharist; churchpeople were divided between shock and admiration. MOW itself was ambivalent, but never disassociated itself from St Hilda's; we had hung on from the beginning to the principle that there were different ways of working in this campaign, and many of that congregation every Sunday would be MOW members, lay and clergy, men and women. Gradually, as St Hilda's produced prayers and liturgies which answered a deep need in many parts of the Church, that creative development was able to be acknowledged as their book became known. The Community itself were welcomed by the neighbouring Bow Road Church, a church with both Anglican and Methodist congregations, so they moved across the road, where they continued to meet for four more years. They then moved to the West End, meeting monthly and continuing to spark off fresh thinking about worship in their own and other groups.

Together in the garden

Every MOW branch could tell its own story of milestones: the first big diocesan meeting, the first vigil or quiet day, the best party, the moment when the bishop first really gave support and the times when, through picnics, walks, or even by letting off balloons to welcome the new Archbishop, friendships were renewed and strengthened. And at the same time, the week-by-week undramatic pegging away, the turning up at meetings, the prayer, the stuffing of envelopes and licking of stamps.

I think it is true that in many ways MOW worked very differently from more established organizations. At least, it seemed to *feel* different. For a start, there were more younger people closely involved than in many Church organizations. And although we were working hard to achieve synodical objectives, we knew that that had to be done through persuading in a whole variety of ways. As time went on, we realized that more and more people were saying 'I do support women's ordination in principle, *but...*'. They were holding back, not out of conviction but because they could not yet feel completely happy at the prospect of a woman vicar. That was understandable, since most people still had little experience of women as deaconesses or Readers, preaching and taking services, or later as deacons. We had to help people to feel good about deciding to vote for this change, and that could only be done if we were not only convinced about our work but actually enjoyed what we were doing. Just slogging away would never be enough. One day Chris Bard compared the Church to a party, some of which is going on in a garden: 'Gradually the people inside will notice the door's open, they'll say "What on earth are we doing stuffing in here?" and they'll go out through the door and find how good it is to be together in the garden.'

As the voting figures began to come in from the deanery synods and the diocesan synods, we saw that the support we knew was there in the Church of England was indeed being translated into votes. Analyses showed the percentages hovering around 66% for the laity and 68% for the clergy. Gradually people were indeed beginning to 'feel good' about voting for women priests and the publicity was enabling them to acknowledge their support openly, even that they had changed their minds. The party in the garden was going well.

Priests for Women's Ordination

But all the time we needed sustenance for the road. One source was the support and research of organizations such as Women in Theology (WIT), many of whose members were also part of the Catholic Women's Network; the Modern Churchpeople's Union encouraged us in various ways, as did, latterly, the Open Synod Group. New support was also forthcoming from the National Alliance of Women's Organizations. In 1990 their AGM passed an Emergency Resolution[6] urging the General Synod to move as quickly as possible to ordain women to the priesthood. A copy of this Resolution was sent to every diocesan bishop; Jane Grant, the Director of NAWO, received a number of pained replies.

Perhaps the most crucial support of all came from Priests for Women's Ordination. PWO was launched in 1984 and consisted of a list, diocese by diocese, of male clergy supporting women's ordination to the priesthood. Unlike MOW, it had no subscription, and few meetings, but those priests did an enormous amount of letter-writing to General Synod members and to MPs. Several times they organized events to maintain a feeling of solidarity among its supporters. All these encouraged MOW greatly. The first was the vigil in the crypt of Canterbury before the 'Joining Hands' service; the second was again a vigil at Canterbury, before the Lambeth Conference; and the third was a Candlemas Service in Coventry Cathedral in February 1991. To this service Cathy Milford brought from the diocese of Dunedin, New Zealand, a miner's lamp lit for us by Penny Jamieson, the new bishop, at her first Eucharist celebrated in Dunedin Cathedral. From it huge torches were lit and given to PWO representatives for one diocese after another. Hundreds of tapers were lit from the torches, and finally a great procession streamed out of the cathedral carrying these lights, the smoke filling the temple in every sense.

In May of that year PWO joined with MOW in a service in

Westminster Abbey, 'Partners in Christ'. Again people gathered from all over the country, bringing their banners of 'Women of Faith', meeting at St Martin-in-the-Fields and processing all the way down Whitehall to the Abbey. Although the police had insisted that we walk only in tens down Whitehall—no 'march' being allowed in that area—by the time we had risked life and limb on two crossings, the groups inevitably joined up and were soon transformed into a fine procession, deacons and priests in their cassocks, crowds of others in support. And when we arrived it felt very good that the Dean and Chapter, robed, were present with us in the Abbey.

Cathy Milford has described the effort that went into that service to emphasize the theme of partnership. MOW—unlike Women Against the Ordination of Women—had never been a women-only organization, and we were always searching for ways of exploring collaborative ministry. However much women needed to be affirmed in the Church—and we were more, not less, conscious of that need as every year went by—our hope was still for an equal partnership in ministry, where the gifts of both women and men would be released in a new way. This, unfortunately, was not regarded as interesting by journalists, the BBC only wanting to know if fur would fly in the dialogue sermon between the theologian Sarah Coakley and Richard Holloway, Bishop of Edinburgh. The *Church Times* did not cover the event at all, and it was left to *The Tablet* to print a fine article by Monica Furlong, reprinted in *Chrysalis*. Her reflections could apply to any of our gatherings in that last two years—to Coventry in 1992 or indeed to the crowd in Dean's Yard on the day of the vote.

It was good to see face after face—women and men—who had laboured year after year in the Church of England's struggle. This one I had stood beside as we held up our 'waiting' banners outside Church House, this one I remembered from a demonstration at St Paul's, that one had been on countless committees with me. This one had worked valiantly through the endless red tape of Synod, that one had been threatened with legal action by her bishop. This woman deacon had been forbidden to take part in a procession, that one to take a funeral. This bishop had taken up the women's cause with a rare courage and a grasp of its importance for men as well as women, that dean had endured a lot of flak for permitting an American woman priest to celebrate Communion in his

house. All these faces, now older and tireder than when I first
remembered them, told their own story. They were still holding on, not
lost to post-Christianity, now bowing to the intimidation of those who
threatened to split the Church, not bitter, not cowed, but attending
closely while women break the silence of centuries in the churches.
What they all know is that merely for women to be seen standing at the
altars and in the sanctuaries destroys a taboo terribly relevant to the
human sickness.[7]

New strategies, new power

As the voting results from deanery and then from diocesan synods
began to sweep in to the MOW office and were relayed to the
branches, the leadership of the Movement experienced a fresh
surge of life. The Executive had learned to work together, and
now a concerted effort was planned. This was to make sure that
the expressed wish of churchpeople would not be delayed or
dissipated by 'them above'. By now we were looking beyond the
General Synod to Parliament who, if Synod passed the Measure
as we expected, would have to vote on it as ecclesiastical legislation.

In 1991 three new Moderators were elected by postal ballot.
The result showed that both the radical and conservative elements
in MOW's thinking were still alive and well across the country.
Emma Nicholson, Conservative MP, long-standing member of
MOW and founding member of the all-party 300 Group (whose
aim is to achieve 300 women MPs), became a Vice-Moderator,
as did Chris Baker of MOW's Radical Group, known to many
as a male deacon who had refused to proceed to priesthood until
women could also be ordained priest. Cathy Milford was re-
elected Moderator.

At the beginning of the following year, on the invitation of
Emma Nicholson, an 'extended Executive Committee' met in the
House of Commons. I thought of Una Kroll's plea to Betty
Ridley, long ago in 1975, that those at the centre of our society's
structures must in the end bring this change about. For many of
those present, meeting in that place was a highly significant symbol
of MOW's acceptance at the heart of the Establishment. At the
same time I was conscious of the other kind of power which had

got us to this point, the vigils, the meetings, the writing, the praying, the big occasions, the celebrations.

After twelve years of working on this issue, the leaders of MOW were well aware of the hidden influences that affected decision-making. We had seen bishops weaken dramatically and unexpectedly, and we knew MPs to be very conscious of the rights of minorities and of the importance of public opinion. We understood the importance of the press and media at local as well as national level. All this had to be translated into a final concentrated effort to bring high-level support out into the open, and to stiffen up the convictions of key figures in the Church, in politics, and in the media. In the long term, we were perhaps more successful in the two latter than with the bishops, as we shall see from the events which followed the final vote.

The 'think-tank' worked hard in all these areas, much helped by John Oliver, Bishop of Hereford, who had become an episcopal consultant along with the Bishop of Bristol, Barry Rogerson. John, like Stanley Booth-Clibborn and Ronnie Bowlby before him, was entirely open in his diocese about his support for women priests and believed that this should not make people trust him any the less.

'Moving in the Light of Christ'

The summer of 1992 wore on. The insufficient vote in the House of Laity at York in July jolted any somnolent branches out of their complacency. Thoughts focused again and again on the forthcoming vote in November. The press and media interest was growing daily and Christina Rees, a lay member of General Synod, had been enlisted as Press Officer. Caroline Davis and Jenny Standage in the office were keeping a great number of enterprises going, including a final last gathering in October, this one for our own sustenance, our last 'special rations' for the journey. It was to be at Coventry Cathedral, by request of the Provost and Chapter, and it did just what it set out to do.

'Christ Before Us' was the theme. Busloads arrived from all over the country. Donald and Jean Coggan were already there, a precious encouragement in their gentle smiling selves, not just as Lord and Lady Coggan, formerly of Canterbury.[8] In the ruins of the old cathedral we waited, then moved into the new, a long, long procession. All that Monica said about the gathering at Westminster was true of Coventry too. What riches, what gifts, I thought, looking at the faces; the Church has been mad spending all these years examining its own anxieties, nurturing its fears.

Cathy Milford and Rowan Williams, Bishop of Monmouth, explored the concept of 'waiting' and the emotions attached to it. 'We wait between fear and expectancy', said Rowan. 'The end of a long journey coming; and we know that, if our God is the God of Jesus, then whatever happens it will be difficult at first to tell birth from death . . . There can be a brick wall in front of prayer and imagination, a stone. Who will roll it away?' Cathy's response, very strong, very deliberate, went right to the heart:

> In my bones I feel that our particular stone, the stone of deep prejudice against women, has been rolled back. Not in the sense that there is not still plenty to be worked through, but in the sense that prejudice has been exposed for what it is. There is a clarity about the issues involved, there is an understanding that the ordination of women is not an isolated issue but that it is connected to and interwoven with the needs of the world today. There is a groundswell of understanding of the far reaching implications of the change that cannot now be stopped.

The Coventry gathering gave us that certain knowledge at last. We could see with a new clarity that women's ordination cannot be stopped; it is part of that vision of God which includes all people in the dance. It was as if, however the vote was going to turn out, we were already there. We had been given a new strength, a new song.

Notes

1 Diana McClatchey, speaking during the General Synod debate of July 1988.

2 The first moving spirits in enabling the Radical Group were Monica Furlong and Canon Stephen Burnett. Stephen, with his clear, radical mind and his undimmed vision, was a loved and respected figure in MOW from the beginning. When he died in 1992 MOW lost an important influence.

3 GGK, 76 Dean Street, London W1.

4 Monica Furlong, 'A "Non-Sexist" Community', Introduction to the St Hilda Community, *Women Included* (SPCK, 1990), p. 6.

5   Monica Furlong, ibid., p. 7.
6   The National Alliance of Women's Organisations includes a number of
    church-related women's groups including the Mothers' Union, two
    women's committees of the Council of Churches for Britain and Ireland,
    the Catholic Women's Network and the National Free Church Women's
    Council. At their Annual Conference in May 1990 the following Emer-
    gency Resolution was passed unanimously:

> Having heard with pleasure the news that the Church of Ireland
> (comprising both the Republic of Ireland and Northern Ireland)
> has passed legislation to allow women to be ordained to the
> priesthood and to the episcopacy, this Annual General Meeting of
> the National Alliance of Women's Organisations urges the dioceses
> and the General Synod of the Church of England to regard the
> passing of similar legislation now before them as a matter of urgency.
> We look forward to the time when all churches give the lead in
> abolishing all forms of discrimination.

7   *Chrysalis* (July 1991), p. 5, by permission of *The Tablet*.
8   After this service, Lord Coggan was moved to write a letter to every
    member of the General Synod, an initiative which may have contributed
    significantly to the shift in opinion among Evangelicals.

11 *Hurling the mountain into the sea*[1]

> The church overall finds it so hard to believe that there can be a new future that is truly faithful to what has been already given. Yet that is what resurrection is.[2]

Restless sleep and a short night for me and no doubt for many others, the night before 11 November, the day of the final vote. An added and joyful reason for my sleeplessness: at 20 minutes past midnight our first grandchild was born. So the day started well, with relief and rejoicing. Then three or four hours sleep, a taxi, a train, and I was in Dean's Yard by 9 a.m.

Already quite a big crowd was gathered on the grass. My joy over the grandchild had to be shared, and lifted other spirits too. Hope and apprehension everywhere. Curiously perhaps, I was convinced that the vote would go through. Over the past three or so weeks, in spite of all the gloomy prognostications, I had lived with this very strong feeling, which is not really possible to explain, that I would be sitting in the gallery and would hear the words we were all longing for, that the Measure had been passed.

The steps to Church House were already crowded. Monica Furlong in a wheelchair, having broken her ankle, the Catholic Women's Network with their encouraging banner, and some women deacons carrying cards reading READY AND WAITING. It felt like a relief just to be together. The Bishop of London, David Hope, looking anxious and saying 'I'm with you most of the way', seemed quite happy to have his photograph taken with the deacons of his diocese.

Caroline Davis was everywhere, calm and encouraging. Among other things she was able to pass on some of the greetings and good wishes which had been coming in to the MOW office during the past few days. Vigils were being held and the debate remembered in prayer all over the world: in Dunedin, New Zealand, a vigil would just be finishing. Helene Mann, a Dunedin priest, had written in a way that expressed the support and love of countless women and men throughout the Anglican Communion:

> Please tell the others that a R.C. sister is one of the organisers for our vigil . . . I will be celebrating the Eucharist in my parish at a time which should coincide with your voting . . . Please believe me when I say that when I approached priesthood, I took the pain of all of you into it and it remains with me. The most touching thing for me is to see so many NZ women, who have never been to England, bear your pain with them too. I feel very conscious of a metaphorical stretching of hands across the miles—we'll get there together.[3]

Part of that continuing prayer, in this country, had been the vigil outside Lambeth Palace which had been maintained through rain and cold for four nights and three days. Margaret Orr Deas, who as Chair of London MOW had activated the vigil, has said that everyone who came to join in arrived rather depressed and left full of hope and strength. 416 people from 44 parts of this country or beyond took part. Every day at 6 p.m. there was Evening Prayer, then Night Prayers at 10, Morning Prayer at 8 a.m., and 'Incomplete Eucharist' at 12 noon. On the Monday night they were briefly joined by 'Nobody's Friends', arriving for dinner at Lambeth and including the judge who had joined us at the very first Southwark Cathedral vigil, a lifetime ago. All the time, in fact, there were people dropping by, rain or no rain, to keep them going.

During those days and nights they kept a notebook for comments. Here are some of them:

Saturday 7th
6 pm Just finished Evensong. 60 or so people, full of joy and confidence.

Although we are told that we must remain together as a Church, and not leave—if the vote is against, it will be very difficult to stay. As a male ordinand this would mean totally re-thinking my whole life.

It's 11.20 at night and still noisy. I go to rest full of peace after having shared and received so much from the two services. One cannot help but be uplifted by those who come to join us for a service, or call by to offer help, or just chat—oh, that the Church were as warm and friendly!

Sunday 8th

6.30 am. Now the waiting resumes. There's nothing we can do except BE HERE, but how important that active waiting is. What stays with me is the sense of serious, expectant, hopeful prayer from last night.

4.20 pm. Lights are starting to come on along the Thames. A few cars have come in and out of the Palace, but their occupants, separated from us by glass, are unwilling to meet our friendly glances.

Monday 9th

3.30 am I only meant to drop off a sleeping bag to one of the women staying outside Lambeth Palace, but was so caught up by the community there that I'm still here . . . That's what 'church' is all about.

7.20 am The elaborate bedding arrangements were desperately unsuccessful. We only slept for about 5 minutes at a time and after an hour and a half gave up—pretty wet and cold . . . Much better now it is light.

Tuesday 10th

1.30 am A red van pulls up, a driver briskly jumps down: hedgehog haircut, leather jerkin, he cheerfully announces 'Got two flasks, one with sugar, one without. And I'll take the one I left last night.' One of Nerissa's parishioners, on his way to new Covent Garden to buy veg. for his stall . . . Some chatter, some feet stamping and hand warming, then sleep and silence . . . A man delivers the papers to the palace gate . . . Bags are packed and blankets shaken. The morning traffic starts up.

Wednesday 11th

After 8 am prayers, LBC did a live interview, cars and lorries listening to the programme hooted as they went past. So, all packed up, sodden, covered in ash from the brazier, off we went to Church House.[4]

And there indeed they were, after this remarkable achievement, looking amazingly chirpy. It had been an extraordinary shared experience. The hope was that the Archbishop of Canterbury, George Carey, would recognize this as a strong gesture of support for his stand on women's ordination.

The historic debate

Eventually, feeling extremely torn-in-two, I left the crowd outside Church House to go inside. I was weighed down by a huge candle in my pocket. If my inner conviction was wrong and the vote should fail, I thought I could just about bring myself to stand up in the gallery holding up this lighted candle. I knew I couldn't shout, but at least there would be some gesture for the women. Because of the security bag search, the candle was hidden in my big mackintosh pocket, draped over by a scarf, and no one saw. I began to climb the wide winding staircase to take my seat in the gallery. Not being someone who wins things in ballots, I was astonished to be told by one of our Norwich Synod members that my name, which she had put 'in the hat', had been drawn. Former Synod stalwarts like Christian Howard and Diana McClatchey had been allocated complimentary seats, along with Oswald Clark, staunch opponent over many years. They were further round the semi-circle, and opposite I could see Caroline Davis, with the press, reporting for *Chrysalis*. It felt very strange that Monica Furlong had not got a seat.

The gallery was packed, with extra places taken up by the press, even though they had an overflow press gallery elsewhere in Church House with closed-circuit television. Struggling into my numbered seat, I found that my neighbours were friends. Through the long day we supported each other, through the nerve-wracking moments and the cramps that develop from sitting knees to chin in those ungenerous gallery seats. At some points there was a horrible familiarity about the debate; I felt I had sat up there and had heard so much of it before, time after time.

The Bishop of Guildford, Michael Adie, a tall, gentle, determined man, had the task of presenting the Measure. He reminded Synod that the legislation had been shaped by the Church's determination to stay together: 'The strength of the Church of England ever since the Reformation has been its ability to hold together Catholic and Reformed—not in uneasy juxtaposition but in interaction.' He spoke of the enrichment of the Church by women authorized as Readers, deaconesses, and deacons: 'Those of us on both sides of the debate who have observed and experienced that ministry want to say to those women that they have enlarged our minds and won our respect for what they have done and are doing in a Church that does not make life easy for them.'

The rest of his speech considered Scripture and tradition, often quoted to prevent any kind of church change. The incarnation of Christ as a male did not mean that we would have for all time a one-gender ministry of the same sex as that of Jesus. 'For centuries we have accepted men in the priesthood as the automatic consequence of God taking human nature, but then for centuries it was only men who enjoyed education, political leadership, the vote and so on, and these have only gradually, even grudgingly, become available to women. What God has made clear to us in our century is that women are not inferior to men, nor are they identical; men and women are complementary; together and equally they make up humanity. That simple but fundamental truth which God has shown to us in his world now resonates with a new understanding of the Scriptures.'

And then, tradition: 'The ordination of women to the priesthood may be contrary to tradition in the sense that it has not happened before; it is not contrary to tradition in the sense of truth as it has been handed down to us. Indeed, if we are to be faithful to tradition in the light of contemporary truth, this development is required of us.'

The main opposing speech followed, then more arguments and counter-arguments. Some objectors focused on detail of the legislation, talking about 'theological confusion and pastoral mayhem'; the Bishop of London, David Hope, declaring he was not and never had been one who believed it was impossible for a woman to be ordained, was very concerned as to how the legislation could possibly work, ending, however: 'Having said this, I shall try to respect, with as good and generous a grace as I can, whatever decision is reached at the end of this day, praying that God will give me the necessary grace and wisdom to continue in communion and fellowship with all in my diocese, whatever their views, and, I desperately hope and pray, they with me too.' The Archbishop of Canterbury followed him: 'This debate is not about excluding anybody but about enlarging the sympathies and generosity of our Church in line with the generosity of God himself.' And, earlier in his speech: 'We are not departing from a traditional concept of ministry, we are talking about an extension of the same

ministry to include women. Christianity is all about God liberating, renewing, and drawing out what has been there implicitly
from the beginning.'

Of the speeches by women deacons, one of the most notable
came from June Osborne (London) describing her experience of
vocation as like a developing photograph. The Synod was moved
by this speech and especially perhaps by her ending: 'We are
asking how we may allow the personality of God to be made
transparent by our life together, for a calling to ordination is built
on the grace of God—and I long for you to allow me to minister
the grace of God through priesthood. In the mercy of Christ and
for the sake of our Church, I ask you: please test my vocation.'

The morning ground on. One leading opponent, Fr Peter Geldard, in a flight of rhetoric, compared the Church of England to
a village oak tree which was just about to be cut down, and made
an impassioned plea that Synod would put down its axe. John
Selwyn Gummer appealed to his Evangelical friends, and spoke
about 'the fullness of the Catholic faith'.

At this point Stephen Sykes, Bishop of Ely and academic theologian, leapt up, tall and magisterial, and warned Mr Gummer
that he would find in the Roman Church an even greater compre-
hensiveness than existed in the Church of England. He had been
besieged at a conference at Louvain by groups of Roman Catholics from France, from Germany and from Belgium, urging
him to support this legislation. 'That is the real Roman Catholic
Church . . . I would like to tell Synod how much I affirm the
truth that the argument in favour of this proposition rests upon a
theological grasp of the doctrines of Trinity, Incarnation and
Atonement which lie at the heart of our faith . . . it is not fashion,
it is not civil rights, it is not the drive for self-fulfilment which
undergirds the proposition among those of us who support it, but
it is faithfulness to the doctrines of the Trinity and Incarnation,
to our Anglican tradition which permits us to judge, as Richard
Hooker has said, of times and seasons, that *"now is a new grown
occasion"* when churchpeople may affirm the proposal before us
as fully consistent with the faith of the one holy catholic and
apostolic Church.'

This statement underlining the theological reasons for women's
ordination was of fundamental importance in the debate. It also

strongly reinforced the earlier speech of Mark Santer, Bishop of Birmingham, who spoke as a co-chairman of the Anglican–Roman Catholic International Commission (ARCIC). This was perhaps the most crucial contribution of all, and one that had been awaited with much interest.

After quoting two particular arguments against, which Roman Catholic colleagues in ARCIC had put to him, he went on: 'The fact that Roman Catholics should be so deeply concerned by our Anglican debate is itself a sign of our growth in love and communion in recent years. If they did not feel a close bond with us they would not bother to express their concern. This makes it all the more painful to express a contrary view.' At this point supporters gripped their chairs. Was the chairman of ARCIC really going to tell us that he had moved in favour? The rest of the speech was short and to the point. 'In the long run we must believe that God will show us a way to find one another in one communion in Christ; but in the short run we must make a decision one way or another. It is clear that . . . the thoughtful, praying majority of our clergy and lay people believe that women as well as men ought to be ordained to the priesthood. I used to believe that it was possible for us to wait for further consensus to develop; I have come to see that continued delay is in fact debilitating the life of the Church . . . One cannot argue forever from the letter of Scripture alone or from precedent alone. We have to ask ourselves if it makes sense to the Christian mind . . . We must also ask if it makes sense to unbelievers . . . I cannot see any way in which the liberating power of the Gospel of Christ is commended to an unbelieving world by the assertion that only men may be priests. That for me is the conclusive argument.'

Perhaps it was conclusive to some waverers too. If someone who was so committed to the Anglican–RC search for closer unity now felt that further delay was wrong, then one cause for hesitancy was removed at a stroke.

The Evangelical standpoint had an equally powerful proponent in Dr Ruth Etchells, former Principal of St John's College with Cranmer Hall, Durham: 'Is the dividing wall of gender not susceptible to the same marvellous grace which could and did wipe out that deepest of divisions between a holy people and the rest? Could Christ redeem Gentiles but not gender?' Sister Carol CHN

(Community of the Holy Name), representing the religious communities, was well aware of the damaged witness of the Church:
'Our work today will be good news if it helps the Church to be
a sign of the reconciled, transfigured, redeemed society on earth.'
Some women spoke against—it would be irresponsible and negative to pass this, it would be legislation for schism; one described
it as theological arrogance and blasphemy, as ruinous legislation.

David McClean, the architect of the legislation, held no brief
for these latter views. Quiet and impressive, he patiently laid out
once again the ways in which those who would remain unhappy
about the priestly ordination of women would be given 'not mere
assurances, but legal rights, clearly stated and entrenched'. His
layman's tribute to the ministry of women was moving: 'For too
long the special gifts of women, gifts from a generous Creator
God, have been under-used and under-valued. We have locked
their talents away. We have refused to women the chance to
respond to a call to use their gifts in lives devoted to the priestly
ministry of Christ's Church. Today, this very afternoon, may we
in this room take the marvellous opportunity that we have to
unlock those gifts, to enrich the Church and to strengthen it in
the service of God.'

The afternoon wore on. By now the debate was being televised,
the lights were blazing, the press gallery ever more packed. The
Archbishop of York supported the legislation, reassuring Synod
that 'As Christians we ought not to be worried about differences.
There have always been differences in the Christian Church . . .
What I cannot abide is the sort of conspiracy theory which
imagines that behind this legislation people are plotting. Conspiracy theories always assume a far greater degree of cunning
than most of us possess. Frequently I read in the newspapers
about what I am supposed to have done, and I marvel at my own
ingenuity.' Cutting nearer to the bone was the Bishop of Southwark, Roy Williamson, with his plea on grounds of justice: 'I
cannot with any degree of integrity challenge the injustices of
society and turn a blind eye to the apparent injustice within the
Church which prevents women from testing their vocation to the
priesthood.' Reminding the Synod of recent decisions in other
Provinces, he said, 'If the Church of Ireland has got on with the
job as has the Anglican Church in South Africa, in two lands

where people's lives are being shattered by violence day after day, it may very well be that in those kinds of circumstances they get even a thing like this into perspective . . . If there is injustice to be removed the only time to do it is now.'

By the time these speeches were made, a five-minute limit had been imposed, then a three-minute limit followed. In this historic debate, the agreement was that anybody standing had the right to speak. Since more than 200 requests had been received in advance, there was need for self-restraint and brevity. New Synod-observers in the gallery noticed that speakers are identified by their number flashing up in rather theatrical lights, and that if they exceed a time limit they can be bowled out by the Chairman's bell. Many speakers stood repeatedly, were not called, and then, finding their points had been covered, gave up. Christine Farrington, a deacon on the General Synod, said afterwards: 'The tension was extraordinary—real, and vibrant. I'd been hoping to speak, standing up, the adrenalin running, sitting down again, hearing the debate and rewriting in one's head. That was what was going on inside.' In the end 39 spoke, 26 men and 13 women (an interesting development from the 1988 General Approval debate where 23 men and five women were called to speak.)

Everyone knew that the hope was for a vote about 4.30 in the afternoon; by 4 p.m. some members were calling for a vote to be taken, but others were still standing to speak. Finally all was quiet; not a single member of Synod on their feet, relief visible on the face of the Chairman, the Archbishop of Canterbury. Now was the moment for the summing-up of the debate, the last two speeches supporting and opposing General Synod's final approval of the Priests (Ordination of Women) Measure.

First David Silk, Archdeacon of Leicester and long-time opponent of every Measure concerning women's ministry, Chairman of the House of Clergy for many years and leader of the Anglo-Catholic opposition. He described the day as 'wearisome' and added that 'most of us have appointments later on'. An unfortunate impression was given that the day had been a rather tiresome interruption to life and there were better things to do in the evening. Michael Adie, the proposer of the motion, replied. Both took up points made during the debate. Michael Adie ended: 'We need to make this decision not on a wave of emotion, though this is an emotive occasion, not even, I dare to say, out of compassion for women who yearn to test their vocation, though those people are never far from our minds, but on the grounds of Scripture, tradition and cool reasoning. A majority of our Church is waiting for us to make this decision. So I ask the Synod to take a step forward into the future, God's future, confident that he will lead us into this truth.'

The debate was over; it had on the whole been marked by the high quality of speeches. Dreadful things which used to be said on similar occasions about women had not been said, and on the whole it was conviction, not politicking, that came across. The atmosphere was intense, but not actually hostile. There was a sense of people pleading with each other as they made their points; however academic these might be, in the true sense of that word, the involvement of the speaker was never in doubt.

Everybody stood up and a deep silence fell; then the Archbishop said a prayer. Then, unusually, he asked members to exchange the Peace—a greeting or handshake which is customary during the service of Holy Communion. Somehow this was extraordinarily moving; it felt absolutely right. Then the call was heard, 'Divide', and members began to make their way to the doors they would walk through for their vote to be counted, whether 'Ayes' or 'Noes'. In the gallery we could only wait, and pray. I thought of Una Kroll and her cry 'We asked for bread and you gave us a stone'; it still seemed intolerable that if the Synod turned the women down yet again, there should be no gesture, nothing on their behalf from the public gallery. Immediately behind me were sitting three women deacons. Feeling sorely in need of support, I wrote, in the dreadful moments of waiting, on a scrap of paper: 'If this vote fails, I am going to stand up with a big lighted candle; would you support me?' Liz Baxter, nearest to me and the one I knew best, read it, smiled, handed it to Ulla Monberg and the others, and they all nodded, quite firmly. I fingered my son's cigarette lighter and prayed I wouldn't have to use it.

Christine Farrington again: 'It was quite impossible to tell, going through the doors, then standing outside before we were allowed back in, what the result would be. Very peculiar conversations went on as you simply passed the time with whoever you happened to brush up against. And then back into the Chamber, finding our seats ... I had worked out the arithmetic, so the moment the Archbishop read out the first laity figures I knew absolutely that a two-thirds majority had been achieved in each House. And I still couldn't believe it. Until he said in that gentle way that the Measure had been carried. It was right that the result was received in silence, but one could hear great intakes of breath, especially from the gallery. I felt very numbed, feeling "It's actually happened, but we've been encouraged to be good girls, not to show emotion"—however there was a lot deep inside. It was when we were walking out of the Chamber that some of it was able to be shown, and that felt very good.'

Between people of opposing views, after the result, there were gestures of support. In the gallery, Christian Howard went and sat silently beside Oswald Clark. Downstairs also there were efforts at rapprochement: 'One of the first was a priest in our diocese whom I knew had voted against, and he immediately came up to me and said "I'm so pleased for you because I know how much this matters to you, and you can be absolutely sure that I accept this to be part of the Church's order, and I shall want to be there, Christine, for your priesting." This was wonderful immediate support, and out there in the corridor people were hugging, were in tears, while we were waiting, because soon after we had to go back in for the next bit.'[5]

Outside, a huge crowd had gathered on the steps and on the grass of Dean's Yard. A television screen outside the entrance had been relaying the debate and now the result. One MOW member catches that moment: 'An intake of breath and a wild shout of joy goes up. They've done it! We've done it! We turn to each other, mouths open, eyes wide, hardly able to take it in, then there is hugging and kissing and faces alight with joy and streaming tears of relief. Someone with a superb sense of timing lets off a single rocket into the sky, and its starry ascent captures for a moment all our hopes and aspirations.'[6]

That whoop of pure joy sent the starlings of Dean's Yard whirling up to the Abbey pinnacles. One Synod member has expressed what the majority must have felt: 'It was when we went right outside of Synod at the end of that day's business that those enormous waves of joy swept over us from the folk who were outside singing—candles, flashbulbs and so on; and some of us

were still feeling very numbed. It was quite overwhelming, all
that, one wanted to be part of it, but somehow also just to slip
away—and be somewhere quiet . . . A very strange feeling. And
walking out with us were some people who were desperately hurt
and upset.'

The bishops were already very aware, apparently, of that aspect
of the question; even then they were finding it hard not to be
taken over by the opposition. 'We *longed* to meet with our diocesan
bishops', said one senior woman deacon 'and for them to say
"Isn't this wonderful, I look forward to ordaining you"—but
almost all of us found that we couldn't get eye contact with
our Bishops, or any form of contact. They were so immediately
concerned with how they would cope with all the hurt people:
"Oh no, I can't be in joy with you who are feeling joyful, because
I've got to be with those who are feeling sad." I just longed for
him to say "I'm so pleased for you" . . . but he couldn't. That
felt hard, and a number of women deacons said the same. It felt
as if from then on, for the next few weeks, we were being told
"You must be very well behaved girls, you've got to understand
how hurt people are"—and most of us anyway were only too
aware of what the pain was.'

But that evening, in the darkness, the joy went on: 'I've never
seen so many grown men in tears', said somebody afterwards.
The Roman Catholic women on the steps had adroitly changed
their placard, which now read 'Congratulations sisters—Catholic
women next'. Everyone was milling about; some of us began
dancing gently on the grass; reporters were catching this person
and that for comments in various languages, and on the screen
one was vaguely aware that interviews were going on, though
drowned out now by the singing of 'Jubilate Deo—Alleluia!', on
and on and on. Some people slipped over to Westminster Abbey
for quiet prayer; most were making their thanksgivings there and
then in the crowd.

After a while Synod members began to emerge, and were
cheered for their long years of patient work. Stanley Booth-
Clibborn, Bishop of Manchester and MOW's first Moderator,
remembers that moment, the culmination of much that he had
worked for, coming in the very last days before his retirement.
'There was a rather sombre atmosphere in the Chamber itself . . .

but coming outside, afterwards, as we got down below and came out into the evening air, it was a most fantastic sight; I will never forget the warmth with which MOW members applauded me personally. Partly because of my illness, of course, and consequent struggle to keep on the scene, but this was deeply moving . . . There was a tremendous atmosphere of joy and rejoicing and one felt that was a real seal of the Spirit on the proceedings.'

In the enormous press coverage which followed, Margaret Hebblethwaite's article in the *National Catholic Reporter* (4 December) was among the most perceptive; she saw very clearly the theological issue at the heart of the whole debate:

> The Church of England's decision on Nov. 11 to ordain women was important for reasons that go far beyond the desirability of having women at the altar in one European offshore island. It has become symbolic of something bigger, but how much bigger is still coming into focus. The most fundamental level of the recent vote was a historic decision in favour of cleaning up the doctrine of the incarnation . . .
>
> What both Anglo-Catholic and Evangelical opponents to women priests had in common was a belief that Jesus related more closely to men than to women . . . Either that was because men derived headship from Christ where women did not. Or it was because men could represent Christ in a way women could not . . . Without the re-clarification that Jesus—as God incarnate—relates equally to men and women, Christianity would have fallen into the indignity of a truly sexist religion, which could not carry weight for anyone who regarded the equality of men and women as a fundamental truth.
>
> Nor was the Movement for the Ordination of Women unaware of the far-reaching theological implications, for a novena of prayer leading up to the vote contains many reflections on the incarnation.
>
> Members of MOW sang by the light of candles for one and a half hours outside the synod their thanksgiving to God, 'Jubilate Deo—Alleluia'. If their mood was one of victory, it was not victory over their opponents; it went much deeper than that . . .
>
> Among those joyful singers was a more religious sense than anyone could have anticipated. Only after the vote did anyone really begin to discover how important that decision felt. The feeling was that at long last we had good news (that is, gospel) to proclaim to the nation. It was not the victory of women over men, but of equality over injustice, of truth over confusion. The real victor was the doctrine of the incarnation.[7]

The stone of indecision rolled away

For a time we all felt more or less dazed. As the realization gradually began to sink in, one was aware of feelings of enormous relief; not so much of victory, but certainly of the deepest thanksgiving—that the Church had actually dealt with the burden of indecision it had been carrying for so long and now was being greeted with joy in messages from all over the world.

They certainly poured in, those messages—the MOW office awash with faxes and the Ansaphone jumping off the desk. Greetings from Penny Jamieson, Bishop of Dunedin; from other bishops of the Anglican Communion; and from Archbishop Peers of the Anglican Church of Canada: 'The ministry of women priests will allow the Church of England to discover blessings they do not yet know, as all of us in Canada have.' From the Episcopal Church Center in New York; from the diocese of Auckland, New Zealand: 'MOW members have put in many years of hard visionary work ... With prayers as you face the outcomes of the decision.' *Uppity*, that sharp lively irreverent newsletter which supports sharp lively reverend women,[8] reported the news that at New York's General Theological Seminary they had rung the bells in the chapel and even played 'God Save the Queen' in solidarity with English women.

The greetings from all over the Anglican Communion were far too many to number here. Equally encouraging were the messages from Roman Catholic groups and individuals, and from the World Council of Churches; and best of all, perhaps, were the letters which arrived over the next week with news of general rejoicing. The experience of one deacon, writing from Walthamstow, may have been typical: 'I returned home to find a bottle of champagne on my doorstep and the phone didn't stop ringing for 24 hours. One call which particularly touched me was from a local policewoman to whom I'd recently made a statement after an incident. She said "I'm not part of the Church, but I think the vote is bloody marvellous!" '

Everyone involved in the struggle will have received letters and cards. Few of mine were as perceptive as the one from Stephen Verney, former Bishop of Repton, steeped in love and knowledge of the Orthodox, and of St John's gospel, friend of many years:

I wanted to share with you the amazing experience of the vote in Synod. First I wept. Then I opened a bottle of champagne. As the days went by, it seemed that something very big had happened. As the symbol at the heart of the church had changed, everything had changed with it. Man and woman, now partners, and with that breakdown of the wall of partition all sorts of other walls were tottering and falling.

Then came the sense that those who had 'lost' in the vote had in some deep sense 'won'. Now the Catholic truth can be proclaimed and welcomed in the C. of E. We are no longer drawn up in battle array. We can proclaim the glory of God together, through forgiveness and compassion. Alleluia!

Notes

1 'Jesus answered them, "Have faith in God. I tell you this: if anyone says to this mountain, 'Be lifted from your place and hurled into the sea', and has no inward doubts, but believes that what he says is happening, it will be done for him" ' (Mark 11.22–23 NEB).
2 Rowan Williams, Bishop of Monmouth, speaking at an MOW service in Coventry Cathedral, October 1992.
3 Helene Mann, from a letter to Penny Nairne, Oxford.
4 *Chrysalis* (January 1993).
5 The Synod had to follow the successful passage of the main Measure with a vote on the Financial Provisions and a miscellaneous series of amendments.
6 Maggie Butcher in 'Diary', *Chrysalis* (January 1993).
7 Margaret Hebblethwaite, 'Anglicans Presage Catholic Women Priests — Later', *National Catholic Reporter* (4 December 1992).
8 *Uppity*, a series of occasional newsletters published by Uppity Women, 21 Blurton Street, London E5 0NL.

12 *Changing the Church*

> You can't kill the spirit
> She is like a mountain
> Old and strong
> She goes on and on.[1]

That 'Alleluia!' and the thoughts behind it resonated day after day. Not only churchpeople, but the world at large, in so far as it was interested at all, rejoiced at the knowledge that the Church had at last done something which seemed so obviously right. People look back now and remember exactly where they were and what they were doing when the news came through. Una Kroll, visiting a dying person in hospital, coming out and on her car radio hearing the result—'a moment of pure joy, because I was alone and had been working . . .'; Betty Ridley, also alone, in her flat in Winchester, having listened to the debate all day found that the hopes, carefully controlled over years, the prayers of decades, overflowed at last: 'I'm not an emotional person but to my amazement, when the vote came through I just wept and wept.' Penny Jamieson, just about to preside at the Eucharist in Dunedin: 'It turned out to be a real celebration and thanksgiving—what marvellous, stupendous, absolutely splendid news!' Liz Canham in the US: 'I was driving back from my parish . . . and almost went off the highway—Hallelujah!' Alan Webster, outside in Dean's Yard: 'I thought of my father and my grandfather, country parsons both, struggling to introduce change, and also to cherish tradition, praying, writing, arguing, hoping, and I was sure they were rejoicing with me. Even more I thought of my mother and my foremothers and their many talents given to the communities and churches where they lived. And as I looked at the faces round me, the faces of the future, I knew the Church was being refreshed and we were experiencing resurrection.'[2]

And yet it is difficult to write about the rejoicing because so much of it was immediately spoiled or taken away. Those who had been most opposed to women's ordination moved in with strong statements about their pain and anxiety. Claims were staked out, rifts announced. The alleluias were described as triumphalist and the song of joy was almost drowned by the unhappy, destructive jangle of those who could not face the idea of women priests.

We seemed to enter a new and curious world. We had apparently walked through a looking glass into a place where everything was upside down. The conviction of two-thirds of church-going Anglicans was being set aside while all eyes were fixed on a vociferous minority. The women, who over so many years had been told that they must not speak about their pain and frustration, were now faced with the spectacle of the pain of the opponents being publicized with considerable effect. The working-out of November's important decision seemed to arouse little interest and instead there was a focusing on the 'breakdown' or 'schism' which no doubt some commentators would have been quite happy to see. I remembered wryly how, at the beginning, we would be told that we were a minority, the Church wasn't ready yet, this or that bishop could not publicly support—and yet supporting the minority seemed now to be the flavour of the month.

In its newsletter of December 1992 *Uppity* did not mince words:

> Not only are we being asked to pretend to feel less angry than we are, not only are we being asked to act as if healing has already happened when it shows no sign of having begun, but, *mirabile dictu*, we are being asked to *feel sorry* for opponents who continue to traduce our intentions and insist that we are 'just' secular feminists who are simultaneously trying to reinstate the cult of Isis; a tricky combo, that one.

The very public reaction of alternately bullying and wringing their hands was distasteful to many who, while 'unhappy' about the vote, were now prepared to accept the Church's decision. We all knew people who were feeling puzzled and upset but were going to remain loyal to the Church of England and not try to break things up. They were the ones who earned respect.

The bishops could have done more to support those priests who were trying to resist pressure and maintain some sanity among the ranks of the disaffected. But they went back to their dioceses apparently focused on how to care for those who were fulminating about the vote. Some exhausted themselves on trying to make deals. There seems to have been scarcely a word of joy with the women deacons or others to whom the vote was the culmination of years of waiting. At the MOW office, amid dozens of letters and phone calls just two letters and two postcards arrived from bishops. Cathy Milford received one or two episcopal phone calls and a joyful letter from the Bishop of Hertford, Robin Smith: '... At last God has cleared the way for all that we have hoped for. I am still reeling from the impact of yesterday's vote and find myself constantly offering up prayers of thanksgiving and relief. Yesterday I was proud to be a member of the Church of England and it has been a privilege over these last 13 years to be associated with MOW, with you and all your colleagues ... With warmest greetings for all that lies ahead.' The Bishop of Hereford, bringing a bottle of champagne to a meeting next day, gave the same kind of message. These were all the more welcome in view of the silence from their brother bishops.

The press and media suddenly lost all interest in the women or their future, or in any positive developments in the Church that might result from the advent of women as priests. Comment and speculation centred on problems that might ensue. *The Times* headlined with 'Joy, Dismay and Warnings Greet Synod Vote', and allocated inches to 'Irreconcilable leaders show signs of rift that could split the church'. The *Daily Telegraph* headlined 'Turmoil Over Synod Vote'; the *Guardian* and the *Independent* were more dispassionate with 'Synod Accepts Women Priests' and 'Women Win Priesthood Vote'; but even they moved into further headlines about grave obstacles, threats of resignation and so on. The *Church Times* reported at length on the formation of a new umbrella organization 'to provide a way forward for those unable to accept women priests' and planning to meet 'almost weekly from now on'. This organization, formed through the Church Union, took the name Forward in Faith. All this led to much speculation in the press, and articles on the demise of the Church of England.

On New Year's Day, however, Clifford Longley, an experienced observer of the Church of England, prophesied in the *Daily Telegraph*:

> The archbishops and bishops of the Church of England now have to guide the Church out of the wilderness of the debate on female ordination into the promised land of a new priestly ministry of women . . . This is the task crying out to be done as 1993 begins . . . The majority of bishops do genuinely regard the approving of women priests as one of the best things the Church has done this century. But while the debate was on, they minimised their enthusiasm so as not to antagonise their opponents, including those among their fellow bishops. Their temptation now, out of habit, is to minimise what happened on 11 November, when in truth the time has come to maximise it. There is no risk they might further alienate the traditionalists, who are now well beyond being placated by mere words.

But the bishops gave every appearance of being painfully torn in two. The conflict which they had been trying for so long to avoid was now fairly and squarely in front of them. Far from everything settling down after the vote, conflict ramped and roared as the opponents of women priests laid down conditions and sought to extract more and more concessions. Some bishops have said that they were completely unprepared for 'the ferocity of the attack'; in fact, it was only what had been rumbling underground for decades, for centuries. In the past it was directed at the women; now for the first time it was aimed at the bishops.

Since 1984 the House of Bishops had supported the ordination of women priests. Even in 1978, influenced by the Lambeth Conference, the majority had voted in favour. But they wanted that support to be consistent with a quiet life, and for many of them the policy had been to sidestep the questions at the heart of the matter. The concept of being a 'focus of unity' in the diocese was often interpreted in terms of not declaring a clear opinion. This was especially true before the dioceses had voted. It was not until 1991 that 16 or so bishops, gathered by the Bishop of Bristol, actually met with MOW's Executive to think about the future.

A comment here from Stanley Booth-Clibborn fills in the background: 'I think the bishops consciously or sub-consciously saw this as an immensely divisive issue; so that even when with their heads they were persuaded of the rightness of ordaining women, they were over-cautious over the speed with which this should come about and their own particular part in it.' He added that this had important things to say about leadership in general. 'Some people have interpreted episcopal leadership as meaning that the bishop should not take strong stands on controversial issues; but I think that that path simply enfeebles episcopal leadership. People respect more the kind of leadership where it's quite clear where the bishop stands.' He went on: 'I think, looking back, I would have to be critical of Bob Runcie as Archbishop. Because his view over the early period was crucial. He was very very slow to move over the whole issue . . . It would have been helpful for the Church of England if he had taken a higher profile at an earlier stage in favour of this change.'[3] Stanley himself, in spite of taking a firm stance on a number of issues, made sure that in his diocese all voices were fairly heard, and indeed that was one of the tributes paid to him on his retirement.

Two months after the vote, in January 1993, the bishops met in Manchester. Most of their time was concentrated on the episcopal care and pastoral oversight of those who said they could not accept women priests in the Church of England. They were deeply concerned also about their own unity as a House of Bishops and hoped to find some way of avoiding 'no-go' dioceses (the term for a diocese in which no woman would be able to officiate as a priest, not simply one in which the bishop would not himself ordain). They managed to come to a common mind and all signed the 'Manchester Statement'. There was a spelling-out of further 'safeguards' for those who were opposed; but there were to be no no-go areas. Every bishop agreed to make arrangements for women to be ordained and to work as priests in his diocese.[4]

This was important, the bishops would say crucially important, and indeed they sang the Doxology when they reached agreement. One senior woman deacon, looking at the document, said 'Of course, it stands out a mile that there was no woman present. In the end they functioned so much as a group of men, their unity became all-important.' A male cleric added 'Male solidarity always seeks to preserve itself even at the expense of something else. A feminist critique would say this was men bonding together to preserve the status quo.' I asked Barbara Harris about this three months later, sitting in her bishop's office near Boston Common. What about the Men's Club, I asked, the focus of unity, the concern with *not tearing the fabric?* She replied: 'I suspect that for men there is that subtle pressure not to tear the fabric, to meld in, to blend in. For me and now for Jane Dixon, we will never blend in—we will never be full members of "The Club" in that old respect. I don't think that women need to try to do that, I don't want to be one of the old boys, I can't be, and the old boys don't want me to be!'

The English bishops in the meantime, while hoping and believing that they had saved the Church of England from painful division, were finding themselves again harassed by Forward in Faith, who continued to campaign. They wanted the Church to go on for them exactly as before, as if nothing had happened. Fresh threats, this time financial, were made. John Broadhurst, a member of General Synod and Chairman of Forward in Faith, at their Conference for Lay People in the Diocese of London, declared: 'Until now we have been holding people back and telling them to act with restraint. It only needs us now to say "Go for the jugular" and the Church of England will break up.' The Additional Curates Society, a long-established non-sectarian charity founded to support clergy in areas of need, immediately wrote to its beneficiaries indicating that grants would be stopped if the parish was in agreement with women priests. Discussing all this, one bishop said to me 'Of course, they've all been very naughty', a surprisingly flippant turn of phrase in the circumstances.

Instead of saying 'Thus far and no further', the bishops allowed themselves to be beaten from pillar to post. Some were beginning to see how unpleasant things had become for the women deacons, and made an effort to support them. But the continuing row on their doorstep, and the problems arising in Parliament's Ecclesiastical Committee, caused them to produce another document, an Act of Synod which went even further in accommodating the opponents of women priests. Only the Bishop of Salisbury, John Austin Baker, did not sign it. As soon as that appeared, of course,

Forward in Faith demanded nothing less than turning the Act of Synod,[5] a morally binding agreement, into legislation.

There were also anxieties about the Ecclesiastical Committee, responsible for examining church legislation and sending it forward to Parliament. The 30-strong Committee consists of MPs and members of the House of Lords who offer themselves for this work and are selected by the Speaker and the Lord Chancellor respectively. In this group three peeresses served but not one woman was included from the House of Commons (did none offer?). The publicity for this next stage of the long process was unprecedented and much was made of the rocks ahead. The Committee was deluged with letters from supporters of women priests; never had the Committee experienced anything like it. Plaintive calls wafted across Westminster: 'Can't you do something to stop it?' But this extraordinary expression of hope and faith was a much bigger thing than a MOW bright idea, and thousands of letters continued to pour in.

The Archbishops of Canterbury and York gave evidence in favour, Canterbury saying that he looked forward to women bishops when the Church had had experience of women priests. The Bishop of Guildford and Professor McClean were called, as prime movers of the Measure in the Synod, along with other witnesses in favour and, in a departure from normal practice, witnesses against the Measure. Questioning to the Bishop and David McClean was intense and often hostile. Once again goggle-eyed bogeys[6] were produced, but the testimony supporting the Measure was patient, expert and ultimately convincing. On 19 July, after eleven lengthy meetings, the Committee voted by 16 votes to 11 and by 17 to 10 that the Ordination legislation and the Financial Provisions, respectively, were 'expedient' and could be presented to Parliament.[7]

All in all, 1993 was a very curious year indeed. As far as hopes and fears, anger, disappointment and relief were concerned, it was one long, rather unpleasant roller-coaster ride. In January, the bishops' Manchester Statement appeared. In April the Ecclesiastical Committee started to meet. In June the bishops produced their Act of Synod. Some bishops spoke of the Archbishop of York having pulled off a *tour de force* in his scheme to keep the dissidents in the Church. Was John Austin Baker alone in seeing

how they were shifting their position in response to pressure?
The Act included the statement that ordinands could still be
selected and trained even if they believed that women could not
be priests.

In August *Uppity* wrote to all its subscribers, coming out
strongly against the Act. This was supported later by a letter
from Monica Furlong and Margaret Orr Deas. MOW's Executive
Committee had given limited support to the bishops' first scheme,
but issued in October a statement voicing grave reservations about
the Act of Synod, seeing it as undermining the Measure which
the Church had discussed and agreed, and building in future
division. At the same time people were still anxious about the last
hurdle. Parliament had to turn the Church's desire into the law
of the land, and that could not happen till the autumn.

The Spirit flies in . . . to London, Sheffield, Windsor

While all this was happening, after the vote and through 1993,
women deacons were trying to hold on to shreds of joy. Some
memorable services of thanksgiving for the vote were held, notably
at St James's, Piccadilly, and in Sheffield. One MOW member,
Rebecca Hodel, celebrated by bicycling to every cathedral in
England (including the Isle of Man!). The deacons began to
prepare themselves for their new work. One series of consultations, held at St George's House, Windsor, a training centre
for clergy, proved to be particularly significant. Alan Coldwells,
Canon of Windsor, had the sensitivity to see—long before the
vote—the need for women clergy to have space to think together
about the future. He acted as a strengthening, encouraging mid-
wife, making space and time at Windsor for seven consultations
on 'Women in Ordained Ministry'. The seventh of these was held
a fortnight after the vote.

Initially they were for women deacons only, then later male
clergy were invited, the ratio in November 1992 being roughly
50–50. This one was seen as the beginning of a new stage. It was
the largest consultation ever held at St George's, and was completely over-subscribed by August. Although the male clergy
included a number who were quite ardently against women
priests, a great deal of honest, searching work was done to plan

for the new vision to come into reality. Instead of concentrating on the anxieties of those who were unhappy, there was a feeling of excitement and commitment to making the change work, and work well. They also recognized the difficulty of the women being seen as a problem, as if viewed from the wrong end of a microscope, or seen as in some sense 'special'. They saw that the real need was for women and men to have space to be themselves, working together and supporting each other. 'We were still in shock, and also euphoric; but it was humbling for us all, we were honest very quickly.'

They gave time both to the immediate concerns, such as the ordination liturgies for the women deacons, and also to questioning what it means for a woman to be a priest, what are the qualities and skills needed in a training incumbent, how to face and resolve conflict, how to exercise care in the use of language. One group's summary: 'We welcome women into a priesthood we know, which will lead to a wholeness the shape of which we do not know.'

These conclusions were affirming and significant. They knit the women together in a very powerful way. Even before the vote they were able to move from feeling inhibited to a new freedom. As one of them said, 'A conference where the male clergy received, but did not produce the report had a very different feel to it'. When they went back to their dioceses, the initiative continued, even if in a rather patchy way and rather hampered by the realization that their bishops were hearing other voices and were in a different place altogether. The women had to plough on on their own as usual. But at those meetings at Windsor they engaged with their own power, their own abilities and gifts, with all that they were offering as they prepared for priesthood.[8]

... and to Santiago de Compostela

September 1993 was a busy month for women theologians. The fifth World Conference on Faith and Order (the previous one being held as long ago as 1963 in Montreal) was held at Santiago de Compostela. Faith and Order has been described as 'the theological arm' of the World Council of Churches and in the past has been the province of mainly male theologians. But women now serve 'the queen of the sciences' with quite as much distinction as men, and in a World Council of Churches setting that fact is recognized.

Mary Tanner had been Moderator of the Faith and Order Commission since 1991 and she moderated, or chaired, the World Conference. Two Vice-Moderators were women, from Africa and Latin America, and three were men. Mary Tanner has commented on how good this felt, and also how impressive were all the contributions from women.

In Montreal 30 years ago there were only three women among the official delegates appointed by the different Churches; Christian Howard was one of the three. In 1993 in Santiago 32% of the official delegates were women. Of the consultants invited by the Commission, 54% were women. Not only that, the women played major leadership roles: Janet Crawford, the New Zealand priest who had celebrated at MOW's Swanwick Conference eleven years ago, led the team responsible for worship; the daily Bible studies in Galatians were led by Frances Young, Edward Cadbury Professor of Theology at Birmingham University; presentations to the whole assembly were given by Elizabeth Templeton of Edinburgh, and other women; a major statement on the future of the ecumenical movement was made by a Lutheran lay woman from Denmark; and the final sermon was preached by a Latin American woman minister. But Mary's point is that all this seemed totally natural and normal: 'There was a maturity about it, and a lack of self-consciousness. At last we felt like a community of women and men in the Church.'

Hearing this, I reflected that the World Council of Churches has managed to cover more difficult terrain more quickly than the Church of England. I remembered taking part in a remarkable consultation on the ordination of women held at Cartigny, Geneva in 1970. The Roman Catholic and Orthodox Churches were represented by Catharine Halkes of Nijmegen University and Bishop L'Huillier of the Russian Orthodox church in Paris. At the final Eucharist, celebrated and sung by a Swedish woman priest, all the members of the conference were able to participate and the Orthodox bishop, who did not receive the elements, gave the blessing at the end. So it was not entirely true to say that women's ordination was simply not within the Orthodox consciousness.

The WCC Conference at Santiago broke new ground in several ways. Although Roman Catholics are only observers at full WCC meetings, they are now members of the Faith and Order Commission, and so for the first time were able to contribute during the sessions. This is the side of the Roman Catholic Church which some Anglicans like to ignore, that majority of Catholics who welcomed the enormous upheavals of Vatican II, and supported the women's religious orders who spearheaded these reforms. The new community of women and men in the Church may still be something of a dream but at the conference at Santiago it touched reality.

... and at York

The Spirit's wingbeat could also be felt in York where 400 people met for four days in September as part of the growing movement of Affirming Catholicism. This marked a significant development in the history of the Anglo-Catholic branch of the C of E. It was reported with phrases like 'Anglo-Catholics Direct Their Energies in a Positive Direction' (*The Church of England Newspaper*) and 'Anglo-Catholics Welcome the Future' (*The Tablet*). More interestingly, 'The Waiting Game Is Now Over' was the headline of the *Catholic Herald*.

The organizers had gathered Anglicans from a variety of traditions, and from their own strongly Anglo-Catholic but forward-looking position had arranged four days of joyful and positive commitment to the changing Church. David Hutt, Vicar of All Saints, Margaret Street, said 'There was a spirit of spontaneity, of being personally revitalized, of understanding the Christian faith in a way that was no longer burdensome. Compared with our previous conference two years ago, the pain and anxiety has been assuaged. It was very generous, very unselfconscious. People there weren't making dramatic statements against things, they were keen to get on, look at an agenda for a much larger, more generous Church.' There was a conviction that this now represented mainstream Catholic opinion in the Anglican Communion: 'Our agenda is a renewal of spirituality and witness to the entire

Church.' Isenda Maxtone-Graham commented in the *Catholic Herald*: 'What Affirming Catholicism seeks to keep alive is the awareness that the word "Anglican Catholic" does not necessarily imply "anti-ordination of women", "traditionalist" or "Rome-seeking". It can also imply universality, wholeness, and delight in every aspect of creation.'[9]

Parliament approves: Synod adjusts

On 29 October 1993 the Measure came before the House of Commons and was debated for most of a day. Then, after five hours, the House, in a remarkable show of concerted support, voted the Measure through by 215 votes to 21.

As was expected, some MPs focused on the minority of clergy opposing women priests and on the financial provision for any deciding to leave the Church, causing Michael Alison, Church Commissioner responsible for the motion, to devote much time to reassuring members that the provisions were just and generous. (As one member agreed, 'More generous than after the dissolution of the monasteries!') Emma Nicholson, a Vice-Moderator of MOW, put very clearly the Church's fundamental case for ordaining women priests. Opposing the Measure, John Gummer was restrained and serious. Ann Widdecombe damaged their cause with what the *Independent* described as 'a rant at full gallop'.

Behind the debate hovered unseen presences—of parents, for instance. Tony Benn, John Gummer and others recalled their mothers or fathers. Others looked to the future. Jean Corston, a Bristol MP, described her daughter's feelings of exclusion from the Church and a Conservative churchman spoke with approval of his niece marrying his son—the niece being a deacon. Above all, there was an awareness of the women deacons, of whose gifts and endurance Glenda Jackson spoke with eloquence.

Four days later a packed House of Lords defeated by 135 votes to 25 an amendment urging further delay, and went on to accept the main Measure without a division. A notable and surprising speech came from the former Archbishop of Canterbury, Robert Runcie, who commended the ordination of women priests as a route back to a model of the priest as 'the Good Shepherd, rather than as the successful graduate of the management training school ... Their ability to bring men and women to God is tempered by the kind of tough gentleness which nourishes families and challenges the overbearing, neither authoritative nor submissive.' I saw this as marking the end of his long hesitation, which had been so hard for him and for others. His successor, George Carey, put the theological arguments and praised the patience of the women who had waited so long, speaking of his confidence that they would enrich the priestly ministry of the Church.

After this massive support in the Commons and the Lords, the Queen gave the Royal Assent three days later.

The following week Synod met for the last debates concerning the ordination of women as priests. They had to discuss the controversial Act of Synod, put before them by the House of Bishops. Opinions were still strongly divided. Could it be right so to emphasize the need to 'give space' to the opponents of Synod's decision of a year before, that opposition could become entrenched, seeking ordination and promotion while still refusing to acknowledge some colleagues as priests? Many people, especially outside the Synod, were outraged at this official permission to deny the priesthood of women colleagues.

They also saw the notion of special bishops being consecrated to officiate for those opposed to women priests as colluding with the notion of 'taint' (that bishops who ordained women thereby became tainted and unacceptable). However much this was denied, it seemed to many that the 'episcopal visitors' scheme was influenced by this thinking.[10]

But the Act of Synod was strongly presented by the Archbishop of York as a necessary generosity, even as common sense. Synod applauded the emphasis on keeping the Church together which, it was said, the Act would achieve. In the end the overwhelming majority of members, even those with reservations, voted for the Act. In the gallery Monica Furlong, Margaret Orr Deas and four others held up a black banner showing in letters of white the one word 'Shame'. Quietly this was chanted from the gallery — 'Shame — Shame — Shame'.

The year 1993, therefore, from the point of view of those concerned with the Church's decision for women priests, was hard in the extreme. In one year we saw a series of moves and counter-moves, proposals, objections, threats, and

accommodations. We had laboriously helped to push the Church
of England bicycle up a long hill, and had paused at the top for
a brief moment of joy at the vista ahead. But then angry sad men
jumped out of the bushes, handed out spanners and watched
while our episcopal leaders, singing their Act of Synod hymn,
loosened the bicycle's nuts and bolts. Quite a crowd gathered to
watch it wobble on its way. The question was, could it now hang
together and gather speed.

'All church work is slow'[11]

Why should it have taken so long and been so difficult for the
Church of England to come to a decision and then act upon it?
Is there something in the make-up of committed Anglicans which
makes it especially hard to contemplate change? Is this tied up in
some way with the difficulty most Christians have in dealing with
the prospect of conflict? We would do anything, it sometimes
seems, rather than have a row on our hands; and yet the inability
to handle conflict only leads to further problems.

Perhaps the system of decision-making, based so closely on
Parliament, is not helpful in coming to a common mind. It can
be adversarial, and has to be managed through 'the proper procedures', which give infinite scope for procrastination or even wreck-
ing. In this instance, however, the delays have been more than
simply procedural. They were part and parcel of the long history
of devaluing women which the Anglican Church (and the Roman
Catholic) have inherited. 'The tradition' of these Churches may
be like a climbing plant; when the bindweed intertwines, new
shoots are nearly choked.

Many people have used the word 'damage' about the effect of
the long-drawn-out process. Damage to the Church, according
to Stanley Booth-Clibborn. Damage to people, inescapably. There
have been casualties among the women in waiting. When anger
is unacknowledged it can cause havoc. But anger can be creative,
too, helping us to see the truth beyond, a source of energy, even
a release into humour, or into prayer. I have learned that anger
is my friend and not my destroyer. 'Anger is one of the sinews
of the soul', says Thomas Fuller.

But it is impossible for anyone not herself called to priesthood to assess or describe the feelings of those convinced of that call who, year after year, have been barred from having their vocations tested. While some were able to cope with that situation — 'Well, we just got on with what we could' — others found the week-in-week-out strain almost intolerable. In addition to those women called to be priests who have suffered, far more women than most of us realize have given up the Church in despair.

In 1975 Una Kroll wrote:

> Suffering is a price people must pay in pursuing their goals. There are many different paths towards the goal of freedom. Along the way some dream dreams, some fight, some pray, some think it right to resist oppression and some think it right to restrain growth. Some find that 'pain rooted in hope'[12] becomes a liberator, if they allow that pain to take root in their lives. Personally I have learnt that I can oppose only those whom I have first learnt to love.[13]

That was written in the year when the Synod agreed to 'no fundamental objections' and then threw out 'remove legal barriers'. There would be one more defeat three years later and a further six years to wait before Synod voted to ask for legislation to be prepared. A long nine years, followed by nine more years for the legislation process. If MOW has done anything, I believe it has helped people make sense of the pain, and to move through it. Even 11 November 1993, the date of the passage of the Act of Synod, about which MOW had such serious reservations, saw the start of fresh celebrations filled with determination and joy as the women prepared for priesthood. On that evening the service was, appropriately, in the London Area of Edmonton, a nerve-centre of clerical anxiety. So although we were often disheartened, always new energy was discovered, energy we didn't know we had, a creative fizzing as we planned, dreamed, got angry, laughed, belonged.

Some were convinced that once the Church had seriously embarked on the moves towards women's ordination the time lapse was a help, allowing the process of 'reception' to go on as people gradually let the idea take root and then accepted it. This may have been important, given the hesitancy of the C of E about moving into change, but anxiety about 'unseemly haste' was always inappropriate. Perhaps, for those who worried most about the

Church rushing things, the point simply was to observe the water as it ran under the bridge, and the interesting games of Pooh-sticks which people were playing. Do not let us become impatient or angry, they would say, these things take time and it is important to play a seemly game with all the rules observed. Others used the time to get to know the other people on the bridge, started interesting conversations, exchanged opinions, explored attitudes.

Joining the exploration

So what does it all amount to? What is going to happen after all these years of slog and prayer, tears and laughter and fizz? This ordained Christian priesthood—what difference will incomers make? And will lay people be enabled, be allowed to claim their own power? Most MOW members would say that their aim has not been to slot women into the familiar parsonical role; they long to see different attitudes and ways of working so that men themselves are freed from their stereotypes.

Something new and profound has started moving in the Church. The Spirit of God is seeking to open us to fundamental questions, forcing us to think more carefully and deeply about God and the incarnation, about the Gospel, about sexuality, about the meaning of priesthood and ministry. And looking at the Bible afresh has forced us to think about tradition and the Church. All this has been going on as the issue of ordaining women has been emerging over years as a crucial decision before the Church. Concepts of authority, of tradition, of leadership have changed as stereotypes and expectations have been re-examined.

Mary Grey, at the end of her book *The Wisdom of Fools*, describes a number of communities engaged in this search— Women in Theology, St Hilda's, Catholic Women's Network, and others—and then she reflects:

> But it is in the Movement for the Ordination of Women (MOW) that the anguish and the courage has been most clearly expressed. It is important to draw out, now that the long travail has reached a successful conclusion, what the struggle has been saying to us about ecclesiology. Contrary to all that is being said about the supposed threat to Christian unity—which is insulting to those Churches in which women have ministered for a considerable time—the struggle within the Church of

England to ordain women is loyal to authentic Church, the Church of 'the discipleship of equals', which Fiorenza claims is the original inspiration of the Jesus movement ... Women are not trying to be 'the innocents of history'—forever identified with nature and not with culture—but to bring their experiences of a different manner of relating, a different experience of how power can be shared, a different articulation of life's deep experiences, to the moulding of renewed Christian community.[14]

But is all this just fine words? Is it conceivable that new ways of exercising and sharing power can be reached? In a paper on collaborative ministry and ways of communicating, David Hutt takes a scalpel to what for him has been a bogey word:

And then there is feminism. Why do I feel personally threatened by feminism? Perhaps because I do not really understand what other people, especially women, intend it to mean. Observing pain and anger in women who find themselves genuinely oppressed and denied what to them seem to be human rights and dignity fills me with embarrassment and shame. Because I am not a woman I feel I am somehow to blame, part of a male conspiracy which keeps me in power (a power I neither relish nor want) and, as if this was not enough I know I am afraid ... I'm over-anxious not to get it wrong but even more I'm fairly desperate to avoid the kind of criticism which can threaten my acceptance of how things are because it threatens my sense of identity, the very person I *am*.[15]

This kind of honesty would open up quite new lines of communication, and would require a true and searching response.

Soon 'women priests' will no longer to be thought of as 'an issue'. Though some people may still be uncertain, the women are there now, ordained, in post, actual women, presiding at the Eucharist, being with other human beings, discovering how to work in new ways with their colleagues. If there is to be some fresh understanding, a new covenant, the burden must not be placed all on the women. We must work at this together, as Christ's body. The exploration may be dangerous, painful, insecure, but it will not be a boring or deadening way to walk and we shall walk it in company with others. Women have had enough of being burdened with expectations and then left to get on with it; we have to grow out of the Angel Gabriel Syndrome (feeling that everyone expects me to be perfect).

The experience of so many thousands of people who have been connected with MOW and those other serious, lively groups has already brought something to the life of the Church. For we have all changed. The different experiences described in this book have welded something stronger than just the temporary goodwill of those involved in a common task—deeper than that and not exclusive. Can the experience be fed into the Church: the suffering, the waiting, the fun, the experience of conflict and dealing with it, the staying together, the valuing of each other even when views diverged? Above all, the discovering over the years of new ways of worshipping, of fresh language, of circular patterns in worship rather than always a pyramidal hierarchical structure. The symbols we have used in worship—oil, yeast, grapes, flowers, rock—are the symbols of a new Christian life.

The important questions about ministry can no longer be put into trays marked 'Too Difficult' or 'Not Yet'. The windows are open, the papers are blowing about, we have to work in a different way. Perhaps for a time we should abandon desks and reference books, put diaries in the fridge, and Canon Law in the oven, while we continue with our exploration.

It has been going on a long time, this exploration, this quest, and people join it as they can. It goes along the banks of the river of tradition, and we have watched the river unfreeze. Great floes have crashed along, bumping into others and making a powerful music as they go. The river has all the strength it had before, is to be respected and loved, but the frozen surface has cracked, the energy below has been released.

Notes

1 Song by Naomi Littlebear Morena from record *We Have a Dream* (One World Peace Songs).
2 *The Tablet* (21 November 1992).
3 Stanley Booth-Clibborn in an interview, July 1993. See also Diana McClatchey, 'A Listening Archbishop Speaks' in *Robert Runcie: A Portrait by His Friends*, ed. David Edwards (Collins, 1990). In this section Runcie's attitudes to the ordination of women are explored, mainly through a careful examination of his speeches in the General Synod.
4 House of Bishops, *Statement by the House Following Its Meeting in Man-*

chester, 11–14 January 1993 (Church House Communications Unit, 14 January 1993).

5 Episcopal Ministry Act of Synod, 1993 (Draft) was presented to Synod on 13 July and debated on 9 and 11 November 1993.

6 See *Ecclesiastical Committee Report*, p. 115 and the suggestion of Peter Bruinvels that 1,000 clergy could resign and the Church of England be involved in costs of £150 million. Professor McClean described these figures as grossly exaggerated.

7 *Reports by the Ecclesiastical Committee upon the Priests (Ordination of Women) Measure and the Ordination of Women (Financial Provisions) Measure* (HMSO, 1993).

8 The Windsor Consultations on Women in Ordained Ministry: Report of November 1992 meeting, *Changing Perceptions of Ministry*.

9 *Catholic Herald* (17 September 1993).

10 Prebendary Donald Barnes, long-standing member of Synod and of MOW, lightened the proceedings by suggesting that the media term 'flying bishops', if unacceptable, should be replaced by 'errant bishops'.

11 Thomas Fuller (1608–61), Anglican historian.

12 Phrase quoted from Melano Couch, theologian from Argentina.

13 Una Kroll, *Flesh of My Flesh* (Darton, Longman and Todd, 1975), pp. 126–7.

14 Mary Grey, *The Wisdom of Fools* (SPCK, 1993), pp. 126–7.

15 David Hutt, 'Men and Women Working in the Church Together—the Challenge of New Opportunities' (private paper).

Bibliography

Peter F. Anson, *The Call of the Cloister: Religious Communities and Kindred Bodies in the Anglican Communion* (SPCK, 1964).

The Revd Joyce M. Bennett, *Hasten Slowly* (Little London Associates, 1991).

Kathleen Burn, *The Calling of Kath Burn* (Angel Press, 1988).

Lavinia Byrne, *Women Before God* (SPCK, 1988).

Lavinia Byrne (ed.), *The Hidden Tradition* (SPCK, 1991).

Lavinia Byrne (ed.), *The Hidden Journey*, (SPCK, 1993).

Elizabeth Canham, *Pilgrimage to Priesthood* (SPCK, 1983).

Jennifer Chapman, *The Last Bastion* (Methuen, 1989).

Concilium 1991/6: *The Special Nature of Women?* (SCM Press, 1991).

Rupert E. Davies, *The Church of England Observed* (SCM Press, 1984).

Susan Dowell and Linda Hurcombe, *Dispossessed Daughters of Eve: Faith and Feminism* (SCM Press, 1981; revised edition, SCM Press, 1987).

Jacqueline Field-Bibb, *Women Towards Priesthood: Ministerial Politics and Feminist Praxis* (Cambridge University Press, 1991).

Sheila Fletcher, *Maude Royden: A Life* (Basil Blackwell, 1989).

Brenda Fullalove, Preface to MPhil thesis, 'The Ministry of Women in the Church of England 1919–1970'. See two Fullalove articles under this title in *Modern Churchman* XXIX, nos 2 and 3 (1987).

Monica Furlong, *Feminine in the Church* (SPCK, 1984).

Monica Furlong, *Mirror to the Church* (SPCK, 1988).

Monica Furlong, *A Dangerous Delight* (SPCK, 1991).

Carol Gilligan, *In A Different Voice: Psychological Theory and Women's Development* (Harvard University Press, 1982).

Mary Grey, *Redeeming the Dream: Feminism, Redemption and Christian Tradition* (SPCK, 1989).

Mary Grey, *The Wisdom of Fools: Seeking Revelation for Today* (SPCK, 1993).

Janet Grierson, *The Deaconess* (CIO Publishing, 1981).

Mary Hayter, *The New Eve in Christ: The Use and Abuse of the Bible in the Debate about Women in the Church* (SPCK, 1987).

Brian Heeney, *The Women's Movement in the Church of England 1850–1930* (Clarendon Press, 1988).

Richard Holloway (ed.), *Who Needs Feminism?* (SPCK, 1991).

R. W. Howard, *Should Women Be Priests?* (Basil Blackwell, 1949).

Julian of Norwich, *Enfolded In Love: Daily Readings in Julian of Norwich*, ed. Robert Llewelyn (Darton, Longman & Todd, 1980).

Ursula King, *Women and Spirituality: Voices of Protest and Promise* (Macmillan, 1989).

Mary Levison, *Wrestling with the Church* (Arthur James, 1992).

Florence Li Tim Oi and Ted Harrison, *Much Beloved Daughter* (Darton, Longman & Todd, 1985).

Robert Llewelyn, *With Pity, Not With Blame* (Darton, Longman & Todd, 1989).

Ann Loades (ed.), *Feminist Theology: A Reader* (SPCK, 1990).

Sara Maitland, *A Map of the New Country: Women and Christianity* (Routledge and Kegan Paul, 1983).

Elisabeth Moltmann, *The Women Around Jesus* (SCM Press, 1982).

Janet Morley, *All Desires Known* (MOW, 1988; expanded version, SPCK, 1992).

Janet Morley and Hannah Ward, *Celebrating Women* (MOW/Women in Theology, 1986).

Jocelyn Murray, *Proclaim the Good News* (Hodder & Stoughton, 1985).

David M. Paton, *'R.O.': The Life and Times of Bishop Hall of Hong Kong* (Diocese of Hong Kong and Macao and Hong Kong Diocesan Assn, 1985).

Rosemary Radford Ruether, *Sexism and God-Talk: Towards a Feminist Theology* (SCM Press, 1983).

Rosemary Radford Ruether and E. McLaughlin (eds), *Women of Spirit: Female Leadership in the Jewish and Christian Traditions* (Simon & Schuster, New York, 1979).

St Hilda Community, *Women Included* (SPCK, 1991).

Elaine Storkey, *What's Right With Feminism?* (SPCK, 1985).

Mary Tanner, *Christian Feminism: A Challenge to the Churches* (Loughborough University Chaplaincy, 1986).

Tierl Thompson (ed.), *Dear Girl* (The Women's Press, 1987).

Pauline Webb, *She Flies Beyond: Memories and Hopes of Women in the Ecumenical Movement* (WCC Publications, 1993).

Brian Wren, *What Language Shall I Borrow? God-Talk in Worship: A Male Response to Feminist Theology* (SCM Press, 1989).

Reports

The Ministry of Women: Report of the Archbishops' Commission (Church Assembly Publications Board, 1935).

Gender and Ministry: Report of the Central Advisory Council for the Ministry (Church Information Office, 1962).

Women and Holy Orders: Report of the Archbishops' Commission (CIO, 1966).

Women in Ministry: A Study. Joint Report of ACCM and CWMC (CIO, 1968).

What Is Ordination Coming To? Report of a Consultation on the Ordination of Women, held in Cartigny, Switzerland, September 1970, ed. Brigalia Bam (World Council of Churches, 1971).

The Ordination of Women to the Priesthood: Consultative Document for the General Synod (GS 104), ed. Christian Howard (CIO, 1972).

The Ministry of Deacons and Deaconesses: Report by ACCM (GS 344, 1977).

The Ordination of Women: A Supplement to the Consultative Document GS 104 (GS Misc. 88), ed. Christian Howard (CIO, 1978).

The Ordination of Women to the Priesthood: Further Report to General Synod (GS Misc. 198), ed. Christian Howard (CIO, 1984).

The Ordination of Women to the Priesthood: The Scope of the Legislation (GS 738, 1986).

The Ordination of Women to the Priesthood: A Report of the House of Bishops (GS 764, February 1987).

Making Women Visible: The Use of Inclusive Language with the ASB. A Report by the Liturgical Commission of the General Synod (GS 859; CIO, 1988).

The Ordination of Women to the Priesthood: A Second Report by the House of Bishops (GS 829, 1990).

The Ordination of Women to the Priesthood: Reference of Draft Legislation to Diocesan Synods 1990. Memorandum by the Standing Committee and Background Papers (GS Misc. 336).

The Ordination of Women to the Priesthood: The Synod Debate 11 November 1992. The Verbatim Record (Church House Publishing, 1993). (See p. 132, note 7.)

Reports by the Ecclesiastical Committee upon the Priests (Ordination of Women) Measure and the Ordination of Women (Financial Provisions) Measure (HMSO, 1993).

House of Commons Hansard, vol. 230, col. 1083 (HMSO, 1993).

House of Lords Hansard, vol. 549, col. 1001 (HMSO, 1993).

Episcopal Ministry Act of Synod 1993 (GS 1085).

Voting figures in debates on women's ordination as priests in the General Synod of the Church of England 1975–92

1975

Motion that 'There are no fundamental objections to the ordination of women to the priesthood' carried: For 255, Against 180. Motion to remove 'legal and other barriers' lost.

8 November 1978 Motion to remove legal barriers lost.

	Ayes	Noes
House of Bishops	32	17
House of Clergy	94	149
House of Laity	120	106

Abstentions: 3

The motion was lost in the House of Clergy.

15 November 1984 Motion: 'That this Synod asks the Standing Committee to bring forward legislation to permit the ordination of women to the priesthood in the Provinces of Canterbury and York'.

House of Bishops	41	6
House of Clergy	131	98
House of Laity	135	79

Abstentions: 5

The motion was carried in all three Houses.

5 July 1988 'General Approval' of the legislation.

	Ayes	Noes
House of Bishops	28	21
House of Clergy	137	102
House of Laity	134	93

Abstentions: 1

The motion was carried in all three Houses.

Draft financial provision was also generally approved.

7 November 1989 Revision of the Measure

House of Bishops	30	17
House of Clergy	149	85
House of Laity	144	78

On referral to the dioceses the voting was as follows:

Deanery synods	Diocesan synods
Voting by Houses	
Clergy 73% in favour	86% in favour
Laity 89% in favour	95% in favour
Total overall votes cast	
Average 67.66% in favour	Average 67.29% in favour

11 November 1992: Final Approval

	Ayes	Noes	In favour
House of Bishops	39	13	75%
House of Clergy	176	74	70.4%
House of Laity	169	82	67.3%

The motion was carried with the necessary two-thirds majority in each House.

Further details are available in *The Ordination of Women to the Priesthood: The Synod Debate 11 November 1992* (Church House Publishing, 1993), pp. 88–91.

Index